The A–Z of Buddy Holly

This book is dedicated to all Buddy Holly fans throughout the world –
past, present and yet to come.

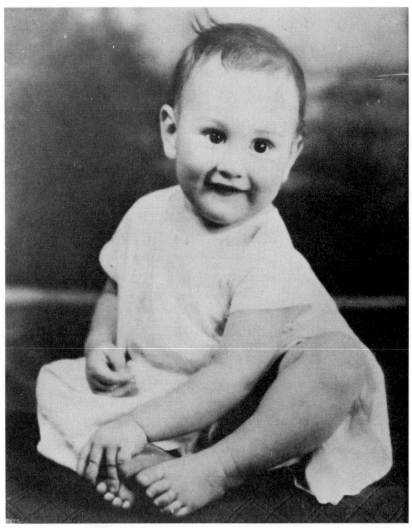

Charles Hardin Holley aged 12 months, and long before any musical sounds were made. (Courtesy of Bill Griggs.)

The
A–Z of
Buddy
Holly

First published in Great Britain 1996
by Aurum Press Ltd, 25 Bedford Avenue, London WC1B 3AT
© 1996 by Alan Mann

A catalogue record for this book is available
from the British Library.

ISBN 1 85410 433 0

2 4 6 8 10 9 7 5 3 1
1997 1999 2000 1998 1996

Typeset by Dorchester Typesetting Group Ltd
Printed and bound by Hartnolls Ltd, Bodmin

Introduction

By John Beecher

It's been a long time since 1957 and 'That'll Be The Day', although to some of us it seems like only yesterday; especially if you've had all the mirrors removed from your house in case you catch a glimpse of someone over 50. But the fascination for rock'n'roll and all things 1950s has remained strong even for those born long after that decade. In fact there are probably more rock'n'roll records and books available now than ever there were when the establishment was telling us that 'jungle music' would never last.

When Alan Mann told me he was putting together a book called *The A–Z of Buddy Holly* for his 'retirement thesis', I wasn't surprised for if ever there was to be a real labour of love, this would have to be it. Alan was a founder member of the Buddy Holly and The Crickets fan clubs in the early 1960s and his enthusiasm for the music and unearthing information about those artists has never diminished. This enthusiasm comes alive through the entries in this book and Holly fans can be certain of a 'good read' all the way from Abba to Zager and Evans. In between you're sure to discover all sorts of things you never knew, had almost forgotten, or didn't realize you ought to have known in the first place. In any event Alan's book is going to be a useful addition to the Holly and The Crickets bookshelf and I for one am happy he's got it together.

Preface

The A–Z format is used extensively these days and this probably fits the hi-tech world in which we live. Perhaps the rush towards the millennium fuels our urge to tabulate and package all we see. To tidy up the 20th century in readiness for the 21st?

Whatever the reason, an A–Z listing is a particularly good way of chronicling the life and musical times of Buddy Holly. It allows us to delve into every aspect without the clutter of footnotes, which might dog a standard biography.

The criterion has been readability. That 400 entries sometimes overlap is unavoidable but the aim has been to avoid a dry work of reference. Holly's music is alive and vibrant so if a little of that spirit is captured within these pages...

A last practical word: if the reader seeks even more Holly-related information then several addresses are listed (with permission) under SOURCES within the text.

Buddy

A brief word of explanation about the 400 or so entries that follow. Readers making the whole journey to Z will absorb a wealth of biographical data along the way giving them much greater insight into the life and legend of Buddy Holly. Along the way they will also learn details of Holly's backing group, The Crickets, as well as reading pen-pictures of contemporaries from Texas and far beyond.

Most of the singers who influenced Holly are apportioned space from the country end of the spectrum to the R&B side. In turn many imitators or soundalikes are catalogued together with a whole roster of those who, although not sounding like Buddy Holly, nevertheless manifest a musical influence in some way.

Also encapsulated within are full details of every recording made by the singer in his short life. In addition entries are included for artists where Holly is known to have been on the session – usually playing lead guitar.

The most unlikely entries in the book are the one that follows and the final one under Z. In between there is much to fascinate both the casual reader and the most avid of fans.

Copyright

Permission to reprint pictures has been sought and obtained as appropriate. As to songs, care has been taken not to quote lyrics and infringe any publishers' copyrights.

A

ABBA

Believe it or not there is a tenuous link between Holly and the group who used a palindrome for their name. Stockholm-born Benny Andersson, the keyboard player with the Swedish group, was originally a member of The Hep Stars, who recorded a rather ponderous English-speaking version of 'Tribute to Buddy Holly' in the early 1960s. It was a minor success. There are no other connections although Bjorn, originally with The Hootenanny Singers, would doubtless have performed Holly material as many folk artists do on stage.

Adverts

The music of Buddy Holly has now entered our collective subconscious so it is little surprise that it has been used almost continually to advertise products via our TV screens.

The products have been as diverse as jelly baby sweets and video cassettes. Most readers could name their own examples. Possibly the most memorable occasion was in 1988 when Terry's All Gold used Holly's recording of 'True Love Ways' and the reissued single went back into the charts – just 30 years after it had been recorded.

Recently a Korean car manufacturer adapted 'That'll Be The Day' to advertise their product. But of course Holly and The Crickets had already pinched it in the first place! See THE SEARCHERS entry.

'Ain't Got No Home'

Demo. Probably recorded late 1956 at Venture Studio, Lubbock. Personnel: Buddy, Jerry Allison and others unknown.

This novelty track was the first US Top 40 hit on Argo for its composer Clarence Henry in late 1956 and led to him permanently adopting the nickname of 'Frogman'. It was almost certainly cut by Holly as a demo using Jerry Allison on drums and an unknown bass player, shortly after Buddy returned from his last abortive Nashville session. It

1

peaked at 20 in Billboard. The Henry number would have been quite familiar to Buddy and the boys.

The Frogman was born in Algiers, New Orleans on 19th March 1937. Seemingly a one-hit wonder he eventually had other chart success in the early 1960s. However, his 1957 sequel disc 'I Found A Home' didn't get anywhere.

When Holly's version was first released (1969 'Giant' LP) it was heavily overdubbed under the direction of Norman Petty thus creating a stereo master. The undubbed mono version first came out in the UK during the 1980s on Rollercoaster Records.

Albums

In the text of this book every known individual recording of Buddy Holly/Crickets is listed under its song title. Additionally, each significant album release is discussed briefly under its individual title, e.g. 'The Chirping Crickets', etc., and a track listing is included.

Extended Play records are not listed separately but are discussed selectively under the heading: EXTENDED PLAY RECORDS.

'All For You'

This Buddy Knox recording has, through the years, been listed as having Holly on the session together with several other musicians who regularly passed through Clovis.

However, Holly historian Bill Griggs gives a recording date of 22nd February 1958 for the song and points out that Holly was on a tour date in Florida at that point. If correct he couldn't have been present. (But Holly & Knox were close friends – see entry BUDDY KNOX.)

Buddy Holly was a very busy Clovis session musician during 1957 and 1958 when he wasn't out on tour and around a dozen artists are listed herein where he definitely was involved on their recordings.

Steve Allen

Steve Allen was the bespectacled US host from the early days of TV who founded *The Tonight Show* in 1954 and later had his own highly rated *Steve Allen Show* on NBC. A lot of up-and-coming rock'n'roll acts made their national TV debuts on his shows around 1957 but, unfortunately, The Crickets were not featured although rumours persisted for years to the contrary. Amongst those definitely appearing were Jerry Lee Lewis and the Johnny Burnette Trio.

Allen was a jazz aficionado who occasionally fronted a big band and also had a solo piano hit in 1955 with 'Autumn Leaves'. As a performer he made one of the numerous covers of the hit Disney song, 'The Ballad of Davy Crockett'.

Steve Allen was member of the musical establishment in the 1950s along with the likes of Ed Sullivan and Mitch Miller. They were to see their influence on the entertainment scene eroded as rock began to take over.

Jerry Allison

Jerry Ivan Allison, known as J.I., was born on 31st August 1938 and co-founded The Crickets with Buddy Holly in early 1957. Whilst he usually played drums in a conventional way he also switched to beating out the rhythm on a cardboard box or even by slapping his knees when the occasion demanded. As if that wasn't enough he's also a highly proficient guitarist and no mean songwriter. (He helped to write many of Holly's best compositions even if he didn't always get composer credits. Since 1959 he has co-written much of the material for the latter-day Crickets).

Buddy and Jerry first met at school in Lubbock *circa* 1952 when Jerry was drumming with a small country outfit name Cal Wayne and the Riverside Ranch Hands. Thereafter they played together more and more, even performing as a duo if necessary. Buddy played a strong rhythm-cum-lead guitar, and with Jerry's busy drumming patterns they created a full sound using amplifiers that would look puny in today's hi-tech world. Not much employment for a roadie in those bygone days.

Jerry has worked with a veritable who's who of artists down the years when his Crickets activities have allowed. It's well-known that he and Sonny Curtis played on Eddie Cochran's last studio session and in the early 1960s Jerry toured with the Everly Brothers. For a time he was an in-demand West Coast session drummer backing artists such as Johnny Rivers and Johnny Burnette. He also toured or recorded with Ray Stevens, Bobby Vee, Waylon Jennings and the late Roger Miller in a long and ongoing career that saw him gravitating to

Nashville and also fitting in a bit of farming.

A talented and humorous individual, Jerry is totally unlike his celluloid counterpart in *The Buddy Holly Story*, which came out many years ago. In fact the biggest disappointment of his career to date, after the loss of his musical partner, must surely have been not being consulted or used in the making of the film. (In the previous decade Jerry was also overlooked, this time by Norman Petty, when overdubbing Holly's remaining unissued material.)

Jerry has also had a short solo career as a vocalist – see entry under IVAN. Other cross-references are too numerous but do see PEGGY SUE GERRON and THE CRICKETS.

Remember, Jerry Allison and Buddy Holly were almost soul-mates and many of this book's entries apply as much to Jerry as they do to Buddy.

Keith Allison

No relation to Jerry Allison, Keith filled in on drums/vocals with The Crickets in the late 1960s during a short period when his namesake was drafted into the Armed Services. Later, he became a highly photogenic member of the US group, Paul Revere and the Raiders before eventually going solo and later moving into the production side of the music business in the 1980s.

The Allisons

This young duo of (apparent) brothers rocketed to the top of the charts in 1961 with their self-penned Eurovision composition 'Are You Sure', an opus very much in the style of the late Buddy Holly. It went on to sell a million.

Later the news broke that the two were unrelated and that the duo comprised of 21-year-old (John) Brian Alford and 19-year-old (Bob) Colin Day. They quickly followed their single with an album that included such Holly/Crickets covers as 'It Doesn't Matter Anymore' and 'That'll Be The Day', but the album failed to chart.

They had a couple of other minor chart singles but within 12 months their meteoric career had nose-dived. Other artists who were

influenced by Holly often carved out more lengthy musical careers.
Worth seeing SOUNDALIKES entry.

Tommy Allsup

Born in Owassa, near Tulsa, Oklahoma on 24th November 1931,
Tommy was, for years, the unknown Cricket despite playing superb
lead guitar on several 1958 recordings. Tracks such as 'Heartbeat', 'It's
So Easy' and 'Love's Made A Fool Of You' all feature Tommy. He had
met Buddy Holly when both were at Norman Petty's studio in Clovis
and was a natural choice to tour with Holly on those fateful 1959
shows; the first tour undertaken by Buddy without having Jerry and
Joe B. alongside him since he had become fully established. Other
backing musicians were Waylon Jennings on bass guitar and Carl
Bunch on drums. Tommy is famous for giving up his seat on the fatal
flight following the flip of a coin with Ritchie Valens. This episode was
shown in a dramatic sequence during the Valens biopic *La Bamba*. Initially Allsup was also believed to have perished in the crash as his
wallet was discovered amongst the debris.

Tommy originally performed in his own group, Tommy Allsup and
his Western Swing Band, before joining up with Buddy in New York
to take part in the ill-fated GAC tour. Although traumatized by the
events of 3rd February, he completed the tour itinerary, eventually
joining up with Crickets Jerry, Joe and Earl Sinks for a brief period.
For further insight into this event see entry THE JITTERS.

Since 1959 he has had a long and eventful career as a session musician (lead, rhythm or even bass guitar), artist manager, AOK label
owner and as a musical 'suit' in Nashville, where he became an A and
R director for a Mercury subsidiary. Perhaps the strangest step was to
open a nightclub called 'Tommy's Heads-Up', which brought him less
luck than the coin flip did! (See RITCHIE VALENS entry.) As if all that
wasn't enough he also recorded five solo albums.

His most satisfying career events were probably producing Western
Swing group, Asleep at the Wheel's first album and also producing, in
1973, the final album for country legend Bob Wills, entitled 'For the
Last Time'. Not long after, Wills was to pass away. In the early 1960s
Tommy teamed up with Jerry Allison, Buzz Cason, George Tomsco
and Lynn Bailey to record an instrumental album, 'The Buddy Holly
Songbook', under Norman Petty's direction. Allsup returned to the
Surf Ballroom, the scene of Holly's last appearance, in 1994 and per-
formed a solo spot as part of the annual Tribute concert. He still
remains active in the music business.

Stranger than fiction? See ZAGER AND EVANS entry.

'Almost Paradise'

This Norman Petty composition was a Top 40 disc for both Lou Stein and Roger Williams back in early 1957 while the original version by the Norman Petty Trio reached only 56. Petty had offered it to RCA but when they rejected it he released on his own Nor-Va-Jak label.

UK Holly fans, to whom the title meant nothing, were bemused to see it listed in the tour programme as part of The Crickets' repertoire. Perhaps an effort to secure performance fees by Norman unless he contemplated doing an organ solo! An unlikely thought.

Needless to say it wasn't featured on stage but The Crickets did perform several titles that they never recorded: 'Keep A-Knockin'', 'Long Tall Sally', 'Be Bop A Lula', 'Sweet Little 16' and 'Jailhouse Rock' have all been mentioned at times.

See also THE NORMAN PETTY TRIO.

American Armed Services

Buddy took his physical in Amarillo around 1958 while *en route* to start a tour and came out with a 4F classification that permanently deferred him from call up for medical reasons.

Several years later the younger Allison and Mauldin were lucky enough to pass their physicals. Sadly in Jerry's case it made him miss one of The Crickets' early 1960s UK tours.

American Bandstand – TV Series

Famous, long-running US TV show hosted by Dick Clark that first put in a local appearance in 1952 but was not networked until 5th August 1957. In an interview taken from The Crickets' appearance on 28th October 1958 Buddy gets tongue-tied talking to Dick Clark explaining how the group were going to travel home separately after the show. The then unpublished news that The Crickets were in the process of splitting up makes the awkward moment understandable in retrospect. *The History of American Bandstand* book lists the tracks performed that day as 'Think It Over', 'Fool's Paradise' and 'Heartbeat', whilst the audible evidence points to 'It's So Easy' with 'Heartbeat' being performed the previous Saturday. (Despite this national exposure 'It's So Easy' never even made the Top 100 in the USA.)

Even earlier The Crickets made their US TV and *Bandstand* debut performing 'That'll Be The Day' on Monday, 26th August 1957; this date being just one week after the song topped the US charts.

There is no film extant of The Crickets appearing on *American Bandstand*, and the footage released on the 1986 Bandstand video is from the Arthur Murray TV programme in late 1957. See ARTHUR MURRAY PARTY entry.

American Graffiti – Film

This was the title of a celebrated 1973 film that was set in small-town America on a late summer night in 1962. It featured a minimum of live music but had a soundtrack of mainly 1950s rock'n'roll classics that translated into a brilliant soundtrack LP. Briefly a hit for MCA when released early 1974.

It was in the 1970s that records that were obviously by The Crickets began to be released as Buddy Holly, no doubt reflecting the fact that Holly's name was well on the way to assuming mythical status. It also made the recordings more identifiable to the musical public and helped separate Holly material from later Crickets' records.

Appearing in the film was the howling, prowling Wolfman Jack, one of America's last great rock DJs. (Sadly the Wolfman died suddenly in 1995 shortly after completing a routine programme.) The film dialogue of *American Graffiti* contained the memorable line that rock'n'roll music had been going downhill ever since Buddy Holly died. The phrase has since been enshrined in rock folklore and most scribes do indeed think of February 3rd 1959 as a musical watershed. On this theme see AMERICAN PIE entry.

'American Pie'

Don McLean wrote and recorded this eponymous track in 1971 and it's true to say that it catapulted him from relative obscurity to chart success in dramatic fashion. 'American Pie' is an eight-minute story in song that charts the path of rock music, using as its starting point the drama of Holly's death on 3rd February 1959 – yet at no point do the lyrics mention Buddy's name. Rock scribes have tried *ad nauseam* to analyse all the nuances contained in the song's lyrics.

In interviews at the time, and to this day, Don McLean has paid tribute to the genius of Holly, and the 'American Pie' album, which followed the single, was dedicated to the Texan. Don McLean certainly helped bring Holly's name back before the American public in the early 1970s when it was in danger of being forgotten.

Although McLean is a folk-related artist he has frequently interpreted Holly material and recorded excellent versions of 'Everyday', 'Maybe Baby', 'Fool's Paradise' and 'It Doesn't Matter Anymore'. The remainder of his material is invariably his own.

Don has appeared at a recent Clear Lake tribute concert reinforcing his links with Holly's name.

See brief biography under DON MCLEAN.

Ampex Tape Machine

Mention is often made in this text of the tape machine that Holly had at his New York flat and on which he taped around a dozen numbers in the last two months of his life. In fact it came from Norman Petty's studio and Buddy had obtained it when Norman decided to update his equipment. The point to be made is that it was not a domestic machine but virtual state-of-the-art hardware.

Carroll Anderson

Manager of the Surf Ballroom, Clear Lake, Iowa, the final venue for three artists on the ill-fated Winter Dance Party Tour. Anderson was the last person to see the artists alive after he drove them to the airport at nearby Mason City for the flight to Fargo, close to the border of North Dakota and Minnesota. The time of the crash is usually given as 1.07 a.m. on 3rd February. Certainly Anderson says the plane was gassed up and ready to fly at midnight.

Anderson had the distressing task of identifying the fatally injured occupants of the plane later that same day. Although the craft came down soon after take-off he was unaware of the crash till he awoke later that same morning. (Ironically it has been said that the crash took place close to the setting for the famed stage musical *The Music Man*.) Anderson stayed on as manager of the Surf till 1967 meeting up with Buddy's parents on several occasions when they went to visit the Surf Ballroom and the accident site.

See also entries under BEECHCRAFT BONANZA, CIVIL AERONAUTICS BOARD, JERRY DWYER and ROGER PETERSON.

Harvey Andrews

UK singer/songwriter who recorded a version of 'Learning The Game' in 1972 and wrote the tribute song 'Please Don't Get On That Plane' a few years later. Of its genre certainly one of the better examples probably because the song was 20 years in germination. One or two tribute discs were maudlin to say the least.

For this and other such titles see entry under TRIBUTE RECORDS.

'An Empty Cup'

The Crickets recording as a quartet. Cut on the road in Tinker Airforce Base, Oklahoma City, September 1957. Personnel: Buddy, Jerry, Joe and Niki Sullivan.

This Roy Orbison composition came Buddy's way via Roy's earlier association with Norman Petty at the Clovis, New Mexico studios, which is how Norman ends up with part-composer credits. Recorded by The Crickets whilst on tour with the mammoth Biggest Show of Stars for 1957 the boys had an enforced break in late September when the white acts on the bill were unable to appear in 'mixed' shows. Norman Petty, on tour nearby with his Trio at that time, was able to meet with the four Crickets and set up his recording equipment in the Officers' Club Lounge on the Airforce Base, in Oklahoma City, and this number, together with three other tracks, were cut. The Picks' voices were later overdubbed back in Clovis and the track duly appeared on The Crickets' first US album, 'The Chirping Crickets'. This masterly album with its superb front cover photo – said to have been taken on the roof of the Brooklyn Paramount Theatre – is often included in all-time 100 best album lists.

In the UK when Coral Records were desperately searching for something to release in 1964 following major Holly hits with 'Bo Diddley' and 'Brown-Eyed Handsome Man', and with other possible titles sidelined because of estate problems, they put out two of the Tinker recordings ('You've Got Love' was the flip) and the disc actually crept into the Top 40 singles chart.

Most Holly recordings have been covered time and time again but this one has hardly ever been. Certainly Holly's plaintive vocal could hardly be bettered. The Picks' vocal backings are either loved or loathed – see entry THE PICKS.

The Angelic Gospel Singers

Margaret Allison, Lucille Shird, Josephine McDowell and Ella Mae Norris.

This US gospel group came from the Deep South; their recording of 'I'll Be All Right' was a Holly favourite. He had a copy in his record collection, and the song was eventually played at his Lubbock funeral.

The number is heavily organ-based and its melody had been referred to as similar to 'True Love Ways'. But the similarity is tenuous and 'True Love Ways' does not really plagiarize the original. Buddy was particularly fond of what was at one time termed 'race music', and his influences are discussed under the heading INFLUENCES.

The Angelic Gospel Singers were well known for their down-home versions of old hymns and gospel tunes. These were sung to either organ or piano accompaniment and for a while in the early 1950s, they were popular artists, recording on both the Gotham and Nashboro labels.

Paul Anka

Born in Ottawa, Canada in July 1941, Paul Anka came to prominence in the 1950s when he penned and recorded the US No. 1 hit, 'Diana'. He continued to have occasional hits and his musical career continues to this day although it includes more and more production work. He is perhaps best known for coming up with the lyrics to a French melody and calling them 'My Way', which remains one of the biggest-selling songs of all time. A prodigious composer, he has written material that has been recorded by artists as diverse as Donny Osmond and Barbra Streisand.

He wrote 'It Doesn't Matter Anymore' for Holly, who included the tune in his last studio session at the Pythian Temple, New York on 21st October 1958. This session was the only one of Buddy's definitely to be recorded in a stereo format. (Although 'Early In The Morning' was reportedly cut in experimental stereo.)

Anka toured Australia in 1958 with The Crickets, Jerry Lee and Jodie Sands, on a bill that included Australian pop artist Johnny O'Keefe, who had a local hit with the part-penned 'Wild One', which was later to be retitled 'Real Wild Child'. Paul Anka and Buddy Holly formed quite a close musical friendship and it has even been said they would have paired up as a song-writing double act at some point. Both were certainly talented composers.

The only sour note concerning Paul Anka is that he has from time to time been quoted as saying he was touring with Holly at the time of the fatal crash. He wasn't. Jerry Naylor has also made a spurious claim to have been a Cricket, with Buddy Holly! See separate entry, JERRY NAYLOR and also 'IT DOESN'T MATTER ANYMORE'.

Apollo Theatre, New York

Virtually every famous black act has played the Apollo, in Harlem, New York at some point in their career. Famous way before the advent of rock'n'roll it nevertheless happily became a venue for rock package shows when they were the phenomenon of the moment in the mid 1950s.

The Crickets played there on the back of their first big hit ('That'll Be The Day') as part of a bill that comprised several major black acts of the day. The scene led years later to Jerry Allison and Tom Drake writing a screenplay, 'Not Fade Away', which nearly got off the ground in 1975. But the scenario of Holly and The Crickets playing the venue was used later to good dramatic effect in the screen biopic, *The Buddy Holly Story*. For the full story of how The Crickets got booked onto an all-black bill see entry NOT FADE AWAY – Film.

Whilst Buddy had strong country influences, such as Hank Williams and the Louvins, he also connected strongly with earthier blues material as performed by Tiny Bradshaw and Muddy Waters. Apart from looking at the INFLUENCES entry it is illuminating to read details of his own record collection under the appropriate heading.

Chet Atkins

One of the supreme country instrumentalists of all time who went on to become a highly respected Nashville producer and record company executive after his initial success as a solo guitarist and sought-after session man. To name-drop, Elvis used him in 1956.

Sonny Curtis quotes Buddy Holly as being a big fan of Chet's guitar playing technique although Buddy's own style was quite different.

Born 20th June 1924 in Tennessee, Atkins still works in the music business. In the 1990s he teamed up to record a superb country album with Mark Knopfler, who has his own connections with Holly. See entry MARK KNOPFLER.

George Atwood

George Atwood, like Tommy Allsup, is one of the unsung heroes of the Buddy Holly story. Seldom listed as a Cricket because he did not tour with the group he played bass on three memorable Holly recordings: 'Wishing', 'Love's Made A Fool Of You' and 'Heartbeat', but only the last of these was to be released in Holly's lifetime.

Born in Tuscaloosa, Alabama on 17th October 1920, he's currently in poor health and living in Jerome, Idaho. In the intervening 76 years he's packed a lifetime in the music and variety business, working with artists in the country, folk and jazz fields. Names that are most identifiable to us include Gene Krupa, the Dorsey Brothers, Norman Petty, Roy Orbison, Eddy Arnold and countless others. Many of the recordings on which Holly played as a session guitarist – mostly lead but sometimes rhythm – also featured George, who was based in West Texas for years.

It would take a book in itself to write George's full story, but the saddest thing to discover is that in January 1959 he had agreed to work with Buddy and others to help set up a new music studio in Lubbock. This project was being lined up for when Holly returned from the Winter Dance Party Tour. Indeed, George has outline plans of the recording complex in his possession and, in addition to rehearsal rooms, it was also planned to have the facility to record studio masters. Would a new musical centre have eventually grown up in the area? Sadly, it's impossible to guess what would have happened.

Australian Tour

The short tour of Australia in 1958 was the first time that Buddy Holly, Jerry Allison and Joe B. Mauldin ever left the continental USA. For Australians also it was one of their first glimpses of major rock'n'roll artists, so the effect on all concerned was quite far reaching. Fan worship has existed down under ever since.

The rock troupe that made the trip comprised of Paul Anka, The Crickets, Jerry Lee Lewis, Jodie Sands, and they were joined by local act Johnny O'Keefe, whose backing group were the Dee Days. British-born Frank Ifield, who emigrated to Australia at an early age, has been quoted as saying he guested on one of the bills and that made him a lifelong fan of Buddy and the boys. Altogether 10 concerts were performed in a 6-day visit.

Australia in the late 1950s was only just appearing on the show-biz map, and it has been extremely disappointing that hardly any archive material has surfaced by way of photo, film, or in audio format. Searches have taken place but it now seems unlikely that anything significant will turn up. In Britain and Australia during the 1950s cameras and tape recorders were still somewhat scarce.

A reasonable-quality interview with Australian DJ Pat Barton has circulated, as have a handful of photos. To the author's knowledge, there is not much else.

For information on other overseas visits see entries HAWAII and UK TOUR.

Automobiles

Perhaps it's of minor interest what vehicles Buddy owned.... So drive on to the next entry if you wish. But mention has been made of at least six or seven different models which seems pretty incredible given the brief timespan involved.

However, Buddy started early, by borrowing and denting his parents' autos. His first car was believed to be a black and white 1955 Oldsmobile, although stories that this was a graduation present seem wishful thinking. Other early vehicles, mentioned by brother Larry, are a 1951 red Cadillac and a Chevrolet – exact models not known. Tinker Carlen also remembers Buddy's father having an old Hudson Hornet for years.

At the time of the last Crickets tour, which ended in October 1958, the group were using a yellow De Soto station-wagon whilst Holly was driving a 1958 Cadillac that he was to keep till the end of his life. He had evidently traded in a Lincoln Continental in acquiring the Caddy.

Perhaps loosely under this heading we can mention the Aerial Cyclone motorbike that Buddy purchased in 1958 when he had just come off a tour. The bike was eventually used by Buddy's father, Lawrence, before ending up being purchased by The Crickets and presented to Waylon Jennings. Further details for bike 'nuts' are given under the heading MOTOR CYCLES.

As a postscript to the above, whilst Buddy Holly never got to own a British vehicle, Jerry, Joe B. and Buddy paid a visit to the Austin Motors factory when in the UK on their 1958 tour. This fact is hardly surprising as Buddy was a fan of speed and had apparently also started flying lessons back home in Texas with the help of brother Larry.

Frankie Avalon

Born Francis Avallone in Philadelphia in 1939, he sprang to fame at age 17 with two Top 10 US hits during 1958. He toured with Holly twice that year on an Everly Brothers' bill and in the Biggest Show of Stars, Autumn Edition and joined the 1959 Winter Dance Party Tour, along with Jimmy Clanton and Ronnie Smith, after the fatal crash took out three of the main headliners. He later went on to make a series of beach movies in the 1960s.

Buddy evidently once remarked to the singer 'Frank, I got to confess I bought only one of your records, "De De Dinah", and that's because it's dee-dee-darned good!' Now, Buddy once said he was a better comedian than Des O'Connor and I'll leave the reader to be the judge on the above flimsy evidence. Alternatively you could read the DES O'CONNOR entry.

Avalon was never a big artist in the UK but he had a string of US hits and strangely, his first US No.1, 'Venus', entered the US charts exactly one week after the Winter Dance Party Tour ended.

He is one of the artists from the 1950s who still looks well preserved and has carried on with a show business career ever since.

B

'Baby I Don't Care'

Recorded at Norman Petty Studios, Clovis, New Mexico, 19th December 1957. Personnel: Buddy Holly, Jerry and Joe.

Jerry Leiber and Mike Stoller wrote this song for the 1957 Elvis movie *Jailhouse Rock*. Jerry Allison has mentioned that the track was one of Eddie Cochran's favourites and that was one reason why they decided to record it when seeking material to complete the first solo album.

Its release in the UK was as an album track on the 'Buddy Holly' LP Coral LVA 9085, where it was listed as 'You're So Square'. It had reverted to the correct title for its 1961 UK single release and it became a sizeable hit, which is surprising considering the modest publicity that surrounded virtually all Holly's posthumous Coral releases over here.

We know that Buddy was heavily influenced by Elvis and this

number is one of seven Presley recordings that Holly either tried commercially or covered as a demo. Buddy's version of 'Baby I Don't Care' is terrific. Play it now and marvel again at the fact that Jerry Allison's drumming is courtesy of a cardboard box! An example of Buddy and the group experimenting to get exactly the sound they required. Vi Petty is listed as playing piano on the track but any piano sounds are negligible.

An overdubbed version with The Picks' added backing vocals was released in the 1980s. See entry THE PICKS.

'Baby It's Love'

Buddy and Bob performance at radio station KDAV, circa 1954–5.

One of a clutch of demo recordings from the Buddy and Bob era that would certainly not have been released commercially were it not for the events of 3rd February 1959. As it was this track and other duets were released in the UK on the 'Holly In The Hills' album in 1965, and such was Holly's popularity here that the album spent six weeks in the charts. (The odd track out of the UK release was the plaintive 'Wishing', a demo dating from much later.)

It is difficult to establish from the dubbed mono release what has been obscured. Undubbed, the original with Sonny Curtis still audible on fiddle, probably sounded more country. Buddy's mother is listed as part-composer on this track but it is rumoured that it was really penned by a J. Fautheree.

Incidentally, undubbed tapes of some 'Holly in the Hills' material do exist but it remains to be seen whether they will be released. Some tracks have appeared on a CD box set, 'What You Been A-Missin'' but not this particular one. 'Baby It's Love' was also one of three titles not included on the US 'Holly in the Hills' album.

'Baby Let's Play House'

Buddy and Bob recording, Nesman studio, Wichita Falls, Texas, 7th June 1955.

As with 'Baby It's Love', this track first surfaced on the UK 'Holly In The Hills' album but it is much more out and out rock'n'roll with Holly on solo vocals. Recorded in mid 1955, Elvis had waxed his version on 5th February of that year, the original on Excello being by the blues singer, Arthur Gunter. When the Holly version first came out it

15

Buddy pictured at a neighbour's birthday party in Lubbock, Texas. (Courtesy of Bill Griggs.)

was given the title 'I Wanna Play House With You', and the country artist, Cy Coben, was listed as penning it. This was corrected on the later MCA box set release. If Gunter did pinch the melody, Johnny Burnette also used it and called it 'Oh Baby Babe' on one of his earliest recordings.

The Holly recording is quite dynamic despite being from a worn acetate and ought to be heard much more often. Deservedly it made an appearance on the excellent Charly double album, 'Buddy Holly Rocks' several years back. The overdubbing is courtesy of The Fireballs on this and on 'Down The Line', which were cut at the same Wichita Falls session. The undubbed version came out in 1995 as part of a box set on the Vigotone label.

'Baby Won't You Come Out Tonight'

Demo made at Norman Petty Studios, Clovis, New Mexico, February–April 1956. Personnel: Buddy, Sonny (lead guitar), Don Guess and Jerry Allison.

Probably written by Buddy and recorded as a demo several times during late 1955 and early 1956. The released version was recorded in 1956 at Clovis but did not surface in the UK until April 1963. Not surprisingly it had been overdubbed by Norman Petty using The Fireballs to create a stereo master.

Sources indicate the track's alternative title is 'Moonlight Baby' although such a phrase does not actually form part of the lyrics! In 1983 Steve Hoffman, then of MCA records, was instrumental in putting out an album of mainly early material that included this track in its pure unadulterated and undubbed mono format. Incidentally, although Holly is listed as composer, Don Guess (see entry), who played bass on the session, used to receive composer royalties. The Buddy Holly songbook has been nothing if not complicated in its time.

In the event that a definitive box set of Holly/Crickets material comes out, then tracks such as an unreleased version of this song – which does exist – would be a natural for inclusion.

Holly was relegated to playing rhythm guitar on this track. A fairly usual occurrence when Sonny was included in the group.

Hank Ballard and the Midnighters

Buddy's brother Larry remembers Holly performing Ballard's 'Sexy Ways' in public, and his own composition 'Rock a bye Rock' possibly bears a passing resemblance to the number. Also, at the very first Nashville session that Buddy undertook, 'Midnight Shift' was recorded and although not a Ballard composition it is definitely a derivative of Ballard's Annie songs.

No one would deny that Holly was one of the most creative of rock'n'roll's innovators but his guitar intro. on 'That'll Be The Day' seems to be almost totally lifted from the Midnighters' 'Switchie Witchie Twitchie'.

All that the above proves is that each and every artist is subject to a multitude of influences, whether or not they are conscious of the fact. Buddy was certainly a fan of Hank Ballard as can be readily heard.

Dean Barlow and the Crickets

Grover 'Dean' Barlow was lead voice of The Crickets. Confused? Well, any self-respecting Holly/Crickets fan knows that the 'other' Crickets were a R & B group from the early 1950s and had no connection with the later hit parade group. But it's a coincidence that there was a black version of The Crickets as Buddy and Jerry had been inspired to

A youthful Buddy Holly aged approximately 13. It was about this time he made a home recording of 'My Two-Timin' Woman'. (Courtesy of Bill Griggs.)

choose the name because of their admiration for The Spiders, a black group who had a record called 'Witchcraft' in the R&B charts.

According to the album sleeve, 'The Crickets' on Jay Dee 5040, their producer Joe Davis earned a considerable cash settlement from the Texan group because of the latter's use of the title The Crickets. This is an intriguing point, but with manager Norman Petty long dead it's unlikely to ever be confirmed.

Anyone with wide musical tastes should seek out recordings by the Dean Barlow/Crickets group. A million miles away from any definition of a Tex-mex sound, they are, nevertheless, very listenable indeed.

John Barry

John Barry Prendergast was born in York on 3rd November 1933 and is a trumpet player, pianist, bandleader and composer. But older fans remember him fronting the John Barry Seven, who began to make their mark in the UK just as rock'n'roll was on the wane.

He used a pizzicato effect on early Adam Faith hits, which he unashamedly based on Holly's string recording of 'It Doesn't Matter Anymore'. In fact, Barry recorded the number himself on his 1961 'Stringbeat' album before moving into the wide world of film scores and eventually relocating to the USA. See entry ADAM FAITH.

The Beach Boys

Probably the most famous of all US bands who came together and played their first major gig at a Ritchie Valens Memorial Dance in Los Angeles, Christmas 1961.

There are obviously not too many links with the Holly legend but the boys did record an excellent cover of 'Peggy Sue' for their 'M.I.U.' album back in 1978, and this also came out as a single. Even earlier in 1966 they had courted 'Peggy Sue' within the lyrics of 'Barbara Ann', which they took to No.2 in the Billboard charts eclipsing The Regents' 1961 recording, which stalled outside the Top 10.

The Beach Boys and the post-Holly Crickets both appeared in a mid 1960s Surfing film *Girls on the Beach*.

Some 30 years on and both groups still retain their popularity and constantly perform.

The Beatles

The Beatles' choice of name was influenced by that of The Crickets, while their early songwriting style was partly inspired by the writing of Holly and his group. There is a lengthy entry under Holly's name in Virgin's *Ultimate Beatles Encyclopaedia*, which spells out several connections between the two groups.

The Beatles' most commercial Holly recording was 'Words of Love', which is a fairly faithful copy of the original. Earlier they had made a private recording of 'That'll Be The Day', which was finally released as part of their 'Anthology' project. In their German period the Beatles had recorded 'live' versions of 'Reminiscing' and 'Crying, Waiting, Hoping'.

Older Holly fans may recall reading in the musical press, *circa* 1968, that The Beatles had ordered a complete set of the MCA MUPS series of Holly's recordings. Earlier, in 1963, The Beatles had sent a congratulatory telegram to the post-Holly Crickets group, who were enjoying a successful second career and continuing to tour.

To old guard rock'n'roll fans it seems somewhat ironic that The Crickets would cover Beatles material but they did so around 1964 when several Beatles numbers were included on their US 'California Sun' LP. A knowledgeable American critic even accused The Crickets of pinching their name from The Beatles! See also entries JOHN LENNON and PAUL McCARTNEY.

19

'Because I Love You'

Demo made at Norman Petty Studios, Clovis, New Mexico, February–April 1956. Personnel: probably Holly, Sonny Curtis, Don Guess and Jerry Allison.

A plaintive ballad that was recorded as a demo in Clovis in early 1956 and which saw its first release seven years on as part of the 'Reminiscing' LP. The album had a long stay in the LP charts and the cover photo was worth the purchase price alone. (For any rare individual who does not have the original sleeve it is a silhouette of Buddy's head against the backdrop of an aeroplane window. The picture had been snapped by Norman Petty when *en route* to Australia.)

The released track was overdubbed under the guidance of Petty and this created a stereo master thus helping aficionados to sort out what instrumentation had been added. 'Because I Love You' was later released undubbed and more recently with additional backing vocals by The Picks.

The song itself is a much underrated Holly composition that has seldom received any attention. A minor coincidence is that Buddy's partner Bob Montgomery (see entry) recorded the same title, different song, in Clovis for a release on Brunswick.

Beechcraft Bonanza

The 10-year-old, red and white, four-seat light aeroplane chartered from Dwyer's Flying Service, registration number N.3794N that was totally demolished shortly after taking off from Mason City airport, Iowa, *en route* to Fargo, North Dakota, 3rd February 1959. Aboard were Buddy Holly (22), The Big Bopper (28), Ritchie Valens (17) and pilot Roger Peterson (21).

For further information see under CIVIL AERONAUTICS BOARD, JERRY DWYER and ROGER PETERSON.

John Beecher

John Beecher is *the* name linked with that of Buddy Holly in UK circles, where he has always been in the vanguard of those fans who have championed Holly's talent at every opportunity. He founded the first UK appreciation society in the early 1960s and did much pioneer work at a difficult time. The media's attitude was generally against the concept of running a fan club for a dead singer. The famous newspaper headline was 'We give the cult 5 years'.

He now heads up Rollercoaster Records, which is his main occupation within the music field. Has had ongoing links with The Crickets over the years and even co-produced their great 1978 single 'Cruise In It'.

Born in 1944, he is fit and well, living and working in rural Gloucestershire.

Chuck Berry

Born Charles Edward Berry, 18th October 1926 in Missouri, Chuck is one of the major figures in 1950s rock'n'roll who is still doing his thing on the verge of 70. He has bounced back from adversity more than once and his place in rock's Hall of Fame is guaranteed both as a performer and as the first poet of rock'n'roll. If he is occasionally criticized for attempting little outside his original songbook the thought has to be 'What a songbook!'

Mention is often made in passing that, when touring, Holly and Berry used to shoot craps together. Certainly Joe Mauldin has been quoted as having very fond memories of Chuck Berry, who was always ready to help in those far-off days. It all seems a far cry from the usual reclusive picture that is painted of Chuck.

Usually, singer-songwriters perform definitive versions of their own compositions, but Holly's demo version of 'Brown-Eyed Handsome Man' rocks and flows far better than Berry's original. Buddy Holly occasionally performed Chuck Berry material on stage but did not record anything of Chuck's apart from the demo mentioned above.

Mike Berry

Mike Berry, real name Michael Bourne, is an ultra-talented singer who has added acting to his repertoire to build a lengthy show business career. He has had two far-flung bursts of chart success spanning nearly 20 years from the 1960s into the 1980s, which got him an honourable mention in Guinness Hit Singles books. In an earlier incarnation he had been Kenny Lord and the Statesman cutting 'Peggy Sue Got Married' as a demo for Joe Meek.

Over the years Holly's vocal style has attracted many copycat artists but none has got closer to the timbre or feel than Mike Berry. Added to that is Mike's known sincerity, which has been there ever since he first auditioned 'Tribute To Buddy Holly' for Holly fans prior to its 1961 release (it also got a US Coral release but wasn't a hit).

Mike's 1985 recording of Lee Jackson's 'Holly' deserved chart success but sadly didn't get enough exposure. Earlier he had re-recorded 'Tribute To Buddy Holly' for the outstanding 'Rock In My Head' album, which allowed him to brush up the lyrics and jettison that irritating opening line 'The snow was snowing …'.

Always happy to remain associated with Holly's name he has recorded much of Buddy Holly's catalogue over the years.

See also SOUNDALIKES heading.

The Big Bopper (J.P. Richardson)

He lost his life in an Iowa cornfield alongside Buddy Holly, Ritchie Valens and the plane's pilot, Roger Peterson. While Holly's wife miscarried, The Bopper's widow produced a son, Jay Perry, a few months after the crash.

The Big Bopper was born Jiles Perry Richardson Junior in Sabine Pass, Texas on 24th October 1930 and one can avoid later dates which are sometimes quoted. He was 28 years old at the time of the Winter Dance Party Tour and, therefore, old in comparison with some rock'n'rollers whilst seemingly youthful alongside the likes of Bill Haley and Joe Turner.

JP had started out as a DJ on Radio KTRM in Beaumont, Texas and was a programme director by the time he was released to tour and cash in on his monster hit 'Chantilly Lace'. He had used his Big Bopper persona from a fairly early date and in his DJ work but initial discs came out with the description, Jape Richardson and the Japetts on Pappy Daily's D label. 'Beggar To A King' (1957) was one such release, but as early as 1954 Richardson had produced a Bopper-type demo 'Boogie Woogie' in Jay Miller's Louisiana studios. Other recordings from that time remain unissued.

The Big Bopper's recordings, which were leased to Mercury, were well produced with first-class fidelity. The music still jumps out of the speakers, like a rock'n'roll version of Phil Harris. (Curiously, both artists recorded versions of 'The Preacher and the Bear'.) Of the twenty or so recordings left by the Bopper, virtually all were his own

The Big Bopper pictured backstage, January 1959, just days before his final concert. (Courtesy of Timothy D. Kerr.)

compositions. He can also be heard to good effect on the answer record by Donna Dameron, 'Bopper 486609', which was held back for release until October 1959. Exactly one year after his death his voice was on the UK hit parade courtesy of his backing grunts to his friend Johnny Preston's big hit, 'Running Bear'.

Although most of Richardson's composition were novelty items he also composed two classic numbers 'White Lightning' and 'Beggar To A King', both country hits for George Jones. In the USA a book came out by Tim Knight cataloguing the Big Bopper's career in words and pictures for in many ways his story was every bit as tragic as that of Holly and the youthful Valens.

Musically the world lost three stars in the early hours of 3rd February 1959.

Blind Faith

One of the shortest-lived supergroups of the 1960s, who comprised of Steve Winwood, Eric Clapton, Ginger Baker and Rick Grech. They recorded a powerful version of Holly's 'Well … All Right', which has cropped up on occasional compilations over the years.

Grech, who died relatively early in 1990 at age 44, was also a member of The Crickets for a few years. See entries RICH GRECH and also ERIC CLAPTON.

'Blue Days, Black Nights'

First Nashville session at Bradley's Barn, Nashville, 26th January 1956.
Personnel: Buddy, Sonny Curtis (lead guitar), Don Guess and Nashville session men.

The obscure 1956 UK Brunswick 45 of 'Blue Days, Black Nights' / 'Love Me' is worth considerably more than the handful of fans remember paying for it aeons ago. £100 might open the bidding. The rarity lies in it being Holly's first release in both the UK and the USA, and it was to be a further year or so before we heard of Holly's name, and even then only as one of a quartet.

From the first Nashville session the track features a prominent, sharp-edged lead guitar performed by Sonny Curtis and with Holly's warm vocal it is one of his better and more underrated performances.

The song was written by singer/songwriter Ben Hall for Buddy with the idea that it would produce his first hit. Instead it failed to make any impact outside of getting played on a few local jukeboxes. Ben Hall himself cut the original country demo around 1955 and it is available on a Rollercoaster CD entitled 'Hep Cats from Big Springs'.

None of the three Nashville sessions led to any overdubbing so we hear the track the way it was put down. The exception is a 1984 version with backing voices added by The Picks. See separate entry under their name for general comments on those performances.

'Blue Monday'

Practice tape. Recorded in Lubbock, late 1956. Personnel: Buddy, Jerry Allison and others unknown.

This number was first recorded by Smiley Lewis in 1953 but failed to make any impact. Later it became a major US hit for Fats Domino in January 1957 having been performed by him in the film *The Girl Can't Help It* just a few months earlier. Holly's performance dates from that time and is very much a home-type version, although probably recorded at a small local studio in Lubbock. As with 'Ain't Got No Home' it was first released in 1969 as part of the 'Giant' album, heavily overdubbed under Norman Petty's direction. Comparing that stereo release with the later undubbed mono release on Rollercoaster Records reveals how comprehensive the instrumentation is on this particular track. In most cases the undubbed recordings are superior but in the case of 'Blue Monday' the drumming is overwhelming although only Buddy and Jerry performed on the demo.

Holly was a big fan of his fellow artist Fats Domino and whilst it is frustrating that he did not make a fully commercial recording of 'Blue Monday', he did fortunately record another Domino/Bartholomew composition 'Valley of Tears' as part of his first solo album. It was a deserved double-sided hit in 1961, spending 14 weeks in the charts.

'Blue Monday' by Fats was so distinctive that covers seemed non-existent at the time. It is surprising to note that 10 cover versions of it are listed in the 1990 book *Who Sang What in Rock'n'Roll*. Amongst the 10 was the latterday Crickets version for their 1962 album, 'Something Old etc.', which is quite listenable but still pales in comparison with the Fats Domino recording. As does the Holly demo.

'Blue Suede Shoes'

Practice tape. Recorded late 1956 in Lubbock. Personnel: Buddy, Jerry Allison and others unknown.

It is an amazing fact that Carl Perkins's 'Blue Suede Shoes' was his one and only US Top 40 record, yet several decades later, he remains one of the great legends of rock'n'roll. The fact that The Beatles recorded several of his numbers is ample testament to his songwriting ability.

Buddy's version is frantic and it was a tune he frequently used on the bandstand in live performances. Dubbed or undubbed the track does not do Holly justice but it is still good to hear early Holly performances of classic rock'n'roll numbers such as this and 'Rip It Up' even if the technical quality of the tapes is poor.

'Bo Diddley'

Hit version recorded as demo/practice tape, Norman Petty Studios, Clovis, New Mexico, December 1956 (approximately). Personnel: Buddy, Jerry Allison and Larry Welborn (bass); unknown second guitar.

1963 was the year that Holly's posthumous career was reactivated and 'Bo Diddley' was a Top 5 entry in June having been released as a follow up to his earlier hit, 'Brown-Eyed Handsome Man'.

No need to list composer credits on this track and Buddy's hit version was recorded at Clovis in 1957 although with heavy overdubbing later by The Fireballs, a hit instrumental group in their own right. This helped create a stereo master. The undubbed mono version sounded a bit sparse without the lead guitar riff and came out on the Steve Hoffman-inspired MCA album, 'For the First Time Anywhere' in 1983. (The album incorrectly lists the recording date as 1955.)

Another, much looser, version of 'Bo Diddley' was recorded in Lubbock by Buddy as a demo a month or two earlier and makes for interesting comparison. Buddy calls out break time to drummer Jerry Allison midway through what is very much a rehearsal-type track. Dedicated fans should endeavour to seek out this hard-to-find original version on the 'Something Special' LP on Rollercoaster. See also BO DIDDLEY, artist.

Marc Bolan

Legendary rock artist born Mark Feld in 1947, who died as the result of a car accident at the early age of 30 and who, like Holly, was largely unfulfilled in career terms at the time.

Ironically, a celebratory pin of 'Everyday is a Holly day' was found in the demolished vehicle. Bolan died 16th September 1977 and has achieved remarkable posthumous popularity after he too sadly made what reluctantly turns out to be the right career move.

Pat Boone

Born Charles Eugene Patrick Boone in Florida 1934, the singer is a direct descendant of frontiersman Daniel Boone and had numerous US hits in the early days of his career (1955 to 1962). He seldom gets a good press when mentioned in rock literature mainly because his earliest recordings were felt to be sanitized version of the earthier originals by others such as Little Richard and Fats Domino.

A cutting remark of Holly's allegedly made in 1957 was that Pat should be in the background on records making the doowop sounds! That humorous but rather flippant remark was surely not meant to be taken too literally. Pat Boone was a stylish vocalist who added his own small contribution to the panoply of rock'n'roll. (But having listened again to Boone's version of Domino's 'The Fat Man' perhaps Holly had a point!)

There is little to connect Holly and Boone, although they were 1950s contemporaries. Pat Boone recorded a decent version of 'That'll Be The Day' on his 'Great! Great Great!' album in the 1960s. The two singers were really coming at rock'n'roll from opposite directions and, of course, Pat Boone rarely got involved on the composing front.

In the 1970s Boone, who had been raised in Nashville, Tennessee from an early date, tried his hand at country music but with limited success. Later his daughter Debbie Boone began a successful country career while Pat moved on into the gospel field. (Goodness knows there were genuine country links, with Pat's late father-in-law being legendary country star Red Foley.)

Jimmy Bowen

Remembered by rock'n'roll fans as a founder of the Rhythm Orchids with Buddy Knox and Donnie Lanier both Knox and Bowen had simultaneous Roulette releases that shot up the US hit parade in 1957. But Knox ('Party Doll') got to No.1 whereas Bowen reached No.14 ('I'm Stickin' With You').

Both artists used Clovis and knew Holly well in the 1950s. Jimmy Bowen was the one who soon moved behind the microphone and ended up a business executive, and most music fans know what became of the two Buddys. Bowen has worked with hundreds of artists and even ended up signing Sonny Curtis to Elektra in the 1970s.

Apart from heading up Liberty Records he became famous for producing and managing the career of Hank Williams Junior. (Bowen has become very hirsute and a party piece is for Hank and him to exchange monogrammed baseball hats at Nashville functions and fool their friends as to who's who!)

Buddy Holly and Bowen met up in New York shortly before the fateful final tour and it's pretty certain the two would have teamed up if fate had been kinder. Bowen was born in Santa Rita, New Mexico in September 1937 and has ended up as an influential figure on the country music scene.

The Bowman Brothers

A quartet of brothers who emanated from Hall County in the Lone Star State and for several years did a lot of recording in Norman's Clovis studio. Although they never backed Holly in his solo work they did all appear together on several recordings where Buddy played lead guitar and the Bowmans performed backing vocals. Details of when Buddy played as session artist are scattered in entries throughout this book.

27

The group eventually had national releases on both the Dot and Columbia labels. Buddy's father, L.O. Holly, also helped produce them for a while after Holly's death. Coincidentally, there is a country comedian who hails from Lubbock and who knew Buddy – Don Bowman – but he is not related to the brothers.

David Box

This has to be one of the saddest entries in this book as David Box lost his life in circumstances uncannily similar to his inspiration, Buddy Holly, while flying near Houston on 23rd October 1964, shortly after completing a gig in nearby Harris County. The very next day he was due to fly to Nashville for a recording session.

Born Harold David Box in Sulphur Springs, Texas on 11th August 1943, he actually got to record with The Crickets in 1960 on his 17th birthday, when he did lead vocals on the back-to-back tracks 'Peggy Sue Got Married' and 'Don'tcha Know'. This was the group's last Coral single and, disappointingly, was not a hit. I remember the great difficulty I had in purchasing the disc, as well-intentioned record shop staff insisted the recording was by Buddy Holly! (His version was still out and had been a modest hit in late 1959.)

His life has been well researched by well-known Holly scribe John Ingman. David Box deserves to be remembered, and some of his recordings do crop up on occasion. (An excellent compilation containing several of his tracks remains in catalogue on Rollercoaster: 'Hep Cats from Big Springs'.) Box never had any national hits but some of his recordings made the Top 10 in the Houston area and he was a first-rate vocalist who, like his idol, wrote much of his own material.

It's a pity his name is not better known.

Owen Bradley

The legendary Nashville producer whose association with artists reads like a Who's Who of country music. Born in Westmoreland, Tennessee in 1915, his work really started back in 1947, and although now retired as staff producer with MCA, he continued producing independently until recently. Having originally produced Patsy Cline, he had the weird sensation in 1981 of producing her two 'duets' with the late country great Jim Reeves. Earlier in 1975 he had been elected to the Country Music Hall of Fame.

He was Holly's first real producer when he had overall

responsibility for three sessions that Buddy cut for US Decca in January, July and November of 1956 at Bradley's studio in Nashville. Certainly the sessions were not a commercial success but the acrimony portrayed in the celluloid movie was pure Hollywood. The music itself was not at all bad and deserves a special, if small, niche in the history of rockabilly.

It is often forgotten that Owen Bradley had a major hit with his combo in 1958 with 'White Silver Sands'. If he hated rock'n'roll he hid it well when he cut an excellent set of instrumentals such as 'Raunchy', 'Big Guitar' and others. A musician, producer and Nashville executive, Owen Bradley is a highly talented individual.

Traditionally all Holly's Nashville sessions are listed as taking place in Bradley's Barn but some sources indicate that the Barn itself didn't come into operation until several years after those 1956 sessions. Earlier, Owen's premises were what has been described as a Quonset hut that was situated nearby. Academic really. What is important is that Buddy Holly got to Nashville and put down those 12 tracks! For further details, see THE NASHVILLE SESSIONS.

Delaney Bramlett

Bramlett was born in Randolph, Mississippi on 1st July 1939. Best known in the 1970s as leader of Delaney and Bonnie (Bramlett), who exploded on the rock scene but quickly became a spent force and went their separate ways.

Delaney was friendly with guitar great Eric Clapton and both joined with members of The Crickets to help out on their Barnaby album 'Rockin' 50s Rock'n'Roll'. He just sneaks in as an honorary Cricket.

'Brown-Eyed Handsome Man'

Hit version recorded as demo/practice tape. Norman Petty Studios, Clovis, New Mexico, December 1956. Personnel: Buddy, Jerry Allison and Larry Welborn (bass); unknown other.

As with the 'Bo Diddley' track, Buddy cut two versions of this Chuck Berry number within months of one another. The earlier, weaker version was a demo recorded in Lubbock late 1956 during which Buddy briefly forgets the words it was not released until the 1980s, on a

Rollercoaster album. The hit version (overdubbed) was recorded in Clovis and the main lead guitar line is Holly's own. It is arguable that the undubbed version (on 'For The First Time Anywhere' LP) could have been a hit, as originally performed. That most certainly would not have been the case with the 'Bo Diddley' track, which, undubbed, lacked the strong guitar hook.

'Brown-Eyed Handsome Man' was the second-biggest solo hit for Holly reaching No. 3 in 1963 and no doubt helped the 'Reminiscing' album, which featured the single, to get to No. 2 and spend almost the rest of the year in the UK album charts.

A copy version is seldom better than the original (and as a demo Holly's was not a copy as such), but Holly's hit version is arguably better than Berry's original, which was the B side of 'Too Much Monkey Business' and not one of Chuck's strongest recordings.

'Handsome Man' is a good example of the music Buddy and the boys performed live in the early days and it's good to have the performance captured for all time on disc.

As a footnote it is worth mentioning that Waylon Jennings (see entry) took the number to No. 5 in the country charts back in 1969.

Dave Brubeck

Born in California in 1920, Brubeck was an innovative, white US jazz pianist whose career stretches back to the 1950s and who is still on the scene some forty years later. He fronted the Dave Brubeck Quartet and had a run of hits in the UK in the 1960s, the most famous of which was 'Take 5'. Pictures of Brubeck from that date show him wearing heavy framed glasses.

Allegedly he had a little-reported friendship with Holly, who he said was very knowledgeable on the modern jazz scene. Brubeck supposedly visited Buddy backstage at the Palladium in March 1958 when he stopped off from an extensive world tour. It must have been quite a horn-rimmed occasion.

Brubeck was reportedly shattered by Holly's death and in a 1962 interview bemoaned the fact that they never got to record together. All this seems rather unlikely, however, and the links between Holly and Brubeck have not been corroborated, and seem somewhat embroidered.

In 1994, *Holly International* editor Jim Carr contacted Brubeck, who seemed not to recall the meeting! It is possible that the story could refer to the bespectacled jazz artist Paul Desmond who just happened to be a member of Brubeck's quartet at that time. Paul Desmond died a few years back.

Buddy – The Musical

The worldwide hit musical opened in the West End of London on 12th October 1989 and bookings are being taken through into the next century. Written by Alan Janes, partly as an antidote to the film biography, the musical still manipulates the story a touch, but all is forgiven in what can only be described as a glorious celebration of Holly's musical legend that is designed to have mass appeal – which it certainly does. Bruce Welch of The Shadows was hired as musical consultant and a high level of musicianship has been evident since the show's inception.

At one time or another Joe B., Jerry, Vi Petty and Maria Elena have all been and seen the musical. It must have been a strange experience to see themselves as virtual characters in a play.

Versions of the musical have now been exported to various parts of the world and it has certainly played its part in keeping the name of Buddy Holly alive as the 20th century ebbs away.

Buddy and Bob

This was an early formation (*circa* 1953) that comprised of Buddy Holley (as spelt at that time), Bob Montgomery and Larry Welborn. The latter was later to become a member of the Four Teens. (See separate entry). Buddy, Bob and Larry performed at functions and on Radio KDAV prior to Buddy getting his big chance to record in Nashville. On one notable occasion in 1955 they got onto a local bill headed by Bill Haley, which helped Buddy's embryonic career no end.

The group's calling card at that time used the descriptive phrase 'Western and Bop' – which is a pretty good summary of the facts. Most of the music they performed in 1954–5 is taken from local radio broadcasts or rehearsals. An album full of Buddy and Bob material came out as 'Holly In The Hills' in 1965. On reflection it's a great pity the album was not released as performed by Buddy and Bob. The LP is quite homogeneous except for the mysterious inclusion of 'Wishing', although it was probably added because composer credits include Montgomery's name. (But see comments under 'Wishing' on this point.)

The group were a legal entity for a time with Hipockets Duncan as manager but they ceased to exist once Buddy went to Nashville. In 1995 several Buddy and Bob recordings finally surfaced undubbed on a Vigotone four-CD box-set.

Buddy and Jack

In 1952 (even before Buddy and Bob) Buddy teamed up briefly as a duo with a Lubbock youngster, Jack Neal, and they performed without great success on a local TV talent show. The performance was much in the style of the Everlys we are told, and included country material such as Hank Williams' 'Wedding Bells' with some gospel numbers thrown in. Evidently Buddy played lead guitar and did harmony vocals while Jack sang and was on rhythm guitar.

Later Jack was replaced by Bob Montgomery and the group became Buddy and Bob. Jack Neal eventually left the music business but retained connections and, surprisingly, made his first commercial recording as late as 1980.

He is not known to be playing on any released Buddy Holly material but he did record two demos, which, he states, feature Buddy on guitar.

See also JACK NEAL entry.

'Buddy Holly'

UK Album: CORAL LVA 9085.

The only solo album issued in this country in the singer's lifetime it came out in July 1958 when Holly and The Crickets were at the absolute peak of their career. The solo aspect was basically an irrelevance as both Jerry, Joe and occasionally Niki are on the recordings. The release coincided with 'Rave On' entering the charts whilst 'Maybe Baby' was on the way out.

Of the album's 12 tracks only 5 had been released at that point, and the remainder were probably recorded with an album release in mind. The album was surely a big seller although national charts weren't compiled until November 1958, by which time sales had no doubt begun to level off.

The sleeve of the album had a colour photograph of the singer *sans* glasses – an image that was to be short-lived. The disc itself stated modestly: Buddy Holly with instrumental accompaniment. For fans of the era the 'Buddy Holly' album was and is an absolute classic.

LISTING: I'm Gonna Love You Too / Peggy Sue / Listen To Me / Look At Me / Valley Of Tears / Ready Teddy / Everyday / Mailman Bring Me No More Blues / Words Of Love / Baby I Don't Care / Rave On / Little Baby

*A rare publicity shot of Buddy Holly – without his glasses – taken in 1957.
(Courtesy of Bill Griggs.)*

'The Buddy Holly Story', Volumes 1 and 2

UK albums: Coral LVA 9105 and 9127.

The original memorial album was available for years after its 1959 release and by 1970 had sold one million copies resulting in Buddy's parents receiving a gold disc. The LP is still well placed on the list of all-time UK chart albums, having reached No. 2 behind the massive-selling 'South Pacific' soundtrack.

The sleeve notes for both US and UK releases were penned by Ren Grevatt of the *Music Business* magazine. Four years later he was to write similar respectful sleeve notes for a Patsy Cline album that followed her death in yet another light plane crash.

The distinctive black and white cover of the first album was a portrait from the final set of publicity photos taken by Bruno of New York. Record collectors should also look out for an alternate cover of the album sleeve. For a short period in the 1960s a fuller face photo was used, which made the album quite collectable.

Although not a greatest hits package as such, the LP included a couple of superb B sides amongst its listing. In 1960 Volume 2 was issued in a colour sleeve complete with touching sleeve notes by Buddy's widow Maria Elena Holly. The follow up was a minor chart hit reaching No. 7 during a 14-week residency.

LISTINGS:
Volume 1: Raining In My Heart / Early In The Morning / Peggy Sue / Maybe Baby / Everyday / Rave On / That'll Be The Day / Heartbeat/ Think It Over / Oh Boy! / It's So Easy / It Doesn't Matter Anymore

Volume 2: Peggy Sue Got Married / Well … All Right / What To Do / That Makes It Tough / Now We're One / Take Your Time / Crying, Waiting, Hoping / True Love Ways / Learning The Game / Little Baby / Moondreams / That's What They Say

The Buddy Holly Story – Film

An Innovisions production made in 1977 and which had its premiere the following year in Dallas, Texas.

A book of the same name by John Tobler came out in the UK shortly thereafter and contains a lengthy illustrated section on the film. A film soundtrack album died the death, probably quickened by an ITV strike that precluded advertising at the critical time. Another factor could have been that the superb twenty golden greats of Holly/

Crickets material had rocketed to No.1 on the album charts for three consecutive weeks and deservedly led to gold records being presented to the Holley family.

It could be argued that the film biography was a genuine attempt to bring Holly to the big screen. But the bulk of Holly aficionados feel it was long on poetic licence and short on fact. One thing not often in dispute is that Gary Busey gives a sincere and hypnotic performance in the title role and was deservedly nominated for an Oscar. But at 33 years of age he was (for some) unconvincing playing someone in the age range 18–22. It must have also been a calculated decision not to use one of the greatest rock voices, Holly's own, on the soundtrack. It was also incredible to release a film of Holly's life without making mention of either Norman Petty, Jerry Allison or Joe Mauldin.

On a sad note Robert Gittler, who wrote the screenplay, committed suicide just before the premiere of the film's release. For those of you who can't stomach the film, play 'The Real Buddy Holly Story' by Sonny Curtis as it's all there on record in just over three minutes of musical magic.

'Buddy's Guitar'

Taped at Holly's New York flat, January 1959.

This is the untitled instrumental listed in the *Remembering Buddy* biography. It is just over one minute long and is based on the Ray Charles number 'Leave My Woman Alone'. Holly would have been familiar with the number, which had also been recorded by his friends Don and Phil.

Holly's tremulous electric guitar strumming was recorded on his Ampex tape recorder during January as he was about to leave on tour. The snippet has never been released officially but is available on unauthorized recordings.

Carl Bunch

Carl was the drummer with Buddy on the last tour but by the time the artists reached the Surf Ballroom, Clear Lake he was already sidelined in hospital at Rhinelander, Wisconsin with frostbite brought on by travelling in a rickety tour bus through the frozen northern states of the USA. According to reports he actually rejoined the tour shortly after the fatal crash.

Tommy Allsup, who agreed to play lead guitar, had been asked to contact a drummer he had met at Clovis one time. This was Carl Bunch a native of Odessa, Texas, who was with Ronnie Smith and the Poor Boys at the time. Bunch has never ever failed to acknowledge that he and Waylon were not true Crickets but just backing up Buddy, who had plans to link up again with Jerry and Joe. (Although equally Holly had plans to work with and produce Waylon Jennings.)

Carl Bunch is today involved in church work and has been quoted as saying that he sincerely believes Buddy Holly's death was brought about by the Devil as Buddy would have eventually led a musical crusade to bring people back to Christ! An amazing comment that may raise eyebrows but who's to judge?

Bunch has led a rollercoaster of a life and has been washed up on several occasions. In between times he has been a drummer with both Roy Orbison and Hank Williams Junior in addition to his short spell backing Holly.

Johnny Burnette (and the Rock'n'Roll Trio)

A legendary rockabilly artist, and no mean composer, who sprang up in the late 1950s and eventually became a successful pop balladeer before his premature death. This was the result of a fishing accident whilst on vacation and it is ironic that this took place at Clear Lake. The Clear Lake in question, one of many in the USA, is in California and about 1,500 miles due west of the Iowa version. His Trio recordings received belated recognition with 'Honey Hush' often quoted as one of the earliest examples of rockabilly.

Although both from the South and both Coral artists at around the same time (1957) it is unlikely that the paths of Burnette and Holly ever crossed. At the time when Holly was doing most of his touring Johnny was in Hollywood trying his hand at songwriting and pitching songs to Ricky Nelson among others.

Johnny Burnette was born on 25th March 1934 in Memphis and died on 14th August 1964 – much too early in the scheme of things. Sadly his brother, Dorsey, bass player with the trio in the early years, also died prematurely in 1979 (age 46) of a heart attack.

The family name carries on with children Billy and Rocky Burnette, who are both in the business of performing and producing records.

James Burton

The man responsible for some of the most memorable guitar licks in rock'n'roll was born in Shreveport, Louisiana on 21st August 1939. His most famous body of work was surely as lead guitarist for Ricky Nelson from 1957 through into the 1960s. Later, he was to hold the same post with Elvis until the death of the King in 1977.

His place in this work is by virtue of his session work with the post-Holly Crickets, which included playing on their surfing records and Beatles' covers. However, he never actually performed nor toured with The Crickets. Quite a few famous artists have picked with The Crickets at different times including Glen Campbell, Peter Townshend and Eric Clapton. A pretty impressive line-up that's for sure.

Gary Busey

Actor Gary Busey played the lead role in the major film biography of Holly in the late 1970s having a few years earlier started rehearsing the part of J.I. Allison for the abortive film *Not Fade Away*. Please see brief entry under the film title.

Busey (arguably too old at 33 to play Buddy) had a musical background and was the drummer for a group called Carp for several years. Later, calling himself Teddy Jack Eddy, he backed singer Leonard Cohen. Busey played his own lead guitar in the Holly film, and the soundtrack numbers were put down live in an attempt to capture the spirit and energy of Holly.

Busey had a serious motorbike accident a few years ago but happily made a full recovery and returned to films. Apparently Busey has paid over a quarter of a million dollars at auction to secure Buddy's leather-tooled guitar.

Whether or not one likes the film biography it has to be said that Busey gave the role his all and tried hard to research the part to get inside the character of Holly. But it has been said that the musical result was more like Gary Busey plays Chuck Berry.

See also entry under film title THE BUDDY HOLLY STORY

C

Glen Campbell

Born 22nd April 1936, Arkansas, USA, Glen Campbell was a contemporary of Holly's, but their paths didn't actually cross. Campbell was to become one of Capitol's major recording artists with solo hits spanning 12 years (1967–78). His inclusion in this volume is through his connection with The Crickets. He played on several of the group's Liberty recordings in the early 1960s, the most memorable of which was the 1962 top 5 recording of 'Don't Ever Change'.

Glen Campbell also had the unusual distinction of briefly backing Gene Vincent (although not a Blue Cap) as well as having a stint with both The Champs and The Beach Boys. He had a prolific career as a session man before embarking on a successful solo career that is ongoing.

Ray Campi

Legendary rockabilly artist virtually unknown in his home country (USA). Usually thought of as a typical Texan he was actually born in New York on 20th April 1934 and his full name is Raymond Charles Campi, junior. He contrived an introduction to Norman Petty at Clovis in 1958 and spent time looking at the set-up Norman had, the hope being that Petty might decide to manage him. Ray was at that time recording for the small Austin label, Domino. In recent years Campi has said that he recorded 'Unchained Melody' at Clovis but this has not been confirmed.

Ray knew of Holly and had also contacted him around that time with songs that he had written, the possibility being that Holly might be tempted. However, nothing materialized at that juncture but possibly something might have done further down the line.

After the accident Ray Campi helped compose two tribute songs and these were commercially released on the D label. The main side was about the Bopper entitled 'The Man I Met' and the backing musicians were The Bopper's own band. The flip was 'The Ballad of Donna and Peggy Sue'. Neither were hits, but they are available on odd compilations from time to time.

In 1959 with nothing much happening for him Ray moved to

California looking for a break as a songwriter. Despite a long career he has never got the full recognition he deserves. How often can that be said of a rockabilly great?

Tinker Carlen

Carlen was a friend of Holly's from Junior High school days. As embryonic musicians they also jammed together. This was in the days when Buddy was also running around with Bob Montgomery, Don Guess, Larry Welborn and others.

Tinker was never a formal group member but (from his version of events) he just kind of 'hung out' – probably cruising around Lubbock looking for the Hi-D-Ho drive-in? In fact, he teamed up a few years ago with Buddy's brother Larry and actually wrote and recorded a song entitled just that, 'Looking For The Hi-D-Ho'. Larry released it on his own Cloud Nine label. (The Hi-D-Ho was established in 1948 and it's still in existence. Sherry Holley, Buddy's niece, has performed there in recent years to keep things in the family.)

Johnny Carroll

John Lewis Carroll was born in Godley, Texas in 1938 and died 18th February 1995 of a liver complaint, aged 57. One of the very greatest of all rockabilly artists who never got the acclaim in his homeland that he deserved. He did, however, appear in an obscure but classic rock'n'roll movie in 1957 entitled *Rock Baby Rock It*. Worth tracking down on video at specialist outlets.

Perhaps the odd man out in this volume but he was a fellow Texan and one of a handful from there actually to get a record released at the hands of Sam Phillips. Rockers from around the Texas area mainly sought their breaks in Clovis or around Dallas. Not that many made the trek through Arkansas to Memphis.

On this theme see SUN RECORDS entry.

Carter-Lewis and the Southerners

The duo fronting this UK group *circa* 1961 were Midlanders Kenny Hawker and John Shakespeare. They wrote and performed prolifically, much of their output being similar in style to that of Buddy Holly and The Crickets. Their debut disc on Ember was cowritten by Geoff Goddard (see entry) but despite much radio exposure, often featuring Holly numbers, they failed to achieve a chart breakthrough.

Their music was so similar in spirit to that of Holly that to mention only under a SOUNDALIKES entry hardly seems fair. Eventually the boys were joined by Perry Ford and as a trio, the Ivy League, finally achieved chart success.

John (Carter) Shakespeare was later involved in The Flowerpot Men and The First Class. The Holly influence surfaced again in 1981 when as The Graduates he released 'I Remember Buddy' / 'Everyday' on the Alacrity label.

Buzz Cason

James Elmore Cason was born near Tennessee in 1939 and had a musical background that sprung from rock'n'roll roots.

Cason joined The Crickets *circa* 1964 following the departure through ill health of Jerry Naylor. He had come up in the late 1950s as part of a group called The Casuals, who were the opening act on local bills, which included Gene Vincent, Brenda Lee, Eddie Cochran and others. Eventually he had a US Top 20 hit himself with 'Look For A Star' as Gary Miles. (The UK version was by the similarly named Gary Mills.)

Buzz worked with Snuffy Garrett on the A and R side of things at Liberty Records, which is how the link with The Crickets initially took root. Apart from performing with the group, Cason also helped out on the production side. He has spent a lifetime in the music business and a year or two back he helped The Crickets on their 'Double Exposure' album.

Along the way he has composed a prodigious amount of music of which the No.1 hit 'Everlasting Love' (revived again and again) has to be the best example.

'Changing All Those Changes'

Alternative title for 'I'm Changing All Those Changes'.

Ray Charles

Ray Charles, blind from glaucoma at an early age, was born Ray Charles Robinson in Georgia, USA on 23rd September 1930. An all-time great of the music business who has travelled a long road since he first made records that were little more than attempts to impersonate his idol Nat Cole.

Holly was a big Ray Charles fan and was certainly familiar with Charles big R&B hit 'I Got A Woman', which Elvis used from the early days. Buddy wanted to link up with Charles and record a gospel style album at some point. Of course it takes two to tango and whether it would have come to pass is a matter of conjecture. But Charles has always been progressive and willing to experiment. So, who knows? Did Buddy and Maria Elena try, unsuccessfully, to call at Ray Charles's home in late 1958? Jerry Allison also remembers Buddy telling him he wanted to record a gospel album with Charles. It was very much on his mind.

Whilst Buddy Holly and Ray Charles never happened as a duo, did you realize that, ironically, there is a tenuous link between the names? It seems that some of the posthumous apartment tape tracks of Buddy's were overdubbed by The Ray Charles Singers, the white hit vocal group of that era, and not to be confused with the Charles's own group, The Raelettes. (The tracks were 'Peggy Sue Got Married' and 'Crying, Waiting, Hoping', which was Holly's first posthumous single in the UK.)

It's amazing to reflect on Ray's career and remember that 'What'd I Say' didn't actually come out until months after Holly's death, and he hadn't had a major pop hit up to that point.

It is just possible that the tracks Buddy recorded in his flat in January of 1959 were numbers that may have been used if he had teamed up with Charles. For more on the Charles/Holly connection see entry JESSE STONE.

The Chipmunks

You may think this an unusual entry, perhaps, in an A–Z of Buddy Holly, but 'The Chipmunk Song' was the No.1 record in the USA in December 1958 and it is certain that the slow version of 'Slippin' And Slidin'', which Buddy committed to tape at $7^{1}/_{2}$ ips, instead of 15 ips, should be played back at normal speed to become an amusing Chipmunks-style track!

This explanation as to why Buddy recorded such a painfully slow version may be bizarre but it came to light in 1985, and might just be true. Perhaps he was messing around with his tape machine to amuse his wife, Maria?

Although David Seville and the Chipmunks means little in the UK, in the USA his 1958 single sold so many that it is one of the Top 10-selling singles of all time.

'The Chirping Crickets'

UK Album: CORAL LVA 9081.

The only album released by the group during Holly's lifetime, it made its appearance in our shops during March 1958. Whilst the music made a terrific impact, the album sleeve, which pictured the group holding their electric guitars also produced an image that left an indelible mark on fans down the years.

The 12 tracks included both sides of the group's first three hit singles together with six new recordings. As with the solo album that followed, it was certainly a hit, although album charts weren't yet in place.

The album has since been in catalogue almost continually since it first appeared nearly 40 years ago. The only slight misnomer was to call it 'The Chirping Crickets' as the quartet didn't actually chirp at that point. Fans were to learn much later that backing vocals were courtesy of an unknown trio called The Picks.

Listing: Oh Boy! / Not Fade Away / You've Got Love / Maybe Baby / It's Too Late / Tell Me How / That'll Be The Day / I'm Looking For Someone To Love / An Empty Cup / Send Me Some Lovin' / Last Night / Rock Me My Baby.

Civil Aeronautics Board Report

An investigation into the fatal Iowa crash under the auspices of the CAB started within hours of the wreckage being discovered.

The basic facts are that the light plane, a Beechcraft Bonanza N-3794N, owned by the Dwyer Flying Service was involved in an accident in the early hours of 3rd February 1959, approximately five miles north west of the Mason City municipal airport, Iowa. The accident resulted in fatal injuries to pilot Roger Peterson and his three passengers, well known entertainers who were headlining a Winter Dance Party troupe.

The purpose of the flight was to take the singers to Fargo in North Dakota upon completion of their show at the Surf Ballroom in Clear Lake on the evening of 2nd February in poor weather conditions. The actual flight takeoff was estimated at 00.55 a.m., 3rd February with the crash time being put at 1.00 a.m. or shortly thereafter. (At the Surf Ballroom the event has been commemorated as taking place at 1.07 a.m.) The demolished craft was found at 09.35 a.m. on the farm of one

Albert Juhl. The ground was lightly covered with snow.

The body of the pilot was in the wreckage whilst the bodies of Holly, Valens and the Bopper were close by. All had, without any doubt, died instantly. For the morbidly inclined more graphic details have appeared in Ellis Amburn's recent biography of Holly.

The final report of the CAB in September 1959 attributed the main cause of the accident to pilot error. Silly stories such as Holly shooting the pilot can be safely ignored. You are more likely to spot Elvis in your local newsagent.

See also entries JERRY DWYER, BEECHCRAFT BONANZA and ROGER PETERSON.

Jimmy Clanton

Born 2nd September 1940, Clanton was a teen idol type (*à la* Fabian, Avalon, etc.), who, surprisingly, came from near the Crescent City of New Orleans. He was drafted, along with others, to replace the dead artists on the fateful Winter Dance Party Tour of 1959. His 1958 release of 'Just A Dream' was to be his biggest, although in a four-year period he had seven Top 40 hits.

Holly and Clanton had met in 1958 when both were on a major package tour: The Biggest Show of Stars. Coincidentally, he had also met Ritchie Valens when both appeared in *Go, Johnny, Go*, the rather tepid 1958 rock'n'roll movie. Publicity stills from that time show a surprisingly chunky Ritchie Valens chatting to Clanton near a Dansette-style record player. The latter looked the archetypal pop star whilst Valens looked, well different. (Certainly nothing like the pelvic-thrusting version in the Buddy musical.)

Jimmy Clanton started performing again in 1993 after a lengthy absence from the business. He had been many things during his life including a church minister and a disc jockey on KHEX in Pennsylvania. Now he's back in Cajun country.

Eric Clapton

The legendary British artist Eric Clapton has always been a self-confessed Holly fan and it is no real surprise that his image as an axeman also includes the obligatory Fender Stratocaster which they both played in inimitable fashion.

In the 1970s two of The Crickets (Curtis/Allison) were to perform backing vocals on the Clapton solo track 'After Midnight' and later

Eric reciprocated and played guitar on some of The Crickets' 'Rockin 50s' album.

Clapton is one of those unique individuals in that he is a musicians' musician yet he has also achieved enormous popular acclaim.

Dick Clark

Dick Clark remains the world's oldest teenager having been born on 30th November 1929. Host of the US TV show *American Bandstand* that started in 1952 and which clocked up well over 30 years before it ran its course, Dick Clark comes over as slick and professional but wisely never nailed his colours solely to the mast of rock'n'roll. This stance, and Clark's longevity in the music business, stands in stark contrast to the life and career of his contemporary, Alan Freed.

Buddy Holly and The Crickets appeared on *American Bandstand* in 1957 and again in 1958. See entry under heading AMERICAN BAND-STAND and for contrast see entry under ALAN FREED.

June Clark

From Lubbock, Texas June was the sister of Donnie Lanier, lead guitarist with Buddy Knox. See separate entry. According to Niki Sullivan, June Clark helped with the backing vocals on the hit 'That'll be the Day' but this seems unlikely according to most sources. However, she did do background vocals on several Gary Tollett recordings, where Holly was used as a session guitarist.

Her other involvement was in allowing Buddy, Jerry and Joe to rehearse in her house in those early days while they were still awaiting a break.

Stanley Clayton

Stanley Clayton is listed as co-writer of perhaps the most unlikely of all Buddy Holly recordings, 'Mailman, Bring Me No More Blues'. The song is, in fact, a 12-bar blues composition and it was no surprise eventually to learn that Clayton was a pseudonym for none other than Coral executive and jazz buff Bob Theile (see entry), whose career became closely associated with that of Buddy.

In the autobiography that Theile completed shortly before his death

Posed early publicity shot (circa 1956) taken at June Clark's Lubbock home, where The Crickets performed. (Courtesy of Bill Griggs.)

he explains that to have used his own name on the sheet music would have led to a charge of conflict of interest. So, as was often the case, a new name was conjured up to circumvent the problem.

It's not just politicians who are devious!

Clovis, New Mexico

Clovis is the name of an ancient French king and – who knows? – perhaps he gave his name to this small New Mexico town where Norman Petty worked his magic.

The original studio at 1313, West 7th Street, Clovis, where Holly and The Crickets cut the bulk of their recordings still stands but is mainly used these days as an historical venue where occasional visitors tour and perhaps ponder on the sounds that once vibrated within the walls. Nearby is Petty's other facility, which he acquired in 1960 and which initially became a radio station. It was eventually opened as a studio in 1968, incorporating a theatre.

Known as America's Land of Enchantment State, New Mexico is

well worth including in the itinerary of any Holly fan contemplating a trip to Lubbock, the border being only 100 miles away due west.

It might not compare in size with its neighbour but with its mountains, lakes and white sand it's a wonderful contrast to the Lone Star State.

Eddie Cochran

Born 3rd October 1938 in Minnesota, USA this classic rocker died 17th April 1960, as a result of a tragic car crash while on a tour of the UK. His friend Gene Vincent was seriously injured in the same accident. Although Eddie appeared on bills in the States with Holly, and they were reported to be close friends no photos of the two together have ever surfaced. There is one of Eddie with the other members of The Crickets that was probably taken by Holly. (Evidently most of drummer Jerry Allison's photos from that time were lost many years ago.) Of interest to fans is a lengthy interview by DJ Freeman Hoover with Eddie, in which Holly is obviously present and laughing in the background at the banter taking place.

Both artists were keen fans of Ray Charles, and Eddie did actually manage to record Charles's classic 'Hallelujah I Love Her So'. Buddy may have also attempted the title and further details are given under JERRY LEE LEWIS. In addition, Buddy was known to feature Cochran numbers in his stage act and certainly both 'Summertime Blues' and '20 Flight Rock' were performed on the Australian tour. It has also been said that The Crickets were shortlisted to appear in *The Girl Can't Help It* film, but the idea was ruled out by Norman Petty – a pity if true.

One of the saddest recordings ever has to be Eddie's version of 'Three Stars', his tribute to the three dead rock stars. The royalties were to be diverted to relatives of the deceased artists. His emotional version did not, in the event, get released at the time but surfaced in the 1960s on a Liberty 45.

Apart from being fast friends with Buddy, Eddie had also developed a friendship with Ritchie Valens, who had just started touring and as result had been offered the Sharon Sheeley composition 'Hurry Up', which was to be released on Ritchie's first Del-Fi album.

It's often stated that Eddie was slated to appear on the Winter Dance Party Tour but dropped out to complete the *Go, Johnny, Go* film. But Valens also starred in the movie *and* did the tour, so this may not be correct. If Eddie didn't get to The Surf ballroom, his backing group The Kelly Four did when they performed there in 1992.

Session guitarist, superb vocalist, multi-instrumentalist, Eddie could do almost anything musically, and his early death at 21 has to be a rock'n'roll tragedy of the first order. If the music did die in 1959 then perhaps the funeral rites took place the following year.

Ed Cohen

Must be included as the man who, as Executive Producer, brought Holly's life to the big screen. The film, *The Buddy Holly Story*, has its critics but it has certainly helped Holly's posthumous career greatly. That big 'plus' must cancel out all the little minus points that the film racks up through the major inaccuracies that litter the script. If necessary see THE BUDDY HOLLY STORY film entry and remind yourself.

Paul Cohen

No relation to the above individual, Paul Cohen was a Decca chief back in 1956 when Buddy was struggling for his first break. At the country end of things he allegedly made the famous quote that Holly was 'the biggest no talent I have ever worked with'.

Cohen was born 10th November 1908 and died 1st April 1971. He was posthumously elected to the Country Music Hall of Fame in 1976.

'Come Back Baby'

Session at Norman Petty Studios, New Mexico, 10th September, 1958. Personnel: Buddy, Jerry and Joe with King Curtis on sax.

One of those little-known Holly recordings that really deserves to be more widely heard. Composed by Fred Neil, a New York songwriter, with Norman's name added, it was one of the two solo tracks that Buddy recorded in late 1958 on the Clovis session, where he enlisted the help of sax great, King Curtis.

The track didn't appear on disc until 1964 when it was one of several new tracks on the 'Showcase' album. Whilst sources indicate the recording is overdubbed the fact that the track is in mono leads to the conclusion that additions, if any, are minimal. (An undubbed bootleg version has surfaced on a European album of Holly material in the last few years.)

It's a real pity that 'Come Back Baby' is hardly ever included on compilations of Holly material as the vocal is first rate even if the composition itself is not Fred Neil's greatest. (He had composed Roy Orbison's 'Candy Man'.)

Sam Cooke

Late great, soul singer who we tend to think of as a 1960s artist, his greatest days dating from 1960 when he joined RCA. In fact he was five years older than Holly and had a string of big US chart records throughout the late 1950s on the Keen label. (It can be said that label boss Bob Keane discovered both Ritchie Valens and Sam Cooke. Quite a duo.)

Originally a gospel singer he fronted the Soul Stirrers before his career took a different direction. It is surprising that Cooke is portrayed in a cameo role in the film biography of Holly and also (by inference), in the Buddy musical as, in reality, the careers of these two famous artists never really interconnected to any great extent although both appeared on the same Ed Sullivan telecast in 1957.

Sam was born on 22nd January 1931 in Clarksdale, Mississippi and died in Los Angeles after a shooting incident, 11th December 1964. Rumours about the strange manner of his death have echoed down through the years, including that of a Mafia involvement, although the court verdict remains justifiable homicide.

One minor link between Holly and Cooke is that both were backed briefly by the great saxophonist King Curtis: Holly during the excellent 'Reminiscing' session, and Cooke during the live 1963 Harlem Club date that led to a memorable album release years after both Cooke and Curtis had passed on.

The Corbin Brothers

Larry, Sky and Ray 'Slim' Corbin were three brothers whose names are intertwined with that of Buddy Holly.

The brothers acquired the KLLL radio station in the late 1950s and it was there that Slim Corbin and Waylon Jennings helped Holly compose, on the spot, a number entitled 'You're the One'. The hand claps which feature prominently on the undubbed version of the song are those of Corbin and Jennings. Sadly, Slim Corbin was to end his days as a murder statistic in Phoenix, Arizona, although earlier he had linked up with Waylon once more and helped on the session that produced the tribute song 'The Stage'. He also recorded several country singles, one of which made the Billboard charts.

Later, brother Larry was instrumental in getting Lubbock to honour its famous son in 1980, when an impressive bronze sculpture of the singer was unveiled.

See entry – RADIO KDAV AND KLLL

Don Cornell

New Yorker born in 1924 and big band singer who had a host of UK releases in the 1950s with 'Hold my Hand' reaching No.1 in 1954. Other notable recordings included 'Stranger in Paradise', 'Unchained Melody' and 'Love Is A Many Splendoured Thing'.

In the USA, one of his 1957 Coral singles was 'Mailman Bring Me No More Blues', which came out on the flip of 'Before its time to say goodnight'. The Holly version on Coral was C61852, while Cornell's version was on C61854! Both came about because of the involvement of Bob Theile, but neither were hits.

'Countrywise' LP

Famous and scarce, 10-inch Dutch album, which came out in the 1960s and comprised of eight of the Buddy and Bob numbers.

Most of these are country in style except 'I Wanna Play House With You' and 'Down The Line', which are closer to rock'n'roll. The album had a small circulation but is worth several hundred pounds these days. It remains very collectable but most fans will have to settle for the counterfeit version, which is easily identified. (Of the many differences between the two, the original sleeve is glossy while the counterfeit one is distinctly dull in texture.)

The superb front cover photo is taken from Holly's last New York Bruno photographic session at the time when Buddy's wife Maria Elena was becoming actively involved in helping to run his career.

Listing: Down The Line / Flower Of My Heart / Door To My Heart / I Gambled My Heart / I Wanna Play House With You / Soft Place In My Heart / You And I Are Through / Gotta Get You Near Me Blues

Eddie Crandall

A Nashville talent scout, long deceased, who was persuaded to watch Holly perform (as the Buddy and Bob trio) on a 1955 concert bill in Lubbock, which, involved Marty Robbins, an act that Crandall himself managed at that time.

As a direct result Crandall requested that Holly send four original recordings to him in Nashville with a view to getting a record contract sorted out. This led to the somewhat abortive 1956 Nashville recordings for Decca. An important step in the story.

Eddie Crandall, Jim Denny and Pappy Dave Stone were all individuals who helped in getting Buddy his first shot at recording with Decca. See individual entries.

Fred Crawford

Texan country singer who had a very active career in the 1950s touring and performing on such shows as the Big D Jamboree and the Louisiana Hayride. However, he never made much impact on records but his Starday single 'By the Mission Wall' does feature Buddy Holly backing him on lead guitar with Jerry and Joe possibly on the same session.

Recorded at Clovis in 1957, the backing vocals were by the Bowman Brothers and the single got a release on the Starday label. The flip, 'You're Not The Same Sweet Girl', was recorded at a different date and does not feature Buddy.

The 'Mission Wall' track has appeared several times over the years on European bootlegs but one wonders if royalties have ever gone the way of Fred Crawford? He has had a long-term recording career doubling as a DJ at Radio KERB in Kermit, Texas and although popular locally he has never achieved national stardom.

Marshall Crenshaw

Latterday US artist who had a lowly 1982 hit, 'Someday, Someday', on Warner, but is little known in the UK although some material has been released here. Holly has been a major influence although Crenshaw's material does not sound remotely similar, but he is certainly a talented singer/songwriter who has had his songs recorded by Robert Gordon amongst others.

In 1987 he played the part of Buddy Holly in *La Bamba*, the Ritchie Valens biopic. He performed only one number in the film (and on the soundtrack), and the choice of material was strange – 'Crying, Waiting, Hoping'. This was one of the New York apartment tape numbers that Holly was working on prior to the final tour but which he certainly did not perform live on stage.

Crenshaw was born in Detroit around 1960 and in the 1980s took part in several US tribute events for Holly.

The Crickets

Let's keep this entry reasonably brief and remember that this book is about Buddy Holly and The Crickets and the group's career post 1959 is not touched upon in depth. To follow the continuing career of The Crickets you can do no better than subscribe to The Crickets' File, which still appears regularly under the energetic guidance of John Firminger, a lifelong fan and friend of the group. His details are given under SOURCES.

Back to the beginning: in 1957 some of us purchased a shellac 78 rpm disc of 'That'll Be The Day', which contained the words, 'The Crickets with Orchestral Accompaniment'. What a deceptive description that was! Early fans had little idea just who The Crickets were and if there was an orchestra involved maybe our ears were playing tricks on us. Eventually, we learnt that the group comprised of four surprisingly young men, Buddy Holly, Jerry Allison, Joe B. Mauldin and Niki Sullivan. (In two errors on the first album sleeve Mauldin was listed as Maudlin and Lubbock ended up as Bullock.) Jerry remembers choosing the name having heard of a group called The Spiders perform a number entitled 'Witchcraft'. The insect label clearly impressed him.

By the time Buddy and the boys were performing in the UK, Niki Sullivan had left and was striving for solo stardom with little success. (He went under the name of The Hollyhawks at one stage so made no attempt to hide his influences.)

There had been an earlier Crickets in the USA and details appear under the entry DEAN BARLOW. Briefly, the black Crickets had disbanded by 1957 so confusion was minimal except in doowop circles. Although do read the *Not Fade Away* film entry.

The Crickets have continued down the years despite splitting from Holly in October 1958, reforming and then breaking up again in 1965. For several years they did not record or tour under The Crickets' banner. You can't keep a good group down, however, and they were recording again in Nashville in early 1996.

More than half of this book's content *could* be listed under a Crickets heading but hasn't been, so as to avoid duplication. I would refer readers to individual entries under group members' names. But remember, there are more Crickets than a dog's got fleas!

'Crying, Waiting, Hoping'

Taped at Holly's New York flat, 14th December 1958. Buddy Holly and acoustic guitar.

This Holly composition was recorded at home on the Ampex tape machine he had purchased from his original mentor, Norman Petty. The simple tape features Holly and his acoustic guitar accompaniment, and this original version still awaits a legal commercial release. It is, however, easily obtainable via European bootlegs.

Holly's vocal was overdubbed by Coral producer Jack Hansen, within six months of the artist's death and as the flip of 'Peggy Sue Got Married' it was a sizeable UK hit in late 1959. Several years later Norman Petty overdubbed the track with heavy instrumentation and without any backing vocals. Both dubbed versions are on the 1979 box set on MCA records.

Unfortunately, stereo masters of this track and 'Peggy Sue Got Married' no longer exist. Not often covered, perhaps the most unusual attempt was the punk version on Stiff Records by Wreckless Eric in 1978.

King Curtis

The basics are that Curtis was born 7th February 1934 and died 13th August 1971. He had been christened Curtis Ousley and he and Buddy were fellow Texans who were both operating out of New York in late 1958. Curtis was an incredibly talented saxophonist who backed literally hundreds of recording artists over a career that spanned many years but which was cruelly brought to an end when he was murdered outside his apartment in Harlem, New York.

John Goldrosen wrote most descriptively in his original Holly biography of how Curtis, Waylon Jennings and Buddy all came together in September 1958 for a recording session that was unique but, in a way, abortive. Norman Petty and Buddy were about to split and this led to Petty physically holding the masters from the session despite Holly owning the recordings.

The gem of the session was Holly's version of 'Reminiscing', which resembles a duet between him and King Curtis. At the time of its release, the composer credits were listed as King Curtis but it has since been revealed that it was a Holly composition passed to Curtis as part of the deal for the session.

The legend of King Curtis is such that up to 20 years after his death a regular newsletter about him was produced entitled, appropriately, *The Boss*. In addition to his session work King Curtis recorded dozens of solo albums although probably his best stuff was on the Enjoy label.

King Curtis was tragically stabbed to death trying to help break up a street fight in New York – a practice not to be recommended, even if you do play a mean saxophone. He is buried at Pinelawn Memorial Cemetery in Long Island, New York.

Sonny Curtis

Where to start such an entry? Basics are that he was born in Meadow Texas, 9th May 1937 and is, at the time of writing, alive and well and back performing with The Crickets. Sonny's career has for most devotees never fully escaped the Holly connection and I don't think Sonny himself would argue that point to any great extent.

The link started around 1954 when Sonny played violin on early Holly demos and then sat in with Ben Hall on the Sunday Party in Lubbock at the same time as Buddy and Bob were appearing on the programme. During the Decca days, Sonny appeared on two of the three studio sessions playing either rhythm or lead guitar. It's worth mentioning that although Buddy and Sonny had country roots they spent part of their formative years listening to a Shreveport radio station that played rhythm and blues music.

To the uninitiated that might appear to be it, but in fact Sonny was a regular member of the post-Holly Crickets, both as vocalist and guitarist. Sonny has visited the UK on a fairly regular basis as a solo performer and time and again demonstrated what an incredibly talented individual he is. Thus far we have not mentioned his song-writing ability, which is quite phenomenal. He wrote the classic Buddy Holly number 'Rock Around With Ollie Vee' and – among a wealth of material for The Crickets themselves – such numbers as 'More Than I Can Say' and 'Baby My Heart'. He wrote the evergreen 'Walk Right Back' for the Everly Brothers in 1961, and as late as 1989 co-wrote 'I'm No Stranger To The Rain'. It is a great shame that Buddy Holly never got to perform The Sonny Curtis Songbook. Something taken from us in February 1959.

On a personal level Sonny Curtis remains an unassuming and

laid-back individual and is one of the nicest people connected with the legend of Buddy Holly. If you haven't time to read Buddy Holly's biography then listen to Sonny sing 'The Real Buddy Holly Story'. It's all there, wrapped up in a 250-word song lyric.

D

Harold Westcott Daily

The legendary Pappy Daily was born on 8th February 1902 in Yoakum, Texas, and he had a lengthy career in the music business working with, among others, Gene Pitney, George Jones, Webb Pierce and through his association with another of this book's heroes, The Big Bopper.

After the end of the Second World War Pappy built up a thriving juke-box and distribution business operating in Texas before becoming a producer with Four Star Records, an expanding independent label. Later, he met up with an individual named Starnes and they amalgamated their names to form Starday. A label that is remembered by country fans as the outfit that first issued records by George Jones as well as other notable artists.

Also known for licensing his own D label product to Mercury he remained in music until retiring through ill-health in 1971. Pappy Daily died 5th December 1987 in Houston, Texas.

Bobby Darin

Born Walden Robert Cassotto on 14th May 1936, in the Bronx, New York, Bobby Darin became quite a legend himself, and it was a tragedy that he was not strong physically having suffered from rheumatic fever at an early age. He eventually succumbed while undergoing heart surgery back in December 1973 at the age of 37. His mother had died in 1959, his father died before Bobby was born and Darin himself did not expect to reach 30.

The paths of Holly and Darin crossed rather briefly in 1958, a meeting that led, fortuitously, to Buddy covering the Darin compositions 'Early In The Morning' / 'Now We're One'. Darin's version of the A side was a hit under artist's name, Rinky Dinks, and both Holly's and Darin's versions entered the US charts in the same week of 1958. For details of the background to Holly recording 'Early In The Morning' see entry under song title.

Interestingly, each recording fell out of the charts during September just a few weeks before both artists joined the same tour, The Biggest Show of Stars, for the 1958 Fall edition. This fact is rather intriguing and has led me at least to wonder whether there was any rivalry between the two singers. The fact, however, that royalties from both versions went to composer Darin makes it unlikely.

At Buddy's Texas wedding in August 1958 his own version of the Darin composition, 'Now We're One', was played. Whilst Buddy never got to collaborate with Ray Charles, Darin, on the same Atlantic label at the time, got to record a whole album of Ray Charles's material.

Before Bobby's death on 20th December 1973 he had also completed at least 15 major film roles and received 2 US Grammy awards. His first wife was the actress Sandra Dee and they had a son Dodd Darin who was born late 1962.

Mac Davis

Mac Scott Davis was born in Lubbock, Texas on 21st January 1942 and is certainly one of the City's most famous musical sons.

First and foremost a country performer, he turned to rock'n'roll briefly after seeing both Elvis and Buddy perform locally. He had to wait until the 1970s before having a series of hit records that led him into films for a while.

A superb composer ('In The Ghetto', 'Watching Scotty Grow', etc.) he has often paid his dues to Buddy Holly in his song lyrics. Probably the best example is, 'Texas In My Rear View Mirror'.

He had major personal problems that led to a temporary retirement from the music scene in 1989. He is now writing and recording again in the country field.

Sherry Davis

Buddy played lead guitar on a session for this artist that produced two songs, 'Broken Promises' and 'Humble Heart', which were released on Ray Winkler's US Fashion label. (It's the same Winkler that wrote Jim Reeves' monster hit 'Welcome To My World'.)

Ms Davis was fairly well known around Texas in the late 1950s appearing as a support act for Elvis on his tour of Texas in October 1956.

Other personal details and current whereabouts are not known.

Skeeter Davis

Country artist who originally performed as part of a female duo, The Davis Sisters. Their promising career ended in 1953 when Betty Jack Davis (no relation) was sadly killed in a road accident that badly injured Skeeter (shades of Vincent/Cochran). At the time of the crash their record 'I've Forgot More Than You'll Ever Know' had hit the country charts.

Skeeter Davis was born Mary Frances Penick in 1931 and, after the accident, opted for a solo career having a major hit in 1963 with the haunting 'The End Of The World'. In 1967 she recorded a tribute album 'Skeeter Davis sings Buddy Holly' on the RCA label, which was produced by Felton Jarvis. Waylon Jennings (an RCA stablemate) played guitar on the recordings, with Buzz Cason helping on backing vocals.

Some critics felt that Skeeter's light voice didn't suit the material and the album wasn't a success. Nevertheless it came out in the 1960s at a time when Holly's name was little remembered in the USA and this project, along with others, did help to ensure that his music wasn't totally forgotten.

We know Holly is fondly remembered by fellow artists and, in addition to Skeeter, albums dedicated to his music have been recorded by Bobby Vee, Denny Laine, Matlock, The Hollies, Don McLean, Jimmy Gilmer, Connie Francis, and Tommy Allsup to list a few at random.

Skeeter has had a distinguished country career and is a member of the Grand Ole Opry.

'Dearest'

Taped at Holly's New York flat, January 1959. Buddy Holly and acoustic guitar.

Composer credits on this apartment tape track are listed as Ellas McDaniels (aka Bo Diddley) Prentice Polk and Mickey Baker. The latter was part of Mickey and Sylvia, a duo who first entered the US charts with the song in 1957. Strangely, the Holly version first saw the light of day dubbed John Barry style as the flip to 'What To Do', which was reissued in 1963 on a UK Coral single. Initially, the record label stated that composer credits were unknown and as a result, the composition was given the unusual song title 'Ummm, Oh Yeah' – which approximates to a phrase in the lyrics.

The undubbed version features just the Holly vocal and his guitar accompaniment, and was included in the MCA box set. Another take, featuring slightly heavier strumming, has come out only on bootleg-style releases.

It is worth pointing out that the original recording is available in three versions, all featuring the same vocal. Firstly there is the undubbed version and then there are two quite different overdubs. Lightly dubbed it was on the 'Showcase' album and a more heavily dubbed version is on the 'Giant' album.

Jim Denny

James R. Denny was born in Buffalo Valley, Tennessee on 28th February 1911 and was elected to the Country Music Hall of Fame in 1966 some three years after his death on 27th August 1963. He was a leading light of the Nashville scene during the 1950s.

He became General Manager of the Grand Ole Opry and he was also a music publisher – he owned Cedarwood. As a booking agent involved with Eddie Crandall and others he helped Buddy get his first recording contract with Decca, in December 1955.

Jim Denny's Cedarwood held the original copyright on the sheet music for 'Modern Don Juan', 'Ting A Ling', etc., although it is doubtful that it earned them much in royalties in the early days. In 1958 Denny had acquired the rights to all Holly compositions dated prior to 1st January 1957 with the exception of 'That'll Be The Day'. At first glance this seems straightforward but as it included Buddy and Bob material it was quite complex, and the legalities took years to sort out.

Denny died over 30 years ago and, unlike some contemporaries, was unfortunately never interviewed in any depth on his role in the Holly legend.

John Denver and Other Folkies

The Rocky Mountain wonderboy was born Henry John Deutschendorf, Junior, in New Mexico and his connection with Holly is tenuous as their careers didn't really overlap.

However, John Denver studied architecture in 1961 at Texas Tech in Lubbock and eventually got round to recording a Holly composition

('Everyday') for RCA in 1972. I have never stumbled across a quote by Denver pertaining to Holly, which is perhaps surprising given that Buddy's vocal style must have been an influence. Many other folk artists have been quick to name the Texan as an influence and have frequently dipped into his songbook, as have a host of country artists.

The following is a short sample of folk artists who have recorded Holly's material in their careers: Phil Ochs, Sandy Denny, Tom Rush, Carolyn Hester, Steeleye Span and Nanci Griffiths. Many other performers have incorporated his material into their acts on a regular basis.

Murray Deutch

Small but important bit part player in the Buddy Holly legend whose name is usually coupled with that of Bob Theile. See separate entry.

Murray Deutch was general manager of music publishers Peers-Southern and was instrumental in helping get 'That'll Be The Day' launched on the road to success. It was he who first received the dub of the song from Norman in Clovis and tried to get it placed with Columbia, RCA and others before finally contacting Theile. The rest is history.

Mentioning Peers the publishers, above, leads me to point out that Elizabeth and Ralph Peer the 2nd, put out what is probably the earliest US Holly biography in 1972: *Buddy Holly, a Biography in Words, Photographs and Music*. Incidentally, Maria Elena Holly was Murray Deutch's secretary, and it was in his office that Buddy and his wife first met.

The Diamonds

Canadian vocal quartet that shot to fame in early 1956 when they made the US Top 20 with a cover of the Frankie Lymon and The Teenagers hit 'Why Do Fools Fall In Love'. Thereafter, they consistently covered recordings by black vocal groups, finally achieving a million-seller with their version of 'Little Darlin'', which completely eclipsed the original by The Gladiolas.

Surprisingly, Mercury issued the Holly composition 'Words of Love' as their follow up and this reached lucky 13 in the Billboard charts. Buddy's version on Coral issued at the same time failed to enter the top 100 or even to bubble under.

Both The Diamonds and The Crickets appeared on the same Alan

Freed package show in the Spring of 1958. Thereafter, The Diamonds jumped on the dance craze and took 'The Stroll' to No.4 in June before disbanding in the early 1960s following several changes in personnel. They later reformed and still perform but none of the original group is involved.

Bo Diddley

Born Ellas Bates in McComb, Mississippi in 1928, he later adopted the name McDaniel. Bo is one of the key figures in the birth of rock'n'roll and he's still doing his thing today – even if a trifle self-indulgently. In his career he had one minor Top 20 hit only and this was his own jive-talking 'Say Man'. However, his composition 'Bo Diddley' was a Top 5 hit on the US R&B charts in 1955.

His name has become synonymous with the Bo Diddley beat and numerous artists have used it to good effect, including Holly and Allison, who wrote 'Not Fade Away' with part-composer credits going, not to Bo Diddley but to Norman Petty. (Whilst Petty's contribution on a number such as 'True Love Ways' seems quite believable, composer credits on titles such as 'Not Fade Away' seem bizarre.)

In a reverse compliment, Bo Diddley recorded a very creditable version of 'Not Fade Away' on a London Sessions album in 1976. Not many connections between these two great artists but Bo Diddley had a hand in composing 'Love Is Strange', which Buddy taped in January of 1959 just days before embarking on the final tour, see song title entry 'LOVE IS STRANGE'.

In recent years a rehearsal of Buddy singing the Diddley composition 'Mona' has become available but not via MCA.

See entry 'BO DIDDLEY' – Song

Dion

Dion di Mucci, born 18th July 1939, was backed by the Belmonts who were on the fateful last tour with Holly and the others. We tend to forget that up to that point, they had not had a major hit, so they were more a supporting act, singing doowop white-boy style. It was in the 1960s that Dion's career really took off and he garnered a string of Top 10 hits, mostly as a solo act, on the Laurie label. He eventually developed a drugs problem, which derailed his career for a time.

The singer was quoted in contemporary interviews as being completely choked at the tragic loss of his good friend, Buddy. The two singers had totally different styles but evidently got on well, with Holly even playing drums for the group when Carl Bunch got frostbite during the tour.

Dion di Mucci is still about, sporting a baggy cap as headgear, and – although often a support act – he remains a good live performer. He toured the UK in the 1990s on a bill headlined by Dave Edmunds, who had produced Dion's 1989 comeback album, 'Yo Frankie'.

He has made a lot of powerful recordings over the years, which, if we must use labels, have ranged from R&B to doowop and gospel.

Fats Domino

Legendary New Orleans artist who was born Antoine Domino, in 1928, and who is still rocking away 40 years after he first entered the US Top 10 (1955) with 'Ain't That A Shame', a track that high school student Pat Boone covered and wanted to release with the more grammatically correct title 'Isn't That A Shame'! He was eventually persuaded to use the original phraseology – much to everyone's relief.

Buddy grew up a big fan of Fats and it must have been a tremendous thrill to end up on the same Paramount bill in New York as a fellow headliner. Holly did a demo of the Domino composition 'Blue Monday' in 1956 and this first surfaced on the 'Giant' album. The only Fats number that Buddy recorded commercially was the excellent album track 'Valley Of Tears' in 1957. This must have pleased manager Norman Petty as the number is heavily organ based, and he performs the solo accompaniment. The track was recorded for the original Coral LP 'Buddy Holly' LVA 9085 at brother Larry's particular request. Incidentally, I still have my original copy of that album with the price marked as one pound fifteen shillings and ninepence.

Held in high esteem by his contemporaries, both Elvis and Ricky Nelson also recorded Domino material in the 1950s. It's impossible to do justice to Fats in such a short entry. He has already recorded a superb body of work, most of which hails from his Imperial days. Apart from Fats' unique vocals, most recordings feature his wonderful piano technique. He also did occasional session work in the early days, perhaps the best example being his rolling introduction to the Lloyd Price million-seller 'Lawdy Miss Clawdy'.

Although Fats had over 60 US and UK Top 40 hits, he never actually reached No.1 in the UK. But he did have the consolation of inspiring a chicken plucker name Ernest Evans to change his name to Chubby Checker!

Lonnie Donegan

The renowned Glaswegian with the Irish name came to prominence when he recorded 'Rock Island Line' at a time when his act was featured as no more than a sideshow within the Chris Barber Jazz Band. It is sobering to remember that the 1956 million-seller earnt Lonnie no more than a small session fee.

Buddy and Lonnie first met at The Crickets' East Ham concert on 13th March and there are several photos of the stars together, although unfortunately these are seldom seen. Holly later went to a midnight concert in aid of the blues legend Big Bill Broonzy at the Dominion theatre, where Donegan was on the bill. Holly and Donegan didn't record the same style of music although both performed with a lot of drive. 'Love is Strange' is the only number recorded by both.

'Don't Come Back Knockin''

First Nashville recording session at Bradley's Barn, 26th January 1956. Personnel: Buddy, Sonny Curtis, Don Guess and Nashville session men.

Buddy collaborated with local Lubbock songwriter, Sue Parrish, to write this track and 'Love Me', both of which were recorded at his first Decca session in early 1956. UK fans got to hear the bulk of those Nashville tracks courtesy of two Brunswick extended-play records that were presumably released directly as a result of Holly's sad demise in early 1959.

In late 1955 Holly had cut a demo version of 'Don't Come Back Knockin'' at the Nesman Studios in Wichita Falls, Texas. A version cut on 7th December 1955 was one of the acetates (see EDDIE CRANDALL entry) and these were released by Buddy's brother, Larry, on an extended play disc on his own Holly House label several years ago. As with the Bo Diddley track, this earlier version is looser and has Holly calling out 'Let's Play It Again Boys, Let's Go'.

The Nashville recording has also been released with added backing vocals by The Picks, *circa* 1984.

'Door To My Heart'

Buddy and Bob performance at Nesman Studio, Wichita Falls, circa 1954–5.

Early demo recording of a Bob Montgomery composition that was released in 1965 as part of the 'Holly In The Hills' album. All the recordings feature some overdubbing but as this release, and all subsequent ones, have been of mono masters just what is added is not certain. At the time of writing the undubbed version has still not been issued, legally or otherwise.

With Sonny Curtis on fiddle, this track, and others, are mostly country-orientated recordings.

'Down the Line'

Demo recording made at the Nesman Studio, Wichita Falls, Texas by Buddy and Bob, recorded mid 1955.

This track is a great slab of rock'n'roll and the nearest Buddy and Bob get to a duet. The composers were Holly and Montgomery themselves. Any visitors travelling across country in Texas/New Mexico will have no difficulty in understanding the inspiration behind the track's title phrase. To get anywhere you need to travel down the line.

The track has finally surfaced undubbed on a four-CD box set by Vigotone, 40 years after the demo was first made.

In addition, a quieter-paced version of 'Down The Line' by Buddy and Bob has also been released on an album not sanctioned by MCA records, which makes for interesting listening.

'Drown in My Own Tears'

Part only, taped at Holly's New York flat, January 1959. Buddy Holly and electric guitar.

This Ray Charles number was recorded by Buddy on his tape recorder in January of 1959 but subsequently the bulk of the track was taped over and the final few emotive lyrics only have survived. This fragment was included on the unsanctioned 'Apartment Tapes' album, which came out on the appropriately named Prism label a few years back. See PRISM RECORDS entry for further background.

A full version of the same song was performed in Fort Lauderdale, 25th February 1958 with Buddy's vocals being backed by Jerry Lee Lewis on piano. This tape is of quite reasonable quality and it is a pity that it has not been made available to Buddy's long-term fans. Perhaps one day it will.

At the same Fort Lauderdale venue Holly also performed a live version of 'Everyday' giving the lie to the assertion that he never sang ballads on stage. Again it is believed a fragment of 'Everyday' and also 'Hallelujah I Love Her So' with Jerry on vocal and Buddy on guitar, does exist.

Hipockets Duncan

William Joseph Duncan was a radio announcer from around Lubbock who was very helpful to Buddy Holly in the very early days. In a seemingly informal way he was manager to Buddy, Bob and Larry Welborn when they were a trio and trying to get spots on local shows. Worth mentioning also is the fact that Duncan was the man who first booked Elvis to appear in Lubbock during 1955.

Hipockets left his job on Radio KSEL in 1953 to set up what was probably the first all-country station, radio KDAV, in Lubbock, Texas. In his later days he ran KRAN radio station in Morton, Texas, which he sold in 1979.

Sadly Hipockets died on 21st December 1981. By all accounts he was a wonderful man who was quite happy to tear up his managerial contract with Buddy when the singer teamed up with Norman and began his trip to the top of the charts.

Jerry Dwyer

Hubert J. Dwyer was the owner of Dwyer's Flying Service from which the doomed Beechcraft Bonanza was chartered by the artists for their abortive flight from Mason City to Fargo, North Dakota.

Understandably, Jerry Dwyer has been reluctant to be interviewed in the years since the crash, which was fully investigated by the US Civil Aeronautics Board, to whom he gave a four-page deposition the day following the accident.

To put things in perspective, whilst the musical world lost three stars in 1959, Jerry Dwyer lost a friend and colleague in pilot Roger Peterson. See entries under the pilot's name and also under CIVIL AERONAUTICS BOARD REPORT.

Bob Dylan

The folk-rock superstar was in the front row at the Winter Dance Party Show, at the Duluth Armory, 31st January 1959. Bob had his own high

63

school rock'n'roll group, the Golden Chords. His biographer, Robert Shelton, says Buddy was Dylan's lasting musical model. Bob began to imitate Holly's sweet, naïve, almost childlike voice. The vocal quality of many Dylan recordings shows his debt to Holly. Try 'I Don't Believe You' (1964). Bob's family noticed a great change in him when Buddy died; he seemed to be living his life in a great hurry.

As teenagers both fell in love with girls named Echo. Bob played piano briefly with Bobby Vee's band in mid 1959 and he said later that the singers and musicians he grew up with transcended nostalgia. Buddy Holly and Johnny Ace are just as valid to him today as then.

E

'Early in the Morning'

Recorded at The Pythian Temple Coral Records Studios, New York, 19th June 1958. Backed by Coral session musicians, including Al Chernet, guitar, Sam The Man Taylor or Boomie Richmond, sax and Panama Francis on drums.

Woody Harris, who had written 'Queen Of The Hop' and 'Pity Miss Kitty' collaborated with Bobby Darin on this number, which, for legal reasons, was released by Darin on Atlantic under the pseudonym, the Rinky Dinks. Holly's version came out at the same time and both were US chart entries in late 1958. It was to be Buddy Holly's last hit there during his lifetime. Darin's same version had also come out just before on Brunswick but using the name The Ding Dongs and it was when this was being withdrawn that the Holly version was rushed out. The identical master recording was used on both these Darin releases.

The vocal has to be one of Holly's most powerful ever and it is complemented by a driving sax sound, with the black gospel group, The Helen Way singers, adding backing vocals as they did on Bobby Darin's version. So whilst we never got to hear Holly cut a gospel-style album, we do get a flavour with this particular number.

Recordings sessions in those days often comprised a minimum of four tracks being cut. On this occasion just two tracks were recorded ('Early In The Morning' and 'Now We're One') specifically for a single release, with Darin's record seemingly sidelined.

As Holly's recording did not reach the Top 10 in the UK or the USA, it is not always included in greatest hits compilations, which is a pity, as this has to be one of his finest-ever recordings.

Rare backstage photograph of Buddy Holly and fellow artists on tour with The Everly Brothers, 19th January 1958. Duane Eddy is on the extreme right. (Courtesy of Dick Cole.)

Duane Eddy

Born New York, USA, 28th April 1938, Duane Eddy is one of the few remaining survivors of the 1950s' rock'n'roll era.

The famous twangy guitarist had a whole slew of hits in both the USA and the UK starting in 1958 with the distinctive 'Rebel Rouser'. Most of the legendary recordings of Duane Eddy are those with the small Jamie label before he signed with the major RCA label.

Holly and Eddy met up on tour in 1958 but never had the opportunity to become closer. Duane remembers his main friendship from that time as being with fellow artist Bobby Darin. If there isn't a close link between Holly and Eddy there certainly has been one with the surviving Crickets.

In his time Eddy has produced recordings for both Phil Everly (one of Holly's closest friends) as well as Waylon Jennings when backed by The Crickets. The Jennings/Crickets grouping were responsible for a particularly fine medley of Holly numbers, which was put out in the 1970s on one of Jennings's albums, and which was also released as an RCA single. (Other Holly numbers from that session remain unreleased.)

Duane Eddy was voted Top Instrumentalist several times in UK polls, and incredibly, Holly himself featured in such polls. This had to be a direct result of Holly's guitar playing, which had been heard up and down the country in March 1958.

Duane Eddy's career is ongoing and there remains in existence an active fan club, The Duane Eddy Circle. In 1995, Bear records put out the ultimate Duane Eddy box set, which contained all his Jamie material.

Dave Edmunds

Following on from Duane Eddy we turn to one of the UK's very best guitarists. Born 15th April 1944 Edmunds has always paid his dues to the rock'n'roll greats such as Holly, Cochran, Vincent, Berry, etc. whilst at the same time managing to keep up contemporary appearances. (His hit records date from the 1960s, beginning with 'Sabre Dance' as Love Sculpture right through to a solo hit in the 1990s.)

Why is he included here? Well apart from working with many of the same artists as Holly over the years he teamed up with US country star Suzy Bogguss in 1996 to cut a scintillating version of 'It Doesn't Matter Anymore' as part of the major Holly country-tribute package.

There will doubtless be other connections to come in the future.

Jerry Engler

Minor Brunswick artist from the 1950s who sadly was never to have a major hit, although, in 1957, he did cut the rockabilly classic 'Sputnik', which has since become a collector's item.

Met Buddy backstage at a Rochester concert and as a result Holly agreed to play guitar on two tracks that Jerry planned to record at Norman's Clovis studio. These were 'What You Gonna Do' and 'I Sent You Roses'. The record session actually took place on 7th September 1958, Buddy's 22nd birthday.

Neither track was released commercially at the time but Jerry Engler did put out one of the titles on a privately released 45 a few years back.

Extended Play Records (EPs)

In the 1950s and in the 1960s in particular, there was a strong demand for EPs largely for economic reasons. In those days fans couldn't always readily afford the more expensive LPs and to get four tracks on a seven-inch EP was the next best option.

Several Crickets/Holly EPs came out on the Coral label over a three-year period which commenced with FEP 2002 in September 1958. There was then a virtual four-year hiatus before Coral issued some six EPs that largely contained earlier less well-known material. Although they sold well they have nevertheless become quite collectable.

Following Holly's death in 1959, UK Brunswick released most of his Nashville recordings on two distinctive EPs. This entry wouldn't be complete without also mentioning a superb EP entitled 'Good Rockin' Tonight', which came out in 1986 on the enterprising Rollercoaster label.

Maxi singles have come and gone since the demise of the EP record but UK Holly releases on 45 rpm seem to be confined to the specialist Old Gold label these days.

Action shot taken at an April 1958 concert in Waterloo, Iowa, during Alan Freed's Big Beat Show. (Courtesy of Dick Cole.)

Don and Phil Everly

Don, born 1st February 1937; Phil born 19th January 1939. It is well known that The Crickets and The Everly Brothers were firm friends. Although the singers all came from the South they actually first met on tour in Montreal, Canada in 1957. Not only did they do one or two tours together but on one occasion Buddy and The Crickets formed the back-up band for the Everlys.

Fortunately (unlike the case with Eddie Cochran), there are several photographs of Buddy with Don and Phil from those early days. The

67

bond seemed particularly strong between Buddy and baby boy Phil, and the two got together in late 1958 jointly to produce a session for little-known singer Lou Giordano. For details, see entry under singer's name. The Everlys also helped Buddy with his image insisting that he go for heavier-framed glasses. (You can look at pictures of Holly over the period 1955–9 and virtually date them from the spectacles being worn.)

Around the same period, Holly and his lifetime friend Bob Montgomery composed 'Love's Made A Fool Of You' and 'Wishing' in the hope that the Everly Brothers would record the numbers. Sadly this did not happen but Holly himself cut superb demos of both numbers. They were finally released in the 1960s.

Both Don and Phil took Holly's death badly and Phil attended the funeral in Lubbock on 7th February. The link has survived Holly's death; Jerry, Joe B. and Sonny backed the Everly Brothers in their 1960 tour of the UK. Around the same time Jerry and Sonny helped out on the recording session that produced the Everly's great 'Til I Kissed You', and, of course, it was Sonny that wrote one of their finest recordings, 'Walk Right Back'.

What are the other essential connections between Holly and The Everly Brothers? Well, the latter recorded superb 1960s' versions of both 'That'll Be The Day' and 'Oh Boy!' before eventually recording an excellent version of 'Not Fade Away' in Nashville as part of their 'Pass the Chicken And Listen' album. (The story is that Buddy had actually pitched the song at the brothers back in 1958.)

Into the 1990s we find ex-Cricket Albert Lee playing lead guitar at Everly Brothers' live concerts, indicating the longevity of the links between The Everlys and The Crickets. It's been a lifelong affair.

'Everyday'

Recorded at Norman Petty Studios, Clovis, New Mexico, 29th May 1957. Trio of Buddy, Jerry and Joe supplemented by Vi or Norman Petty, celeste.

This recording is an absolute gem and, according to Jerry Allison, was recorded quite quickly, at the same session that produced 'Not Fade Away'. Jerry's contribution? – slapped knees! Anybody who has tried to pick this melody out on a keyboard will know how simple it is, but *how* effective. Composed by Holly and Norman Petty, the use of a celeste gives it a distinctive sound. It has become one of the numbers most associated with Holly throughout the years. Although it was never a chart hit (it was the B side of 'Peggy Sue'), it has nevertheless usually been included in his greatest hits compilations. (It was eventually a UK hit courtesy of Don McLean in 1973.) Interestingly, both Vi and Norman in separate interviews claimed they played celeste on the session!

In 1984, The Picks did overdubs to Holly's vocal but for many fans the uncluttered charm of the original was destroyed.

In 1958, Buddy Holly cut a promotional radio jingle for Lubbock radio station KLLL to the tune of 'Everyday' and all 28 seconds of it appeared on a Live Gold album entitled 'The Real Buddy Holly Story' in 1991. See separate entry, JINGLES. It is believed there is also a live clip of this song by Buddy, which was recorded at Fort Lauderdale, Florida when Jerry Lee was present.

'Everyday' remains one of Buddy's greatest recordings and it's a sobering thought that it was written and recorded before The Crickets first charted with 'That'll Be The Day'.

F

Adam Faith

The first most of us knew of the glottal stop or vocal hiccup was when we heard the lead voice of The Crickets back in 1957. UK artists were quick to catch up and one of the very best exponents and vocalists of the era was, of course, Adam Faith.

Born Terence Nelhams on 23rd June 1940, he initially fronted The Worried Men, a skiffle outfit, but was to get his first break with an appearance on the *6.5 Special* TV show before landing a residency with Drumbeat. (There were all of two channels in those days but both the above shows were on BBC.)

Adam became quite a major star with 14 successive Top 20 hits in a 3-year period. With John Barry's pizzicato style backings, his first two hits, 'What Do You Want' and 'Poor Me', were definitely from the Holly-soundalike school.

He has since gone on to pursue a highly successful musical and acting career. See also JOHN BARRY entry.

Terry Farlan

An absolute unknown who cut an album of Holly's songs, which was released on the UK budget Hallmark label in 1969.

The heavy-framed glasses the singer is sporting look as if they are being worn purely for the album cover photo. Terry Farlan was in good company as artists such as Brian Poole, Cliff Richard and John Lennon all had periods in their early careers when they sported Holly-type glasses. Elton John was eventually to take the fashion to the absolute limit.

Terry Farlan could still be about – I'm not sure. He seemed to surface just long enough to cut this album, which, as covers go, was a reasonable effort.

Irving Field

Feld was president of Super Enterprises and with two others formed the General Artists Corporation (GAC) in the 1950s. GAC were responsible in the USA for staging many of the legendary rock'n'roll package shows that often featured over a dozen acts, each performing on two or three numbers.

In the UK, with far fewer stars, we had to tolerate a mixed roster of artists who often appeared on bills that bore more than a passing resemblance to their music hall predecessors. The UK tour that Holly undertook was an extreme example of the phenomenon. The bill, complete with the *de rigueur* compere, Des O'Connor was 100 per cent variety acts. One could be forgiven for thinking that The Crickets were added as an afterthought, but they were not and were the major draw.

Irving Feld remains a shadowy figure and was certainly at the business end of things. There have been rumbles down the years that the fateful tour should have been cancelled after the crash took out all the headliners. Instead it carried on, with a patched-up itinerary, through to the final 15th February date. Artists that filled in on the remaining tour dates have remarked that the atmosphere was quite weird. Feld has long since retired but his son is in the music business carrying on the family name.

Fender Stratocaster

This is the guitar make and model forever associated with Buddy Holly. Down the years guitar greats such as Hank B. Marvin, Eric Clapton, Mark Knopfler and others have also used this solid-bodied piece of electrified equipment that was first launched back in 1954 by its inventor, Leo Fender.

See also entry under GUITARS

Films

We know sadly that Holly never appeared in any of the mainly low-budget rock'n'roll movies that proliferated in the period 1956–9. Maybe manager Norman Petty was approached, but legend has it that he didn't approve of the genre.

Certainly fellow Texans such as Jimmy Bowen and Buddy Knox were signed up as one of the dozens of acts who appeared in *Disc Jockey Jamboree*, a typical film of the period. At that point in 1957 The Crickets had not yet raided the charts and by 1958 they were pretty busy with tours that included Australia and the UK. So perhaps the reason it never happened was simply because of their schedule.

Maria Elena, Buddy's widow, has been quoted as saying the singer wanted to turn to acting and enrol in classes – perhaps with Elia Kazan. She envisaged that he would become a thespian in the Anthony Perkins mould! That all sounds a long way from performing odd musical numbers in film quickies, but his hero was Elvis, so who knows?

If Holly didn't make it onto the silver screen in the 1950s, the latter-day Crickets did in 1962 when they did a musical number in the UK movie *Just For Fun*. Shortly after, they sang 'La Bamba' in a US surfing movie *Girls On The Beach*, which featured Lesley Gore and The Beach Boys.

A few clips of Holly and The Crickets appearing on TV have survived and been seen frequently over the years.

The Fireballs

The original quartet of Chuck Tharp, Stan Lark and Eric Budd were led by George Tomsco on lead guitar and had their first hit in late 1959 when their instrumental 'Torquay' was a Top 40 hit. They had been formed some two years earlier taking their name from the fact that their staple live number, played again and again, was 'Great Balls of Fire'. Although not a UK hit, their instrumental 'Quite a Party' influenced a generation of British guitarists.

The group from New Mexico recorded at Norman Petty's Clovis studios and it is well documented that they came to be involved in a whole batch of posthumous overdubs of Buddy Holly material. Sometimes these overdubs have been criticized for turning Buddy Holly material into 'singalong with The Fireballs'. But it's very much a matter of personal opinion as to whether this was the case or not. What is certain is that the opportunity to include Jerry Allison or Joe B. on

71

such sessions was missed. A matter of perennial disappointment, surely.

The Fireballs did meet up with Buddy Holly fleetingly when both were visiting Petty's Clovis, New Mexico studios in 1958 but their musical liaison did not crop up until after Holly's death.

The Fireballs added a vocalist, Jimmy Gilmer, in 1961 and Chuck Tharp left at that time. Norman Petty was also heavily involved in the career of another celebrated instrumental group, The Stringalongs. Of course, Holly and Allison had recorded two instrumentals 'Honky Tonk' and 'Holly's Hop' but these were more like jams, as part of the group's rehearsals, and were certainly never intended for release.

Although The Fireballs disbanded in the 1970s they got back together in 1989 as part of the Clovis Music Festival.

See JIMMY GILMER entry.

Flatt & Scruggs

Lester Flatt (born 28th June 1914) and Earl Scruggs (born 6th January 1924) were definitive bluegrass performers who were members of the Grand Ole Opry during the 1950s and they were one of many influences on the youthful Buddy Holly growing up in Lubbock, Texas. Two of Buddy's earliest musical instruments were the banjo and mandolin, stringed instruments that Scruggs was certainly the master of.

It is also worth mentioning that for every white, country influence on Buddy (Hank Williams, Bill Monroe, The Louvin Brothers) there was, seemingly, a compensatory black rhythm influence in the shape of Fats Domino, Little Richard, Muddy Waters, etc.

Although when Buddy first teamed up with Bob Montgomery his music was close to bluegrass he eventually seemed to absorb all types of musical inputs and distil these into his own unique sound.

Flatt & Scruggs continued to perform as a duo until 1969. Lester Flatt, the elder by 10 years, died in 1979, but Earl Scruggs continued to record as The Earl Scruggs Revue, although he has latterly moved away from active performing.

'Flower of My Heart'

Buddy and Bob performance at Nesman Studio, Wichita Falls, Texas, circa *1954–5.*

One of a batch of five country, or western and bop, numbers that Buddy and the boys performed in the early days, which were probably recorded as demos at the Nesman Studio in Wichita Falls, Texas. Although not strong commercial numbers they were, fortunately, preserved for posterity. Some overdubbing was added for their release on the 'Holly In The Hills' album. Whether the undubbed version is issueable is not known.

'Flower Of My Heart' was probably written by friends Bob Montgomery and Don Guess and although the number won a school prize, being chosen Westerner Song of The Year, it is not noticeably stronger than any of the other material.

Quite who wrote what on these earliest Holly/Montgomery tracks is very uncertain to say the least. Generally, authors' credits had to be allocated when the recordings were given a commercial release, except in those few cases where a song had already been published.

'Fool's Paradise'

Crickets recording (Buddy, Jerry & Joe) following Niki Sullivan's departure. Cut at Norman Petty's Clovis Studios, New Mexico, probably 14th February 1958.

Norman Petty added his name to this composition by Sonny LeGlaire and Horace Linsley; The Roses were later used to dub backing vocals for the finished release. They were evidently paid a session fee of US $65 each for overdubbing vocals on this track and 'Think It Over'. This was the first time that Petty had switched from The Picks when looking to dub Crickets' material. With the addition of distinctive piano played by Vi Petty the recording is a good one, and it was surprising that it did not appear in album format until the 1971 UK release of 'Remember', which tidied up several loose ends at that particular time (most notably the inclusion of the Norman Petty overdubs of apartment tape material).

The released master of 'Paradise' is take three; the undubbed takes one, two and three have appeared on unsanctioned albums and make for fascinating listening.

Not a song that has inspired frequent covers but Don McLean did do a strong version on his 'Playin' Favourites' album in 1971. 'Fool's Paradise' has been used as the title of several other songs, and of most interest to rock'n'roll fans is the composition by Eddie and Hank Cochran that dates from around 1956.

'Footprints in the Snow'

Home recording at 3315, 36th Street Lubbock of Buddy Holly with Bob Montgomery. Dates from 1953.

There are several home recordings of Buddy that predate the 'Holly In The Hills' material and on which his voice is adolescent. They are most definitely of academic interest only but do help chart the development of Buddy Holly from those earliest days right through to his final efforts in 1959 at age 22.

In the UK, the American Johnny Duncan and his Blue Grass Boys seemed to tour British ballrooms endlessly on the back on this number and 'Last Train To San Fernando'. Footprints has been a tune that has been handed down over the years and would have been staple material for country singers back in the 1940s and 1950s.

If, as has been said, Holly performed 'Gotta Travel On' nightly during the final tour, he *may* also have used the similar styled 'Footprints In The Snow'. Certainly, older fans will be familiar with this song title and for this reason if little other, it ought to be officially released if and when a definitive collection of Holly material sees the light of day.

'For the First Time Anywhere'

UK Album: MCA MCM 1002.

This is the celebrated 1983 album that finally saw a whole batch of Holly performances released in their undubbed original state complete with occasional pops and clicks. The colour sleeve even sported previously unseen photos. Arguably, it is the last great album of Holly's to be released by his original label.

It was compiled by MCA employee Steve Hoffman and it seemed for a while that fans would be treated to several new collections. 'The Stereo Album' and 'Lost and Found' were even mooted as titles. However, Hoffman suddenly left his employers and since then hardly any innovative Holly releases have been forthcoming via his label.

It's hardly surprising that an unofficial four-CD box set on Vigotone has recently appeared, which contains most of the tracks that long-suffering fans have been awaiting, and is entitled 'What You Been A-Missing'. Those are, in fact, the words Holly sang so prophetically during 'Oh Boy!'.

Listing: Rock-a-bye Rock / Maybe Baby / Because I Love You / I'm Gonna Set My Foot Down / Changing All Those Changes / That's My Desire / Baby Won't You Come Out Tonight / It's Not My Fault / Brown-Eyed Handsome Man / Bo Diddley

Lance Fortune

This minor UK singer was born Chris Morris and achieved fame briefly in 1960 with the Hollyish hit, 'Be Mine', which reached No.4.

The record had a pizzicato style backing courtesy of John Prendy (aka John Barry), and to complete the Holly connection it was no surprise to learn that the engineer on the session was none other than Joe Meek.

See also JOE MEEK entry.

The Four Teens

Joe B. Mauldin was the bassist with this rock'n'roll group from the Lubbock area, prior to moving on to join The Crickets.

Larry Welborn also had a spell with The Four Teens, who were little known outside their immediate area, although they did back singer Terry Noland for a spell. The other group member of the quartet was Brownie Higgs on drums. See various entries for further details (except Higgs).

Connie Francis

Born Constance Franconero, of Italian extraction, Connie had an incredible run of chart success in both the UK and the USA in a six-year spell that commenced in 1958 and ended when The Beatles took over the whole scene in 1964.

She has successfully plundered many songbooks for her albums over the years but it was still a surprise in 1996 to learn that her latest collection of songs were by Buddy Holly and entitled 'With Love to Buddy'. The combination works well and we finally get to hear a female version of 'Peggy Sue'!

It seems Francis didn't appear on many package shows and it's unlikely therefore that the stars met.

Freddie and the Dreamers

This UK male vocal and instrumental group shot to fame in 1963 on the back of the Northern beat boom.

Freddie Garrity (born 14th November 1940) was the leader of this distinctive quintet and has been described as a Holly lookalike. If this is the case, then surely a stronger claim could be made by Greek songstress, Nana Mouskouri or even John Major?

Freddie recorded 'It Doesn't Matter Anymore' and 'Early In The Morning', frequently using the former in his stage act. He's still performing these days along with many other hardy survivors of the 1960s' music scene.

Alan Freed

What a sad entry to write. It's absolutely certain that this legendary DJ, who did so much to promote rock'n'roll in its most ethnic form, died as an indirect result of his love of music. Every report indicates he died a broken man not long after the payola scandal (radio plays secured by bribes) had ripped the industry apart and led to him receiving a suspended prison sentence.

If payola was a painful episode for Freed, for Stan Freburg it was another excuse to parody the rock'n'roll scene in his wickedly funny way.

As to Holly and Freed, there's a wonderful photo of them with Larry Williams; the three are sporting bow ties. Considering rock'n'roll had such a rebellious image it is interesting to look back and to see the photographic evidence that most artists were smartly turned out. If asked to say something about the clothes, I suppose it would simply be that they were different.

The Crickets made their first ever US TV appearance when they appeared on Freed's show on 23rd August 1957. There is also an excellent interview with Holly by Alan Freed, which took place at radio WNEX, New York on 2nd October 1958. The interview appears in full on the MCA box set and there is a chilling section where Holly and Freed discuss planes crashing. Another section is mildly embarrassing with Freed trying to set up a humorous punchline with Buddy and failing totally.

Alan Freed had a magnificent speaking voice, which has been captured on such albums as 'Alan Freed's Memory Lane', where he gives brief spoken intros to such legendary artists as The Moonglows and The Flamingos.

While he is often portrayed as a mere figurehead, it is conveniently forgotten that Freed fronted a powerhouse big band that performed on tour bills and also made records. Maybe he ended up with more composer credits than he deserved but this was often the price recording artists had to pay in the 1950s to get exposure from DJs.

He deservedly had a film made of his life, *American Hot Wax* (1978), which was a critical success. Freed, who was of Welsh extraction, was born 15th December 1922 and died 20th January 1965 of uraemia.

Bobby Fuller

Founder, lead singer and guitarist with The Bobby Fuller Four, Bobby Fuller had two sizeable US hits in 1966 on the Mustang label. He was born in Goose Creek, Texas in 1942 and was to lose his life on 18th July 1966, age 23.

Bobby was heavily influenced by the sound of Buddy Holly and The Crickets, and a few years ago a posthumous album, 'Memories of Buddy Holly', was issued on the Rockhouse label pulling together all Bobby Fuller's Holly-related material.

Back in 1962 Bobby and his group had actually recorded in Clovis under Petty's direction after a demo tape sent to Buddy's parents was forwarded to Norman Petty. The two numbers 'Gently My Love' and 'My Heart Jumped' were very Hollyish. Although they were issued on a local label, Yucca, and popular around El Paso they were not hits. He then went on to record material that attempted to cash in on both the surfing and the drag racing craze of the time.

In the mid 1960s Bobby finally broke into the big time taking the Sonny Curtis composition 'I Fought The Law' into the Top 10. His next Mustang release was Holly's own 'Love's Made A Fool Of You', which reached No.26 on Billboard in May 1966. But, come July Bobby was found dead in his car in mysterious circumstances. Whilst suicide was mentioned this seems highly unlikely given his record was still in the charts and his career was on a real high.

Let's finish by listing a few of the similarities between Holly's career and that of Fuller's. Both were from West Texas and both lost their young lives tragically whilst seemingly at their peak. They had both recorded at Clovis and each artist had split with his backing group just before his demise. Bobby's manager was Bob Keane, who also handled the career of Ritchie Valens, who had lost his life in the same crash as Holly. Norman Petty wrote to Fuller in 1966 seeking to persuade him back to Clovis. The similarities are striking!

Billy Fury

Legendary artist who enjoyed a fantastic sequence of UK chart successes from February 1959, when he had his first hit with 'Maybe Tomorrow'.

Born Ronald Wycherly on 17th April 1941 in Liverpool, Fury had heart problems from an early age and actually retired through ill health in the mid 1960s. He returned in the 1970s and appeared in the hit movie *That'll Be The Day*, which starred David Essex.

In the final years of his life he recorded a stream of Holly-like material, which included 'Maybe Baby', 'I'm Gonna Love You Too', 'Well … All Right' and 'Sheila'.

Sadly, he died 28th January 1983, aged only 41.

G

Snuff Garrett

Thomas Lesslie Garrett was born in Dallas on 5th July 1938. He has a long musical CV, having started out as a Dallas DJ in the 1950s moving on to station KDVB in Lubbock in 1955. It was then that he met Holly and began a friendship that lasted until Buddy's death.

If you check out your musical collection you may find you have something Snuffy's been involved with. For example the series of instrumental albums, '50 guitars of Tommy Garrett', was Snuff Garrett. He was musical supervisor for several Clint Eastwood movies, including the *Honky-Tonk Man* film soundtrack, which was just about the last thing Marty Robbins was involved in. He also recorded a quasi-classical album calling himself the 'Texas Opera Company'. Of course we mustn't forget that he produced the hit album 'Bobby Vee Meets The Crickets', as well as supervising Eddie Cochran's last session and many of Johnny Burnette's recordings. For a while he was the Liberty label's star producer.

In addition, Snuffy was instrumental in helping get the Buddy Holly statue erected in Lubbock, Texas, for which fans owe him a debt of thanks. At the time of Buddy's death the two were planning to get together and form a music company called Taupe, which just happened to be the exact colour of Buddy's Cadillac Fleetwood.

Snuff Garrett is still active in the music business, having moved on from his rock'n'roll days, and in his time has produced artists as diverse as Roy Rogers, Frank Sinatra and Cher.

'Giant'

UK Album: MCA MUPS 371.

The name of the famous James Dean movie was shrewdly used by Norman Petty as the title for this 1969 album. In fact, whilst additional Holly material had been discovered over the years this album was to be the last to include significant new material. Coming 10 years after Holly's death it was an exciting release and it is a surprise that the album crept into the UK charts for only one week. Even more surprisingly the single 'Love Is Strange', issued concurrently, failed to chart at all.

One real criticism of the album has to be that of the varied content. 1956 and 1959 demos are placed side by side making for very uneven listening. Comments that the album was overproduced are not really valid although it remains disappointing that former Crickets were not asked to help on the overdubbing project. Petty's sleeve note comment that the drummer used on the overdubbing played with more drive and verve than the original drummer must have irked Jerry Allison somewhat.

But the album remains a great one and few can argue with its title.

LISTING: Love Is Strange / Good Rockin' Tonight / Blue Monday / Have You Ever Been Lonely / Slippin' and Slidin' / You're The One / Dearest / Smokey Joe's Café / Ain't Got No Home / Holly Hop

Jimmy Gilmer

Gilmer (vocalist/guitarist) was born in Illinois and moved to Amarillo, Texas in the early 1950s. He was catapulted to enormous fame in 1963 when his Clovis recording of 'Sugar Shack' spent five weeks at the top of the US charts, and quickly went gold. It may well have been Norman Petty's overdubbed organ that gave the track its greatness.

Jimmy Gilmer had, since 1961, been the occasional vocalist with The Fireballs but without much success until 'Sugar Shack' transformed things. The vocalist had also used Norman Petty's Clovis studios to record his album 'Buddy's Buddy' in the early 1960s. The title was a slight misnomer as the two artists never actually met, and the Holly numbers on the album are all performed in a style that, while much removed from the originals, makes for interesting listening.

Since 1991 he has been regional manager for the SBK label, whose roster includes rap artist Vanilla Ice.

See entry THE FIREBALLS.

Lou Giordano

Little-known US artist who was born Louis Patsy Giordano on 23rd June 1929 and who died, age 40, on 22nd December 1969. As well as performing as Lou Giordano he also used the stage name, Lou Jordan. He had a single produced in New York by Buddy and Phil Everly in late 1958 for the Brunswick label, which was released to good reviews in February 1959 but which failed to chart.

The A side of the disc was the Holly composition 'Stay Close To Me' whilst the flip was a Phil Everly number, 'Don't Cha Know'. It is interesting to note that the apparent 'girlie' group on the latter were, in fact, Holly, Phil Everly and Joey Villa of The Royal Teens. (It was probably Villa that introduced Giordano to Buddy and Phil.) Both of the latter also played guitar on the session.

Giordano had a lightweight voice and it is a pity Holly never recorded his own composition. If it was taped by Holly no sign of it has ever materialized. Incidentally, a superb version of 'Stay Close To Me' was recorded by Mike Berry years later in which he incorporated a sequence of 'Words Of Love'.

As a footnote it is worth mentioning that the two Giordano sides took nearly twenty takes between them before masters were created. We hear the finished tracks and sometimes forget just how much effort has been expended along the way.

'Girl On My Mind'

Second Nashville recording session at Bradley's Barn, 22nd July 1956, which included Jerry Allison, Sonny Curtis and Don Guess. Released version is Take 3.

A pedestrian ballad, it was written by Lubbock friend and bassist Don Guess, who appeared on this and each of the 1956 Nashville sessions. Although it was never a hit, it's interesting to note that it was released as both a 45 and 78 in the USA during Holly's lifetime.

A few years back The Picks released the Holly vocal with their own dubbed backing vocals added. Whilst it helps somewhat it cannot totally transform what must remain, by Buddy Holly standards, a pretty mundane song. The criticism usually levied at the Holly recording is that he is trying to sing in too high a register à la Tony Williams of The Platters. Whatever the reason it is certainly one of Holly's less popular performances.

Glasses

As mentioned in an earlier entry, you can virtually date a Holly photo by looking at the glasses he is wearing. Evidently Buddy had 20/800 vision in both eyes so he needed to wear spectacles from an early age and preferred conventional styles to contact lenses, which he had tried and discarded.

In the USA, a long-defunct magazine once stated that by 1958 Holly had ditched his nerdy Cuban half-rims for bop glasses! However you put it, he certainly turned to heavier frames – evidently after discussing the subject with his friend Phil Everly.

The style he was wearing at the end of his life were on prescription from a New York firm. They were apparently lost in the fateful plane crash but were rediscovered in 1980 when a storage vault in Mason City was being cleared out. Evidently Holly's glasses, The Big Bopper's watch and one or two other personal effects had been stored away and forgotten about.

Coincidentally, a wallet that Holly lost when water-skiing on a Lubbock lake was recovered years later when a routine dredging operation unearthed the find.

Arthur Godfrey

Godfrey was a big name in the States in the 1950s, primarily as a result of his regular *Talent Scout* shows.

It is on record that The Crickets failed an audition in Amarillo, Texas, 11th May 1957 while waiting for one of their recordings to break out. Interestingly, around January 1957 Patsy Cline had appeared on the show, which led to 'Walking After Midnight' being a major hit record for her. The US version of the UK's Hughie Green show, Godfrey's show also helped discover Guy Mitchell, Steve Lawrence and many other name acts.

Before moving on, just reflect that Buddy and the boys were rejected in May some three months after they had actually recorded both 'That'll Be The Day' and 'Words Of Love'! 'Everyday' was recorded that same month.

Maybe Arthur Godfrey should have failed his audition as a talent scout?

John Goldrosen

Author of the trailblazing US biography, *Buddy Holly, His Life And Music*, published in 1975, Goldrosen grew up in Worcester, Massachusetts, USA and graduated from Harvard in 1971. Shortly thereafter he gave up two years of his life to research the book. All Holly fans owe John a great debt as he was able to interview many important players in the Holly legend whilst they were still living. At the time of writing he is alive and well in the state of Massachusetts.

Bobby Goldsboro

Bobby Goldsboro is an American recording artist who had a string of big hits over a 10-year period commencing in 1964. 'Honey' was the big one although the Mac Davis composition 'Watching Scotty Grow' went Top 10.

Earlier he had been a member of Roy Orbison's backing band before teaming up with Buddy's pal Bob Montgomery, who produced all his hits on the United Artists label, most of them in the country idiom.

Goldsboro is a native of Florida where he was born in 1941.

'Gone'

Demo; recorded at The Venture Studio in Lubbock, Texas, late 1956. Personnel: Buddy, Jerry Allison and others unknown.

Buddy, with Jerry Allison, cut a demo version of this country number towards the end of 1956. Earlier, he had completed several southern tours, as Buddy Holly and the Two Tones; and the line-ups featured mostly country acts. It is certain that this number would have been typical of the material featured at such concerts.

The song had been composed several years earlier by Smokey Rogers and Ferlin Husky had hits twice with the same number, under different names. The first time he called himself Terry Preston and he claims he re-recorded it in 1957 after hearing Holly perform 'Gone' on stage in Texas!

The Holly version – overdubbed as so much of that early stuff was – appeared first on the 'Showcase' album in 1964, the album itself being a big seller and proving there was still a voracious appetite for new Holly material.

The song is simple but strikingly beautiful and Buddy's version, despite lasting only 69 seconds, is a good one given the garage-type recording circumstances that produced it. Undubbed earlier takes of 'Gone' finally appeared on an 1986 album 'Something Special From Buddy Holly' on Rollercoaster, which sadly is no longer in catalogue.

'Good Rockin' Tonight'

Demo: recorded at the Venture Studio in Lubbock, Texas, late 1956. Personnel: Buddy, Jerry Allison and others unknown.

First written and recorded by Roy Brown back in 1947, this song was then covered by Wynonie Harris, who had a pretty successful record with it in 1948 on the King label. Even Pat Boone covered it in the 1950s but it was not a hit for him.

However, it was probably the Elvis performance on SUN 210 that Buddy first heard before proceeding to cut his own version at a practice session in late 1956. Never intended for release it finally came out on the 1969 'Giant' album with other unreleased product, all heavily overdubbed to give them a more commercial sound.

Those fans who wanted to hear how Holly sounded in a more raw and undiluted manner finally got to hear the truth when the undubbed recordings of this and other performances were released on the 1986 album, 'Something Special From Buddy Holly'. Any fan not having these garage recordings should do their level best to search them out even if it means camping out at Record Fairs.

Keith Goodwin

An *NME* reviewer for years, the name is sure to ring a bell with popular music fans who are in their middle years.

He met up with Buddy, Jerry and Joe on their UK visit and they spent lots of time in each other's company. It's worth mentioning that they visited the Austin car factory together, the possibility being that the boys might end up buying new sports cars while over here.

Goodwin attended several tour dates and wrote several articles on the group, which appeared in both the weekly *NME* and its monthly companion, *Hit Parade*.

'Gotta Get You Near Me Blues'

Buddy and Bob performance at Nesman Studio, Wichita Falls, Texas, circa *1954–5.*

Long before Holly walked up the steps of the Pythian Temple in New York to undertake his final recording session with Coral he was cutting demos in a small local Texas studio at Wichita Falls. One of these was 'Gotta Get You Near Me Blues', written by Bob Montgomery and one of the most rhythmic of a batch of numbers they tried out in those early days.

Not recorded for commercial reasons it was nevertheless put out in the 1960s with other similar performances on the 'Holly In The Hills' album. All the tracks included additional overdubbing.

The undubbed version came out in 1995 as part of a Vigotone CD box set allowing fans to hear the prominent fiddle of Sonny Curtis that had largely been hidden before.

Billy Grammer

Billy Grammer was born in Benton, Illinois on 28th August 1925, 1 of 11 children. He's not a name that appears in every country reference book these days but that wasn't the case back in 1959 as, months earlier, he had a major hit with 'Gotta Travel On', having been a session man around the Washington area for several years. Thereafter, he became a regular on the Grand Ole Opry and recorded albums continuously right up to the late 1970s. He even found time to invent his own distinctive flat-top guitar.

It is documented that Holly performed 'Gotta Travel On' and 'Salty Dog Blues' during the final Winter Dance Party Tour, and the former's lyrics, with hindsight, are sad but apt. The Billy Grammer disc entered the US charts in early December 1958 for a 15-week stay and it was natural for Buddy to perform this type of number on the bandstand.

Grand Ole Opry/Louisiana Hayride

Both showcases for country music in the 1950s and, of course, the Grand Ole Opry is around even today, although it is now more of a tourist attraction than the mecca for country talent that it was once.

Buddy was certainly a fan of the Opry but would not have been a serious contender to perform on it. However, artists such as Johnny Horton (only marginally more country), did appear of course, as did Elvis Presley, though his performance was unsuccessful. A far better potential venue for Holly would have been the Louisiana Hayride at nearby Shreveport or the Big D Jamboree in Dallas. Buddy and the boys did make an abortive attempt to appear on the Hayride following an introduction by Elvis but, frustratingly, it just didn't work out.

Interestingly, whilst we don't think of Holly in terms of country music it is a fact that he merits an entry in the majority of books on the genre that have appeared over the years. He is also in country's Hall of Fame as a composer. 1996 has also seen the release of a major Nashville tribute album that features many of country's contemporary artists. But Holly never had a record on the US country charts.

Rick Grech

Though British, Rick was born in Bordeaux, France of Ukrainian parents in 1965. He played a variety of musical instruments and was no mean vocalist. Apart from session work he was also a member of such groups as Family, Traffic and Blind Faith in a career dogged by drug-related problems.

He was possibly introduced to The Crickets through Glen D. Hardin in the early 1970s and appeared on their 'Bubblegum Bop Ballads and Boogie' album as well as 'Remnants' before leaving to form a short-lived group of his own, Square Dance Machine.

Evidently, Grech died rather a lonely death in March 1990 at the age of 44.

Lloyd Greenfield

LLoyd Greenfield acted as Buddy's agent in 1958 and claimed to be responsible for helping him with his later image. Certainly Holly had his teeth capped and his hair took on a more stylish look that year. Studying photos and film of the singer over a period of time, a gradual change can certainly be seen. To what extent this was on the advice of Lloyd Greenfield, we will probably never know.

At the time of the New York Bruno photographic session, just prior to the final tour, the change of image was about complete. Sadly, the output from that photo shoot hardly got used during Buddy's lifetime but an example was to be used evocatively for the sleeve of 'The Buddy Holly Story' memorial album that was rush released in March of 1959.

In Ellis Amburn's recent weighty biography of Holly, the name of Greenfield is not mentioned. But Buddy had split from Norman Petty and would certainly have needed an agent from late 1958, even if not a full-scale manager. What is certain is that Greenfield ran an agency in New York in the 1950s with the help of his brother Manny, and Holly visited their office in 1958.

Bill Griggs

Bill Griggs was a well known US super-fan of Buddy Holly. He took up the torch in the 1970s and organized a worldwide fan club, which did a lot of good things. Bill even moved his home to Lubbock, Texas, doubling as a record dealer to finance his hobby.

In an exciting 10-year period lasting into the mid 1980s, he was there to witness Buddy's statue being unveiled and to see Holly's life story turning up on celluloid. Bill helped to mastermind regular Lubbock conventions that acted as a magnet for fans from all over the world for many years.

Certainly this A–Z would be a much slimmer work without the author having access to Bill's pioneering magazines and works that have appeared on a regular basis since 1977. Nearly 20 years on and Bill is still diligently researching the music of Holly and his West Texas contemporaries.

Don Groom

It is not widely known but Don Groom was the first British member of The Crickets when he deputized on drums for Jerry Allison in 1962 on the recommendation of Mike Berry. J.I. had sadly been sidelined by Uncle Sam shortly after the Cuban missile crisis started up.

Don had in fact been seconded to complete the tour from The Outlaws, who backed Mike Berry, and who also had a hit instrumental group in their own right. This also meant that he ended up appearing with The Crickets in the musical film *Just For Fun*, which starred Mark Wynter, Joe Brown and Bobby Vee.

After the tour, Don joined up again with Mike Berry and stayed with him for several years. Don Groom was interviewed a few years ago about his Crickets connection, and, at the time of writing, is believed alive and well.

Don Guess

Born in Aspermont, Texas on 14th May 1937, Don Guess was a contemporary of Buddy Holly whose main instrument was standup bass, although he was also an expert on steel guitar. He composed quite a lot of early material, which was performed by Holly and Montgomery.

He appeared on many of the country 'Holly In The Hills' recordings and also toured with Buddy in 1956 before The Crickets became established. Apart from Buddy himself, Don Guess was the only one present on all three of those Nashville sessions. Guess recorded several numbers in the late 1950s and secured a few releases on small independent labels.

Eventually, he left the full-time music scene to pursue a career in insurance. He died of cancer, aged 55 on 21st October 1992.

Guitars

A lengthy article appeared in the *Guitar Player* magazine back in June 1982, which listed details of the many guitars owned by Buddy. The entry below is based on this and other information.

The first guitar that Buddy owned was a Harmony, made by a well-known Chicago-based firm who specialized in producing basic guitars for the mass market in the 1950s. By the time he met J.I. he was playing a Gibson Les Paul Gold Top, which he possibly found a bit too heavy. He switched to a Fender Stratocaster pretty early on and it's that image that dominates the photos of Holly on the bandstand. (His most famous Strat was stolen from his station wagon in Canada whilst on tour and had to be quickly replaced.) On the acoustic side, Buddy initially used a Gibson J45, the instrument that he hand-tooled in leather after seeing Hank Snow's guitar on a country bill in Lubbock. (Buddy's guitar, with leatherwork, is now owned by Gary Busey.)

In 1958, Buddy designed his own hollow-bodied guitar with the help of Guild and there is speculation that he might actually have endorsed that particular model. In the same year he also had a buying blitz picking up a Gibson J200, a Guild F50 Navarre (both acoustic) and two white Stratocasters. An Epiphone (a Gibson-related make) and a Gretsch have also been linked to Holly. (Not a bad haul and that's not counting the famous Des O'Connor Hofner!)

Down the years, Holly's guitar style has influenced many artists, including Jimmy Page, Eric Clapton, Ritchie Blackmore, Hank B. Marvin and Mark Knopfler to name a select few. Many would-be musicians were permanently influenced after first seeing Holly with his sunburst Fender on that famous March 1958 tour.

In the USA, Jerry McNeish has analysed all Buddy's recordings and decided that, on each number, one of four styles was adopted. These were:

- Open chord strumming, e.g. 'Ting A Ling'
- String lead playing – most records
- Downward fast-chord strumming, e.g. 'Peggy Sue'
- Folk/acoustic (chords), e.g. 'Well … All Right'

I hope the above helps guitar buffs. Incidentally, Holly experts fall out trying to say what amps Buddy used so we'll just mention that on the road he mainly used a 4 x 10-inch Fender Bassman.

H

Bob Hale

Hale was the regular DJ at the Surf Ballroom and was at the show on the evening of 2nd February 1959 spinning a few discs prior to introducing the various acts.

In a 1977 interview conducted by Bill Griggs it was interesting to learn that Holly played drums in backing up both Ritchie Valens and The Big Bopper. With regular drummer Carl Bunch sidelined with frostbite this makes sense.

Another source indicates that at one point in the proceedings the three headliners appeared together, light-heartedly forming a vocal trio. Considering the three different styles that must have been mighty interesting! At the time of writing, Bob Hale is still alive.

Bill Haley and the Comets

Born William John Clifton Haley in Michigan on 6th July 1925, Bill Haley was in the forefront of the rock'n'roll vanguard, and it disappoints to hear, occasionally, criticism of his contribution to the birth of the musical genre that we know as rock'n'roll. The music certainly needed Bill and it is sad that he burned himself out prematurely as the result of a non-stop touring schedule that stretched all over the world.

Buddy Holly, with Bob Montgomery, appeared on a Comets bill in Lubbock, Texas back in October 1955 and this ultimately led to Holly getting his first big chance to make a record. Bill has also been quoted as saying Buddy and the boys once backed him when his Comets were late arriving. Whilst Buddy opened those bills in 1955, in later years he appeared on other packages with Haley very much as an equal.

Both artists had definite country roots, and while Buddy's career was to be cut short, Bill went on touring for decades before, sadly, dying at the age of 55, in Harlingen, Texas on 9th February 1981. His greatest music dates from his lengthy career with Decca although the output from his Essex days (pre 1954) and his later material (Warner Bros, Swedish Sonet, etc.) was always eminently listenable. It is worth adding that Bill was invariably backed by first-class musicians, none more so than the great sax man Rudy Pompilli.

A little-remembered fact is that Bill Haley was a champion yodeller in his youth, a talent for which he actually won awards. In some of his earliest recordings he used the yodelling technique to great effect. It was obviously dropped from his routine in later years as no doubt it would have been considered square. Buddy's mother has said that her son grew up yodelling around the house but no examples ever cropped up in his recording output.

One other footnote: Bill Haley's mother was born in England and emigrated to the USA as a teenager.

Ben Hall

Ben Hall was born at Alvord near Wichita Falls, Texas back in 13th June 1924. Amongst his many talents are listed those of DJ, songwriter and publisher. He also fronted a band, Ben Hall and the Ramblers, and was well known locally in the Lubbock area for many years, becoming involved with both radio KDAV and KSEL.

Buddy and Sonny Curtis occasionally sat in with Ben Hall's group and Holly eventually sought Ben's help in obtaining material to cut at his forthcoming Nashville recording session. 'Blue Days, Black Nights' was the result and it has the distinction of being Buddy's first ever record release on US Decca D29854. Ben, with ace steel guitarist Weldon Myrick, also composed 'It's Not My Fault', one of the very best of Holly's earliest recordings, which got deserved exposure as the flip of the posthumous hit, 'Bo Diddley'.

Ben Hall has recorded his own versions of 'Blue Days, Black Nights' and this and other material has recently been released by Rollercoaster records in this country. He has had an active life in the music business helping to produce The Newbeats' 'Bread and Butter' hit in the 1960s and later produced country superstars Alabama.

George Hamilton IV

This US country artist was born 19th July 1937 in North Carolina and has ended up far more popular in the UK and elsewhere than in his own homeland.

In the 1950s he toured with Holly and others on some of the rock'n'roll package tours that criss-crossed America. He had several teenybopper hits before gravitating to Nashville and appearing on the Grand Ole Opry. He has recorded a prodigious amount of country music (his first love) as well as a large catalogue of church/gospel material. A long and distinguished country career continues for this most likeable and genuine of men.

He also has been somewhat of a worldwide roving ambassador for country music and has always spoken warmly of his occasional meetings with Holly, Cochran and others, never realizing that many would go on to achieve a legendary status.

Not to be confused with his namesake who played the role of Hank Williams, George is still in the music business at the present time as is his son, George Hamilton V. When interviewed for this book, George could remember clearly the last tour on which he met up with Holly and was also able to list all the cast. (It was The Biggest Show of Stars during October 1958.)

Jack Hansen

Producer of the first posthumous overdubbing session of Holly material that led to the single release of 'Peggy Sue Got Married' and 'Crying, Waiting, Hoping'. Thereafter, he was responsible for dubbed versions on the remaining four songs that Buddy had taped in his New York apartment in late 1958.

Often referred to as the Jack Hansen combo (shades of Ernie Freeman) Hansen worked for Coral and had actually been the A&R man at the October session that produced 'True Love Ways'.

The Hansen backings have often been criticized as being too heavy and for including a chorus on the tracks that ends up a bit overpowering. Many fans favour the later, Tex mex sound dubbed by Norman Petty, which, although instrumental only, came nearer the feel of the songs.

But the original Hansen versions are etched in our memories and for that reason will always retain a high level of popularity. Jack Hansen died in 1977.

Charles Hardin

Buddy Holly was christened Charles Hardin Holley and occasionally used the abbreviated format (Charles Hardin) on his composer credits. Evidently, this was done at a particular point in 1957 so that publisher Cedarwood Music/Jim Denny would not readily know the true authorship of some of the Holly/Crickets compositions.

Charles Hardin Holley had no connection with the notorious Texan gunfighter Wesley Hardin, who supposedly shot down 40 people before being gunned down himself in El Paso.

Holly slayed people, but with his music.

Glen D. Hardin

This former Cricket has a long pedigree that starts back in Lubbock, Texas, where he grew up with Buddy Holly. He was born on 18th April 1939 at Ropesville, Texas, and was christened Glen Dee Harding.

His main instrument is piano/keyboard and he can often be glimpsed in footage of Elvis on stage during his Vegas years. Like some other Crickets his relationship with the group has been intermittent. In between times he has worked with a host of other artists although his spell with Elvis (1970–6) was one of his longest involvements, before he left to join Emmylou Harris. A first-rate musical arranger, he is heavily involved in production these days.

Glen D. is not related to Holly in any way despite sharing the name, Hardin. Surprisingly, given his musical prowess, Glen is seldom thought of as a composer, although he has collaborated on over 20 titles. Probably his best composition from Crickets days is the classic 'Teardrops Fall Like Rain'.

'Have You Ever Been Lonely'

Practice tape; recorded at Venture Studio in Lubbock, Texas, late 1956. Personnel: Buddy, Jerry Allison and others unknown.

A favourite of his mother's it was hardly surprising that Buddy attempted this number, which had been quite a successful song for both Jaye P. Morgan and for the Three Deuces in the USA. Back in England there were a host of cover versions, and although the sheet music was a hit the actual records didn't chart. The song was composed by George Brown and Peter De Rose, the latter having also been part composer of the great favourite 'Deep Purple'.

The first release of Holly's recording was on the 1969 'Giant' Album in an overdubbed format. This gave the track a more commercial sound and had the twin benefit of transforming the original mono tape into a stereo release.

Undubbed versions of three takes of the song have been released on vinyl by Rollercoaster and despite the deteriorating condition of the tapes they are essential listening. More recently Vigotone has released them on CD format.

The released master of the song has Buddy calling out to his mother at the end of what was obviously a rehearsal performance.

Hawaii

The night after performing on the US *Ed Sullivan* TV Show (26th January 1958) The Crickets appeared on a stopover date at the Civic Auditorium, Honolulu, Hawaii *en route* to Australia.

This must have been a busy time for the boys as, a few days earlier, they also completed the 'Rave On' session in New York. The troupe that appeared in Hawaii, not in the Union at that point, comprised of the Australian lineup of Jerry Lee, Paul Anka, Jodie Sands and The Crickets.

Some reports indicate that they put in a further appearance in Hawaii on the way back to the USA and before embarking on The Big Gold Record Stars tour in Florida. What is certain is that The Crickets did stop off at the island of Canton, which in those pre-jet-powered days was an important refueling place on long-distance flights.

From a 1950s' standpoint, Holly was somewhat of a globetrotter and it is of little surprise that in 1959 he nightly sang the Billy Grammer hit 'Gotta Travel On'.

'Heartbeat'

Recorded at Norman Petty Studios, Clovis, New Mexico, July–August 1958.
Joe B. Mauldin (bass), replaced by George Atwood for this performance.
Tommy Allsup, lead guitar. Holly played rhythm guitar.

One of Buddy Holly's greatest solo performances and, like 'Everyday', its sustained impact over a period has totally eclipsed its original chart success. It was barely a hit in the UK and only reached a lowly No.82 in the USA. Buddy must have accepted the failure of this single, as the follow up, 'It Doesn't Matter Anymore', had been released in the USA coinciding with the start of the Winter Dance Party Tour.

Composer credits for 'Heartbeat' indicate Montgomery/Petty but it is generally accepted that Holly and Bob Montgomery collaborated on this number. The sound on this track was ahead of its time although in the States it was given the ugly label, 'chalypso'.

Much covered over the years, actor and Holly fan Nick Berry had a major hit with it in 1992, when it was used as the theme tune for a TV series of the same name. There have been other versions by: Humble Pie, Denny Laine, The Hollies, Bobby Vee, Skeeter Davis and others, but not The Crickets! But evidently Holly did perform it on stage during the curtailed 1959 tour.

Buddy's own version has been released with overdubbed vocal licks by The Picks but it doesn't work well and the original recording remains the definitive one, although the powerhouse Humble Pie version is worth checking out.

Caroyln Hester

A folk artist from down in Texas who has toured the UK over the years and who is probably most well known for helping introduce Bob Dylan to Columbia back in 1962. Decades later she helped Nanci Griffith on the road to folk/country stardom.

Carolyn recorded a session at Clovis in June 1958 that produced four numbers, none of which have been released to date, officially or otherwise. Of particular interest to Holly fans is a folk version of 'Take Your Time'. According to UK authority John Ingman she is also believed to have recorded 'Rave On'.

Let's hope the various recordings are prised out of the vaults at some point. Ms Hester has toured the UK in the last 12 months and still occasionally includes The Crickets' unsung classic 'Lonesome Tears' in her act.

Larry and Travis Holley (and other family members)

Older brothers Larry and Travis Holley have continued their support for Buddy's music over the years, eventually coming to terms with the personal tragedy of their younger brother's sudden and cruel death at the age of 22.

It is Travis (born 1927) who is most similar to Buddy in looks and build while Larry (born 1925) favours his mother's side in outward characteristics. Larry's working life has been spent running the family ceramic tile business, which briefly employed Buddy and the boys while they awaited their big break. They even helped lay some tiles at Norman's Clovis studios in an effort to achieve better acoustics! Larry has also run a small independent record label (Cloud Nine) for several years now. He has also put records out on the Holly House label.

Sister Pat (born 1929) has also followed Buddy's career with much pride and recently appeared being interviewed on a TV documentary that featured Peggy Sue, the ex-wife of Cricket Jerry Allison and Donna Ludwig, Ritchie Valens's old girlfriend.

Carrying on the musical torch is Larry's daughter Sherry, who has cut several records and a few years ago had a hit in Europe on the independent charts with her own composition 'The Cost Of Loving You'. As of 1996, Sherry is back in Lubbock busily writing new material and planning for the future.

Mr and Mrs L.O. Holley

Buddy has a wonderfully supportive family who have always welcomed contact with fans and have been his greatest champions down the years.

Charles Hardin Holley was the youngest of four children born to Lawrence Odel Holley (Born 4th November 1901, died 8th July 1985) and Mrs Ella Pauline Holley *née* Drake (Born 29th August 1902, died 20th May 1990.) Brothers Travis and Larry and sister Patricia are alive and well at the time of writing.

Lawrence Holley was born in Cooper, Texas, and moved to Dallas at a very early age. As was common in those far-off days, Mr Holley had a variety of diverse jobs, working as a carpenter, a tailor and even as a cook. By the time their youngest child was born, the family was located at 1911 6th Street in Lubbock and although they were to move it was always within the confines of Lubbock.

Mrs Holley helped write part of the lyrics of 'Maybe Baby' and also contributed other odd musical ideas that Buddy sometimes took up. It is also said she, or perhaps Larry, contributed a whole verse to 'I'm Lookin' For Someone To Love'.

Mr Holley senior led an active life until sidelined by a stroke during 1970. Although Mrs Holley was the musical one Mr Holley had, after the death of his son, helped produce and manage Niki Sullivan when he led a group called The Hollyhawks for a short time.

Lawrence and Ella Holley resided for many years after Buddy's death at their 56th street home, where they continued to do all they could to promote and keep alive their son's name.

After his death, Mrs Holley lived on for several years, although becoming increasingly frail and passing on at the age of 87 after a stroke. Both parents emanated a lot of love and warmth and should not be confused with their celluloid counterparts in Holly's film biopic.

See also LARRY & TRAVIS HOLLEY entry.

The Hollies

One of the very best groups that emerged at the time of the British beat explosion. Many think The Hollies choice of name is derived from that of Buddy Holly although alternatively the link is given as the name for a Christmas decoration.

The Hollies did record a superb album, 'Buddy Holly', for Polydor in 1980, but despite being TV advertised it surprisingly failed to chart. Each Holly number is given an unusual treatment, and they also, refreshingly, tackled lesser-known material. It's worth searching out and is not just for completists.

In 1996 an ambitious Holly tribute album emanated from Nashville and the highlight for many fans was to hear The Hollies help out Buddy Holly with the vocals on 'Peggy Sue Got Married' thanks to a bit of technological wizardry. For Graham Nash and Allan Clarke in particular the opportunity was a dream come true.

Buddy Holly

Vital Statistics: born Lubbock, Texas, on the afternoon of 7th September 1936 to Ella and Lawrence Holley. He was their fourth child. We are told that it was Dollar Day in Lubbock at that time.

Buddy had dark brown hair, brown eyes and – in UK parlance – was a shade under six feet tall and weighed approximately 10st 5lbs (145 pounds). He had poor vision and failed his physical for the armed services.

Music was his full-time career after he left school, but for a time he did a little carpentry and also laid some tiles while awaiting his big break. During his musical career he reportedly had a mild stomach ulcer and avoided alcohol. He was an occasional cigarette smoker and also tried pipe smoking, much the norm for the lifestyle of the 1950s.

As regards ancestry, he is believed to have English, Welsh and some Cherokee Indian blood. In the case of the latter he was in good company as Elvis also had American Indian ancestry, as did other late greats, Marty Robbins and Johnny Horton. Johnny Cash, still with us, can be added to this select group.

Buddy was a practising Christian and a member of the Tabernacle Baptist Church in Lubbock, Texas. He is buried in Lubbock City Cemetery. The grave has a stone with a guitar carved on it.

Maria Elena Holly

Born in Santiago, Maria Elena Holly is Buddy's widow. They married in August 1958 in a ceremony conducted at Holly's parents' house in Lubbock, Texas. It is well documented that Maria was a receptionist at the Southern Music Company in New York when the two met.

What is not so well known is that they actually first met in early January 1958 – a fact published when Maria was interviewed for the US teen *16* magazine in early 1959. Whilst their relationship was short they had actually known each other over a year before the crash that claimed Buddy's life, but this was still a tragically brief period, and it is obvious that she has never got over Holly's sudden death. (She miscarried in that same month of 1959.)

The two of them had temporarily based themselves in New York and had taken several career steps that would probably have borne fruit if fate had not intervened. One was to form a music publishing company, Maria Music, and this and other plans all fell apart in the early hours of 3rd February 1959.

Maria Elena, who is of Puerto Rican extraction was born 20th December 1932.

Buddy Holly pictured strumming an acoustic guitar, July 1958. This is said to be Maria Elena Holly's favourite. (Courtesy of Dick Cole.)

'Holly Hop'

Practice tape; recorded in Venture Studio, Lubbock, Texas, late 1956. Personnel: Buddy, Jerry Allison, drums and others not known.

Buddy Holly never released an instrumental in his lifetime but two recordings have been issued posthumously, 'Holly Hop' and 'Honky Tonk'. Both were recorded at the same practice session held close to Buddy's home on 19th Street, Lubbock.

'Holly Hop' was an untitled instrumental and is probably the jam type introductory number that Buddy used on his local KDAV radio appearances. This number and other material was passed to Norman Petty in the 1960s and it was released, overdubbed on the 'Giant' album in 1969. (With no known composer credits, it was decided to put it down to Mrs Holley, so maybe it should be 'Holley Hop'!)

The undubbed recording was first released subsequently on the Rollercoaster album 'Something Special From Buddy Holly' in the 1980s.

'Holly in the Hills'

UK album: CORAL LVA 9227.

On the face of it this album should not be a favourite as it contains very early material that would never have been released if Holly had not perished. The tracks (apart from 'Wishing') were not recorded under studio conditions, and, with Bob Montgomery often taking lead vocals, they do not in any way compare with the 1957–8 hitmaking recordings.

Many of these Buddy and Bob recordings were made at radio KDAV in Lubbock and as such cut onto metal 78 rpm acetates. Later, these primitive recordings were overdubbed by Norman Petty in an attempt to give the album a commercial sound or at least to hide the strong country feel that the tracks exude.

Nevertheless, the album was packaged with eye-catching artwork and it reached No.13 in the album charts when it came out in 1965.

A few of the tracks have finally surfaced undubbed in the last year on the Vigotone label. The US track listing of the 'Holly in the Hills' album was somewhat different to our own, which meant that various early recordings were unobtainable in the USA for many years.

UK LISTING: I Wanna Play House With You / Door to My Heart / Baby It's Love / I Gambled My Heart / Memories / Wishing / Down The Line / Soft Place In My Heart / Queen Of The Ballroom / Gotta Get You Near Me Blues / Flower Of My Heart / You And I Are Through

Buddy Holly Statue

A larger-than-life heroic bronze sculpture was unveiled in Buddy's hometown, Lubbock, Texas, on 5th September 1980 close by the Civic Centre. It was sculpted by Grant Speed, a well-known American artist who was also born and raised in Texas. He used a unique style known as 'The Half-breed' and visited Lubbock to see the work unveiled at a ceremony that brought together members of the original Crickets and Waylon Jennings amongst others. A limited number of miniature statuettes were also created and have become prized possessions of the lucky owners.

The main Holly statue initially stood somewhat forlornly in a grassy area without any adornment, but at the latter end of the 1980s, an attractive surround was built that incorporates a Walk of Fame. At a ceremony in 1986, former Crickets, Jerry Allison, Joe B. Mauldin, Niki Sullivan and Sonny Curtis were made inductees. Others honoured over the years read like a Who's Who of Texas musicians.

In recent years a monument to Holly and the other fallen stars, including pilot Roger Peterson, was erected close to The Surf Ballroom, Iowa, the scene of the singer's last appearance. It was donated by one-time Surf manager Darrel R. Hein and his family.

At the crash site itself three stainless steel records and guitars have been placed as a marker for those who trudge across the frozen cornfield each February.

'Honky Tonk'

Practice tape; recorded at Venture Studio in Lubbock, Texas, late 1956. Personnel: Buddy, Jerry Allison and others unknown.

It's sometimes hard to remember just how massive the instrumental 'Honky Tonk' was in the States. Part 1 and Part 2 of this number were in their Top 40 for close to six months in 1956. Doggett's version was recorded at the New York Beltone studio, where Buddy was to record Lou Giordano two years later. In the UK, several versions sold well (Ernie Freeman/Bill Justis/Bill Doggett) and the impact was diluted.

The melody was written by members of Doggett's band, and the number featured prominent sax by Clifford Scott. Holly's practice version substitutes guitar for sax, and it works well although it was never intended as a commercial release. It is infinitely better to listen to the undubbed version (the 'Rollercoaster' LP again), where the woops and shouts of Holly and Allison can be heard to better effect.

Johnny Horton

Known as 'The Singing Fisherman', Johnny La Gale Horton was born in Los Angeles on 30th April 1925 and died in Milano, Texas, 5th November 1960.

Buddy Holly and Johnny Horton had little in common except their Texan connections and that each was to die early in tragic circumstances. Although born on the West Coast, Horton was brought up from 1928 in Tyler, Texas, and was to become a regular performer on the Louisiana Hayride, where other illustrious country artists (Webb Pierce, Johnny Cash, Jim Reeves) had also gained exposure. Holly himself, at Elvis Presley's suggestion, tried to get on the Hayride but without success.

Many of Johnny's distinctive compositions were based on historical events although his first million-seller, 'Battle of New Orleans', was a traditional song that had been arranged by country artist, Jimmy Driftwood. He was enjoying his third major hit, 'North to Alaska', when he was killed in an auto accident returning from a show at the Skyline, in Austin, Texas. Hank Williams had coincidentally made his final appearance at the same venue (Johnny had also married Hank's widow).

Johnny Horton allegedly contacted Merle Kilgore from beyond the grave by getting the coded message 'The drummer is a rummer and cannot hold the beat' to him several years after his death.

Jack Huddle

Local Lubbock artist born 1st February 1928 who had a children's TV programme back in the 1950s and also cut a few singles although none of them made any national impact. He knew Holly quite well, and Buddy made his TV debut on his local talent show.

Holly plays a strong lead guitar on Huddle's 1957 single 'Starlight' / 'Believe Me', which came out on both the Petsy and the Kapp labels. (A lot of leasing of product was done in those days.) The A side guitar break is generally felt to be one of Holly's finest and is worth seeking out.

The Spring 1957 session that produced 'Starlight' was split with Jim Robinson, and, once again, Holly, Allison and others helped out as session musicians. Jack Huddle died 3rd January 1973, aged 44.

I

Frank Ifield

One of the biggest-selling UK artists of the 1960s, Frank spent much of his youth growing up in Australia before returning to the land of his birth.

He has claimed that he appeared on the same 1958 bill as Buddy and The Crickets when the group toured Australia. He is not, however, listed on tour posters of the time.

Some of Frank's earliest material was somewhat similar in style to The Crickets before he eventually created a hit-making yodelling style. Later (1964) he was to record an excellent version of 'True Love Ways', which was not a hit.

'I Forgot to Remember to Forget'

The Buddy Holly recording that never happened. In fact Buddy *did* cut a version of this classic song at a local radio station but the acetate was mutilated as it was felt that playing it might infringe his new Decca contract. (The acetate is in existence but is quite unplayable.)

The song is credited to Stan Kesler and rockabilly star Charlie Feathers although it is almost certain that the former was the sole contributor. Holly would have heard several versions but it is probably the Presley version on Sun 321 that influenced him to record it. Holly would almost certainly have performed it himself on his early 1956 tours.

'I Gambled My Heart'

Buddy and Bob performance at Nesman Studio, Wichita Falls, Texas, circa *1954–5.*

A Buddy and Bob performance from early Radio KDAV days that formed part of the 'Holly In The Hills' album released in the mid 1960s. Originally listed as a Bob Montgomery composition, this was later corrected to Holly/Montgomery.

The track is very country indeed and was overdubbed somewhat by

Norman Petty prior to release. While the original version presumably exists it seems unlikely to get a release even from a bootlegger.

'I Guess I Was a Fool'

Demo recorded at Norman Petty Studios; Clovis, New Mexico, February–April 1956. Personnel: see below.

The odd track out of a batch of practice demos recorded by Buddy, Jerry, Sonny and Don Guess in the months between the January and July Nashville sessions. Its oddness lies in the fact that it was the only track not apparently overdubbed and is therefore only available in its original mono format.

A self-composition, the lyrics contain an emotional message and it tends to be a much overlooked recording perhaps because the sound quality itself is less than top class. It was this composition that led to a search for a non-existent Holly recording 'I Tried To Forget', an alternate title for this song. See RUMOURS entry.

There are several earlier demo versions of this number by Holly but only one other recording has been released albeit on an unofficial basis.

'I Know I'll Have the Blues Again'

A title recorded by a little-known group called The Whitesidewalls, who have performed at numerous Holly tribute concerts over the years.

Writers of this song, according to a lead sheet, are Buddy Holly and John Mackey, but no Holly tape of the song exists. It has been said that the royalty splits were 10per cent/90per cent leading to speculation that Holly's involvement was minimal and his percentage was for helping the song get plays.

'I'll Just Pretend'

Home recording by Buddy Holley and Bob Montgomery, circa 1952.

Buddy and school friend, Bob Montgomery recorded this number during the early 1950s. Bob sings lead while Buddy plays the mandolin and sings harmony. The composer may be a Jessie Mae Martin or it may be traditional.

This number and others are taken from practice tapes and were released as collector's items by Buddy's brother, Larry, on his own local Holly House record label.

Never released by MCA it is, nevertheless, available on various unsanctioned releases.

'I'm Changing All Those Changes'

Main version: second Nashville recording session at Bradley's Barn, 22nd July 1956, which included Jerry Allison, Sonny Curtis and Don Guess. Take 4. See also text below re. Clovis version.

In the first few months of 1959, following Holly's death, there were those in the UK who thought he'd sold out rock'n'roll and turned to pop with a capital P. Of course, we were in ignorance of those early Decca sessions, eight tracks of which belatedly got released in the shape of two bland-looking seven-inch Brunswick EPs. Fans were in for a shock because these tracks included several rockabilly gems. Maybe not the wildest rockabilly but, nevertheless, rockabilly by any definition.

The number above, written by Holly, was one such tune. 'Changing All Those Changes' brings to mind the phraseology of 'I Forgot To Remember To Forget' and drives along well with sharp lead guitar from Sonny Curtis.

An earlier, shorter version recorded at Clovis appeared on the posthumous album, 'Reminiscing', as overdubbed by The Fireballs and made for a stereo release. Undubbed, the track appeared on the 'For The First Time Anywhere' album on MCA (1983) in mono.

A further 1955 demo is said to exist but has not surfaced as far as I am aware. In addition, a further take from Nashville has not been released but is believed to exist. (We know of several take numbers from the Nashville recordings but that doesn't mean that they still exist. Almost certainly they don't.)

'I'm Gonna Love You Too'

Recorded at Norman Petty Studios, Clovis, New Mexico on 1st July 1957. Personnel: Buddy, Jerry and Joe.

The sheet music instructions to this say moderato, with a solid rock – a pretty good definition of this rhythmic number that could well have been used as an A side. Instead, it was the flip of 'Listen To Me', a size-able hit for Buddy as a solo artist in the UK, but not in the USA. Both these recordings had double-tracked vocals, an innovation for the 1950s.

If Niki Sullivan didn't get to play on this recording session it is believed a real live insect fleetingly became the fourth Cricket! Turn up the volume on the fadeout and listen to the sound of a chirping cricket, which is clearly audible. (This incident has nothing to do with how the group got their name.)

Composer credits are listed as Joe B., Niki Sullivan and Norman Petty but Holly and Allison evidently had a big part in writing this powerful number. As well as double tracking the harmony vocals, Buddy also overdubbed a second guitar line on the finished recording.

It is not a number that has routinely attracted cover versions. Blondie made a driving version of it when Debbie Harry was the rage in the 1970s.

'I'm Gonna Set My Foot Down'

Demo made at Norman Petty Studios, Clovis, New Mexico, February–April 1956. Personnel: probably Buddy, Sonny Curtis, Don Guess and Jerry Allison.

Despite sharing composer credits, this is evidently a self-penned number that Buddy performed as a demo while he was alternating between practising in Clovis and recording in Nashville. A driving performance, it first appeared on the 'Reminiscing' album in 1963 with overdubbing courtesy of The Fireballs.

Twenty years later the unadulterated track was released, with others, on the 'For The First Time Anywhere' album. Finally, The Picks have released Holly's vocal version with their own chirping background on a double album of Buddy's material. All the three versions mentioned have the same vocals.

'I'm Lookin' For Someone To Love'

Recorded as a demo along with 'That'll Be The Day' on 24th–25th February 1957 at the Norman Petty Studios, Clovis, New Mexico. See text below for personnel.

This number was recorded as a demo but subsequently assigned Master No.102021 and released as the flip of the legendary number that catapulted The Crickets to the top of the hit parade. The master number would indicate this track was the A side, while Holly's most famous recording ever was a potential B side!

Local musicians Gary and Ramona Tollett were used on backing vocals with Niki Sullivan whilst Larry Welborn played bass as Joe B. Mauldin hadn't yet been enrolled in the group. Jerry was, of course, on drums. Written by Holly with help from his family and a credit given to Norman Petty, the number has remained one of the most popular from the days of the Chirping Crickets being featured on soundtrack albums of both the Buddy stage show and the film.

Whilst studio chatter or out-takes from Holly's other recording sessions do exist, all we have from the lengthy session that produced this track and 'That'll Be The Day' is just over four minutes of pure magic. And not a remix in sight.

Influences

It is known that Holly was influenced by several artists in his lifetime but it's more certain still that he was to influence dozens of artists that followed him. Although Elvis was undoubtedly the King of popular music, Holly has perhaps been as influential on others in a variety of ways. As a singer/songwriter, as instrumentalist, as innovator, even as a good old boy! He really has been a phenomenon.

Many names are scattered throughout this book, with individual entries included where appropriate. Others that also deserve inclusion are: Donovan, Bruce Springsteen, Fleetwood Mac, John Cougar, Alvin Stardust and numerous others. Each of the above has happily admitted that that the bespectacled Texan's music influenced theirs. The list is by no means exhaustive.

Under a separate heading of SOUNDALIKES are mentioned artists who actually recorded material that was very Hollyish. Some, like Tommy Roe, carved out a whole career by adopting the style. Others, while not sounding like Holly, have recorded an occasional number that has Hollyish overtones. Four examples will have to suffice: from the USA, 'My Heart' by Gene Vincent and 'So Deep' by Brenda Lee, while home-grown examples are 'Twist Little Sister' by Brian Poole and the Tremeloes and 'You Were On My Mind' by Crispian St. Peter.

John Ingman

Unsung hero of the UK Holly scene, John has spent the bulk of his adult life researching and compiling information relating to Buddy

Holly and the West Texas music scene. At one point he stayed in Clovis and actually got to sort out some of the tape boxes! Meantime, he has given me invaluable help in compiling this present volume.

Recently, in researching his own Welsh ancestry, an entry turned up: Sarah Ingman married John Holley on 7th April 1807! Bearing in mind that Holly has some Welsh roots, this is a thought-provoking coincidence.

Instrumentals

Buddy and the boys never went into the studio to record an instrumental but fortunately they did do a couple of demos that were probably rehearsals and these have since been released. Certainly in their early years before the hits began to flow they would have been likely to include the occasional instrumental in a set.

The two tracks ('Holly Hop' and 'Honky Tonk') make for interesting listening, especially the latter in its undubbed state. Of course 'Honky Tonk' was an absolute classic instrumental from the 1950s whereas 'Holly Hop' is little more than a brief jam. It is possible they played these during their appearances at the Sunday Party on KDAV.

While it is clear that Buddy, Jerry and Joe were highly proficient musicians, the real chemistry involved achieving a really tight sound that revolved around Holly's distinctive lead vocals.

Interviews with Holly/Crickets

Although several interviews have come to light over the years, most are fairly lightweight in content as they date from the days when pop/rock was treated as ephemeral and not something that needed analysing for posterity.

The best of these are included on the MCA box set that first came out in 1979. Also worthy of mention is a fairly lengthy interview with Canadian DJ Red Robinson that surfaced in the early 1980s. More recently, an interview with DJ Freeman Hoover has been released as part of a Crickets CD and makes for interesting listening. (Eddie Cochran is obviously present throughout.)

It was several years after Holly's death before the average UK fan got to hear his speaking voice. Prior to that, the spoken lyrics in 'Listen To Me' were about as near as we got. So it was interesting eventually to hear a clear Texan accent speaking in fond tones of his home town and with a lively sense of humour never far beneath the surface.

'It Doesn't Matter Anymore'

With the Dick Jacobs Orchestra; recorded in stereo at Coral Records Studios, Pythian Temple, New York, 21st October 1958.

Posthumous UK No.1 record for Buddy Holly in early 1959. The track was composed by Paul Anka, and the story goes that the number was only included on the session at the last minute. If so, was another song jettisoned? A quirk of fate led to Dick Jacobs working up an inspired arrangement at short notice. In Britain it became the biggest-selling American recording of 1959 whereas in the USA the weekly Cashbox had it stalling at No.30.

Holly's recording has stood up well to repeated playing over the years and still manages to sound fresh. The title is famous for being one of many ironic song titles that have been the kiss of death for certain unlucky performers. A quick sample includes 'Last Date' / Mike Holliday, 'Welcome To My World' / Jim Reeves, 'Three Steps To Heaven' / Eddie Cochran and Hank Williams's last big hit 'I'll Never Get Out Of This World Alive'. Buddy Knox, probably protected by being born in Happy, Texas, tempted fate by recording 'I Think I'm Gonna Kill Myself' but survives to this day.

Turning back to 'It Doesn't Matter Anymore', Johnny Worth had the Embassy (Woolworths) cover that presumably sold a few copies, their recordings always being cheaper to purchase than the hit parade counterparts. 1996 has seen the release of a very strong country version from Suzy Bogguss assisted by Dave Edmunds as part of a Nashville tribute album.

One minor bit of research that won't be nailed is whether or not Petty was at the 1958 recording session as an adviser? He claims he was but Coral's man, Bob Theile, set up the session and doesn't agree. One person who definitely was present was the composer, Paul Anka.

'It's Not My Fault'

Demo made at Norman Petty Studios, Clovis, New Mexico, February–April 1956. Personnel: probably Buddy, Sonny Curtis, Don Guess and Jerry Allison.

This is a good country number written by Ben Hall and his one-time sideman Weldon Myrick that is short in duration (1 minute 48 seconds) but not in quality. One of many Holly performances that, one feels, deserves greater exposure.

Overdubbed by The Fireballs the original release was on the 'Reminiscing' album. It has also been released undubbed and, more recently, The Picks have added backing vocals. The 21 tracks they overdubbed in 1994 are curiously uneven but this is one of the tunes that works quite well.

'It's So Easy'

Recorded at Norman Petty Studios, Clovis, New Mexico, 25th May 1958. Personnel: Buddy, Jerry and Joe plus Tommy Allsup, lead guitar.

The last Crickets recording to feature Holly as lead singer it flopped as a single in the USA even though Buddy and the boys did their best to promote it. Backing vocals were by The Roses and they actually got to go on the road with The Crickets in 1958.

A Holly/Petty composition, royalties must have flowed in during 1977 when Linda Ronstadt made it a Top 5 record Stateside with a really energetic interpretation.

In 1992, The Crickets, with lead singer Gordon Payne, cut a punchy re-recording of the number with Sonny Curtis on lead guitar. Even the Beatles, as The Quarrymen, used to perform the number on stage. They also used it – unsuccessfully – in a local talent show.

'It's Too Late'

Recorded at Norman Petty Studios, Clovis, New Mexico, 19th July 1957 (approximately). Personnel: Buddy, Jerry and possibly Joe, with Niki Sullivan on guitar.

While Buddy and the Two Tones were out on the Sonny James tour, *circa* April 1956, Chuck Willis was in New York recording a session for Atlantic that included his own composition 'It's Too Late'.

The Crickets cut their interpretation (very similar in style to the Willis version) in mid 1957 for inclusion, on their first album, 'The Chirping Crickets', which was released in November of the same year.

The Picks added backing vocals at a separate recording session, and it is this version that we have heard over the years. A tape without Picks overdubs does exist and is available on unsanctioned releases.

Jerry Allison as recording artist Ivan in a 1958 publicity picture. (Courtesy of Bill Griggs.)

Ivan

Jerry Ivan Allison, co-founder of The Crickets with Buddy Holly, had a single released in 1958 on the Coral label that was put out using the pseudonym of Ivan, his middle name. The A side, 'Real Wild Child', has since become something of a classic and Jerry's version holds up well against all comers. The original recording of the song was by Johnny O'Keefe and had been styled 'Wild One'. See entry under O'KEEFE.

Listening to the track it is surprising how identifiable Holly's voice is amongst the backing vocals. Whilst the record was good and a chart entry in the USA, Jerry decided not to give up his day job as a Cricket. He released a further single on Coral, 'Frankie Frankenstein', but Buddy is not on that one.

These days not only does Jerry do occasional backing vocals with The Crickets, he has even recorded lead vocals, characteristically in a very laid-back manner. See also entries under JERRY ALLISON, PEGGY SUE GERRON, and 'REAL WILD CHILD'.

J

Wanda Jackson

This dynamic country artist was born Wanda Goodman in Oklahoma in 1937 and is still performing today.

In the early days, she was a member of Hank Thompson's band and toured with Holly on early country-tinged tours. She is warmly remembered for being one of the few ladies capable of producing strong rock'n'roll vocals (*circa* 1960) when most of the hit parade was turning to saccharine.

During her rock'n'roll period, her group went under the arresting title of Wanda Jackson and her Party Timers. Later, she drifted back to the country field but has managed to record a wealth of gospel material. Amongst the Holly material she has recorded are strong versions of 'Oh Boy!', 'Rave On' and 'It Doesn't Matter Anymore'.

Dick Jacobs

Dick Jacobs was A&R Director with Coral Records, a subdivision of Decca, which was formed in 1949. Buddy eventually signed for Coral, the irony being that he had originally signed for Decca and his contract had as good as lapsed when early recordings failed to lift off. Holly, along with the Johnny Burnette Trio, remained with Coral even though the subsidiary only dabbled with rock'n'roll and couldn't decide whether or not to build a roster of artists. (Bill Haley was, however, part of the same stable.)

Jacobs produced both the 'Early In The Morning' session and the final New York session at the Pythian Temple, which included 'True Love Ways' and three other recordings. It is quite possible that Dick Jacobs would have continued to work with Holly from time to time as both were contracted to Coral. (Holly, meanwhile, was beginning to formulate his own recording plans viz.Prism Records.)

Several years back Dick was allegedly stabbed by his wife and sustained severe injuries. He survived several years but died on 20th May 1988.

Mick Jagger and the Rolling Stones

Before having his nineteenth nervous breakdown Mick Jagger had, no doubt, been partly inspired by seeing Holly and The Crickets at the Woolwich Odeon during their 1958 tour. Legend has it that he was there in the front row. Although the Stones' early material was R&B their first UK hit some 30 years back was with The Crickets' 'Not Fade Away'.

Group member Keith Richards feels the Holly influence has permeated much of the pop music scene down the years. A view shared by many music critics.

An item of passing trivia: US sax man Bobby Keyes has been featured on several Stones albums and he happens to hail from Lubbock, Texas. He even lived on the very same street as Holly!

Waylon Jennings and Buddy Holly snapped in a photo booth on the final tour, 1959. (Courtesy of Bill Griggs.)

Waylon Jennings

Waylon was born Wayland Arthur Jennings just down the road from Lubbock at Littlefield in Texas on 15th June 1937, just a year after his friend Buddy Holly. They had met first around 1954 when both had appeared on the Sunday Dance Party on KDAV radio.

Eventually, Waylon got to work as a DJ on radio KLLL in Lubbock and after he had made it, Buddy would often drop in at the station and even took time to record jingles advertising the station to the tune

of 'Everyday' and 'Peggy Sue'. Shortly thereafter Holly helped produce Waylon's first attempt at recording on the session that included
celebrated saxophonist, King Curtis. The Cajun standard, 'Jole Blon',
backed with 'When Sin Stops' by Waylon was not released until May
1959 (US Brunswick 55130) and despite reasonable reviews it sank
without trace. This was probably not helped by the fact that, following
Holly's death, Waylon quit the music business temporarily and was
not in the mood to promote the single.

Whilst he toured with Buddy, but didn't officially record with him,
Waylon is still featured in every discography, having helped to compose 'You're The One' and performed hand claps on the informal session at the station where the number was taped.

Waylon Jennings recorded a dramatic tribute record 'The Stage' in the
1960s, which coincidentally was written by Bill Tilghman, co-writer of
'Oh Boy!' and 'Rave On'. Later, a much more subtle tribute, 'Old Friend',
was recorded, which subtly alludes to Buddy. (Holly's name is not actually mentioned in the lyrics, but the message is crystal clear.) Yet another
tribute, 'Buddy's Song', was composed by Waylon with composer royalties from the Bobby Vee recording going to Holly's mother.

Waylon Jennings's video biography, *Renegade Outlaw Legend*, contains a lengthy opening sequence of his Lubbock years with Holly
through to the final Winter Dance Party Tour. He leaves no doubt that
Holly was his mentor.

To bring the connection up to date, Jennings has recorded a moving
version of Holly's 'Learning The Game' with the help of guitar legend
Mark Knopfler as part of a major Nashville Holly tribute. This comes on
the heels of Waylon finally returning to the Surf ballroom some 36 years
after he last rode into Clear Lake on one of those rickety old tour buses.

Waylon has always felt guilty that he gave up his seat on the plane
to The Bopper and also about the last bit of banter he had with Holly.
Buddy said he hoped the bus would freeze up and Jennings reportedly retorted that he hoped his plane crashed!

Jingles

Promotional jingles by recording artists were the norm in the 1950s,
achieving the dual purpose of boosting an artist's current record
release, whilst at the same time bringing kudos to the radio station
whose airwaves were being used.

In the Fall of 1958 Holly sang brief snatches of both 'Everyday' and
'Peggy Sue' to extol the merits of radio KLLL. The jingles have been
circulating amongst fans for years and a legitimate MCA release on
record is well overdue.

Buddy and the boys had also recorded fun messages for Murray Deutch and Bob Theile to the tune of The Crickets' first hit record. See entry under 'THAT'LL BE THE DAY'.

The Jitters

This was a brief cul-de-sac in the history of The Crickets. The name The Jitters arose in early 1959 following Holly's death. With the former Crickets (Jerry, Joe plus new boy Earl Sinks) back in Texas and already beginning to record, Waylon Jennings, Carl Bunch and Tommy Allsup found themselves staying in New York waiting for bookings, the idea being that Ronnie Smith, who had been drafted into the Winter Dance Party Tour, would lead the new group. Perhaps the choice of name wasn't the best in the world!

In fact, neither bookings nor recordings materialized, and the various musicians pretty quickly split and went their separate ways. What happened to each can be worked out from looking at the entries under their individual names.

Ben Johnson

Lubbock pastor who officiated at Buddy and Maria's August 1958 wedding ceremony, which took place at Buddy's Lubbock home. Buddy was a firm Baptist and often attended his local church. Prior to his death he tithed monies from his earnings, which is a far cry from earlier days when he was hard up and for a short period only just kept up with his car payments.

The Reverend Johnson had the sad task of taking Buddy's funeral service just six months later.

George Jones

Famous, much-revered country artist, who could be termed a singers' singer as many artists owe something to George's delivery. His voice sounds lived in, which, given his life story, is hardly surprising.

George Jones was born 1931 in Saratoga, Texas, and he and Buddy often toured on bills together during 1956. As fellow Texans, one assumes they got on pretty well. Jones himself was on a rockabilly kick in those days and had one or two reasonable hits for the Starday label, as Thumper Jones. There is also an apocryphal story that, one night, Jones performed all rock'n'roll material, whereas Holly and his group did pure country.

A more tangible link was that between George Jones and The Big Bopper. Both were Mercury artists and George had country success with a string of J.P. Richardson compositions, most noticeably 'Beggar To A King', 'Running Bear' and 'White Lightning'.

Malcolm Jones

The late-lamented Malcolm Jones wrote the comprehensive sleeve notes on the World Records box set of Holly recordings around 20 years ago. Later, he collaborated with John Beecher on the MCA box set, which, to date, remains the definitive collection (It was first released in 1979; it needs revising!)

He spent most of his working life in and around the record business setting up the HARVEST label for EMI and the small independent, Fly Records, in 1970. A meticulous individual he did not always get the recognition he deserved but is thought of with gratitude by Holly fans.

Malcolm died on 17th February 1990.

K

KDAV & KLLL

The main radio station operating out of Lubbock in the early 1950s was KSEL, which comprised a mainly pop playlist. Around 1953, Ben Hall, Hipockets Duncan and Dave Stone, all associated with the station, got together to form radio KDAV, which was quite certainly one of the first stations to operate an all-country format. It was KDAV that was to run a popular Sunday Party feature on which Holly and Bob Montgomery were to make regular appearances. Much of the 'Holly In The Hills' material is culled from tapes of their performances.

In 1958, another Lubbock station (KLLL) was taken over by the Corbin brothers (see separate entry under CORBIN) and also changed to an all country format. It was on K Triple L, as it was known, that Waylon Jennings went to work as a DJ although he had known Holly from a few years previously. It was there at the station that Holly and Jennings recorded 'You're The One', together, which was composed virtually on the spot – just to prove that it was that easy to dash off a pop song!

The Lubbock station KSEL actually banned rock'n'roll from its airwaves on 21st July 1958 as part of a nationwide Top 40 backlash – so we are told.

See also JINGLES entry.

Ronnie Keene and his Orchestra

Ronnie was musical director of the British tour that featured The Crickets. His 14-piece band, which included a female vocalist, opened each half of the tour bill each night. Their repertoire was big band fare such as 'One O'Clock Jump' and 'Woodchoppers Ball'.

The Orchestra never recorded but did appear with Don Lang in many of the regular 6.5 Special TV shows of the day though not the full-length film.

Some tour posters from 1958 indicated Don Smith and his Orchestra would actually appear. Don Smith had been given the provisional booking but subsequently Ronnie Keene was hired.

Ronnie is now basically retired and lives in West Sussex. Speaking to the author recently he had very warm memories of that famous UK tour.

Mark Knopfler

One of Britain's 500 richest men, Knopfler really came to fame as leader of Dire Straits in the 1970s.

A famous exponent of the Fender Stratocaster, he has always admitted to being a Holly fan. Apart from that influence he became hooked on The Fireballs' classic instrumental 'Quite A Party', which coincidentally, was recorded in Petty's Clovis studio, where Holly made so much great music.

Always keen to collaborate with others, he teamed up in 1996 with Waylon Jennings to record 'Learning The Game' as part of a special Decca Nashville tribute to Holly.

Buddy Knox

Born three years before Holly (20th July 1933) in Happy, Texas, Knox cut the original of his big hit 'Party Doll' at Norman Petty's Clovis studios, New Mexico, in 1957.

Certainly Knox, with his group The Rhythm Orchids (which included Jimmy Bowen), were friends and acquaintances of Buddy and the boys. Holly was rumoured to have played guitar on at least one of Buddy Knox's sessions. There was actually an element of competition, with Buddy Knox managing to get his big break via Roulette a few months before Holly. If, in fact, Holly was not on the 1958 Knox session of 'All For You', it is possible that he was on a 1957 recording 'Swinging Daddy'. If all this conjecture seems strange, remember that written details of sessions weren't always made, so we are tapping 40-year-old memories.

Buddy Knox has a light and pleasing voice and has made many good records, while never having been at the cutting edge of rock-'n'roll. He has lived, during more recent years, in Canada and has intermittently toured the UK.

He tempted fate by recording 'I Think I'm Gonna Kill Myself' in the early 1960s, which session included members of The Crickets. Whilst Bo Diddley invented the riff that became rather famous and carries his name, Knox created his own distinctive rhythm pattern, which is seldom copied but is classic in its own way.

L

Trevor Lailey & Others

There are many individuals who really deserve a separate entry in a work such as this but space prevents that luxury. A brief list must suffice.

Trevor still runs The British Buddy Holly Society, which he co-founded with Ray Needham 15 years ago. Both individuals keep heavily involved with fans while continuing to hold down demanding jobs.

John Firminger runs The Crickets File from his home in Sheffield. It specializes in collecting information about The Crickets on an ongoing basis. He does sterling work.

Alan Jenkins has run a Holly/Crickets Fan Club for a great many years, and this includes organizing the occasional dance or disco. Long may he do so.

New boy on the block, but most welcome, is Jim Carr, who started his ambitious *Holly International* magazine in 1994. Having taken retirement Jim now devotes his daily energies to seeking out fresh photos and a wealth of information all relating to the late Lubbockite.

Addresses of various organizations are given with permission under SOURCES for those who wish to make contact.

Denny Laine

Denny Laine was a member of Wings when he recorded a solo LP, 'Holly Days', aided and abetted by his boss Paul McCartney, who produced the album and was partly responsible for the concept. The 10 tracks are highly listenable, and particularly welcome are the inclusion of some of the less well-known numbers: 'Lonesome Tears', 'Look At Me', etc.

The trend for other artists to record Holly material continues to the present day. Recently, the Lemonheads recorded 'Learning The Game'.

Denny Laine has just reappeared on the music scene and fronts a new group, Reborn.

'Last Night'

Recorded at Norman Petty's Clovis Studios, New Mexico, 12th March 1957. Personnel: Buddy, Jerry, Joe; possibly Niki Sullivan on guitar.

A fortnight after the legendary session that produced 'That'll Be The Day' a further session was held at Clovis but this time the group comprised of the soon-to-be-famous quartet of Holly, Allison, Mauldin and Sullivan. It was at this session that 'Maybe Baby' was attempted using a different rhythm to the more famous recording made whilst on the road at the Tinker Airforce base, Oklahoma City.

'Last Night' was written by Joe B. for The Four Teens, the group that Mauldin had left to join The Crickets. Part of the deal in allowing this number to be recorded was adding Norman's name to the composer credits. Shortly afterwards The Picks recorded the backing vocals and the track was one of twelve that formed one of the greatest albums ever released, 'The Chirping Crickets'.

Both 'Oh Boy!' and 'Last Night' have been released undubbed, i.e. ex-Picks, but only on bootleg-style releases. MCA are perhaps biding their time.

'Learning the Game'

Taped at Holly's New York flat, 17th December 1958. Buddy Holly and acoustic guitar.

'Learning The Game' was the last of six songs that Buddy had written and experimented with on his recorder in their Greenwich Village flat during the run-up to Christmas 1958. Shortly after he and Maria flew to Lubbock for the festivities before travelling back to New York at the end of the year. In January 1959 he recorded further home-produced material, all featuring songs that he had known since his early rock'n'roll days, which do not touch the creative output of the previous month.

Holly's rendition of 'Learning The Game' heavily overdubbed by Jack Hansen of Coral was released as a UK single in October 1960 and was a minor Top 40 hit. All six of Holly's compositions were included on the follow-up memorial album 'Buddy Holly Story, Vol. 2', which joined 'The Buddy Holly Story' in the UK album charts.

'Learning The Game' is a track that is particularly popular with discerning Holly fans and while the lyrics are not meant to be analysed the song title neatly sums up the journey we make through life. All three versions (undubbed, Hansen and Petty overdubs) are available on the MCA box set. It has seldom been covered over the years, though there is a version by folk singer Sandy Denny, and Waylon Jennings and Mark Knopfler have recently collaborated on a fine version.

Albert Lee

One of the greatest home-grown guitarists who started off in Chris Farlowe's Thunderbirds before ending up as a Cricket for several years in the early 1970s. If you accept that Rick Grech is British, then for a period The Crickets were definitely an Anglo–American combo.

Albert's leaning has been towards country rock and he's remained in demand as both a session artist and as a performer on the bandstand. He joined the Emmylou Harris Hot Band and, most famously, was drafted in to join The Everly Brothers for their famous reunion concert.

Has also made a couple of acclaimed solo albums on which not only does he play a fine Fender Telecaster but he also throws in vocals, including a superb 'Real Wild Child'. He wrote 'Country Boy', which has become a showcase for his guitar prowess.

John Lennon

Lennon certainly deserves an individual entry this time around. After watching The Crickets on their Palladium TV appearance in 1958, Lennon was quoted as saying that Holly made it possible for rock stars to wear glasses on stage.

On the composing front there is little doubt that the songwriting talents of Lennon and McCartney owed something to the simple melodies and lyrics that Holly and The Crickets practised.

There are many well-documented connections between The Beatles and The Crickets from their names to the fact that the first demos made by both groups were recordings of 'That'll Be The Day'.

In his solo days Lennon did a powerful version of 'Peggy Sue' on an album largely produced by rock guru Phil Spector. Many years earlier, when still in college, John had similarly performed his party piece impersonation of Holly, which naturally included 'Peggy Sue' complete with hiccups.

Jerry Lee Lewis

Celebrated rocker from Ferriday, Louisiana, Jerry Lee Lewis, born 20th September 1935, is one of the true greats of the music business who is still able to mesmerize audiences even though he is now 60, and long may that continue. He effortlessly manages to balance a rock and country career without alienating fans. Remember, no version of any song is definitive until Jerry has cut it!

The paths of Jerry Lee and Buddy crossed from time to time during the 1950s after they first met up in New York during December of 1957. It is disappointing that genuine quotes by Jerry about Buddy are few and far between but there are two excellent photos of them together, which (naturally) feature The Killer seated at the piano. One of these, used on the reverse of a Lewis album cover, has Buddy playing his Fender and is a classic snap of the period.

A bit of tape from a radio show in February 1958 survives; it features Jerry Lee and Buddy together. The songs include 'Drown In My Own Tears' with Buddy singing and Jerry Lee playing piano. A short snippet of 'Everyday' also exists whilst on 'Hallelujah I Love Her So' it is believed the Killer sings and Holly plays backup. The various items were not recorded under studio conditions and whether they will ever be issued is not known.

Of course, The Crickets and Jerry Lee were both headliners on the Australian tour that had started in Sydney during January and it is also disappointing that a minimal amount of memorabilia (photos, interviews, etc.) has survived from that visit, even if the tour was only a brief one.

In 1996 a new biography of Jerry has appeared in which he speaks warmly of his friend and fellow musician Buddy Holly.

'Listen To Me'

Recorded at Norman Petty studios between 29th June and 1st July 1957. Personnel: Buddy, Jerry, Joe with Holly double tracking vocals/guitar.

Quite incredible to look back and realize that this classic Holly solo recording was NOT a US hit. It was not even released there as an A side – that honour went to 'I'm Gonna Love You Too', which also failed to chart.

Written by Buddy (as Charles Hardin) and with composer credits shared with Norman Petty, it is one of the earliest attempts by any artist to dual track and comes off spectacularly well. Another unusual feature of the track was a rather deadpan spoken segment midway through. No trace of any Texan accent either.

'Listen To Me' was a major hit in the UK and a stand-out track on his first solo Coral LP 'Buddy Holly'. Later reissues of that album were actually entitled 'Listen To Me'. This is one of those recordings that, although recorded in mono nearly 40 years ago, could not be improved upon even with the help of multi-track equipment.

Literature (fictional)

In reference books listing the lives of 20th-century figures, Buddy Holly is categorized as a necromantic love icon. I'm not too sure exactly what that means! What is known is that Holly's persona has been used as the basis of several fictional works over the years. The following are a selective list only:

- *Words of Love* by Philip Norman; juxtaposes scenes of Holly's last tour with British school life of the time
- *Buddy* by Nigel Hinton; a trilogy about a teddyboy father and Buddy Holly fan seeking to bring up a young son
- *Buddy Holly is Alive and Well on Ganymede* by Bradley Denton; Weird sci-fi story of youth conceived at exact moment of Holly's death
- *Jungle Music* by unnamed authors; fictionalized Essay in which Holly is the leader of the Laundromat and Alan Freed is the US President

Such are the inaccuracies in a couple of Holly biographies that they probably qualify for inclusion in the above list of fictionalized works.

'Little Baby'

Recorded at Norman Petty Studios, Clovis, New Mexico, 17th December 1957.
Personnel: Buddy, Jerry and Joe, supplemented by C.W. Kendall Jnr, Piano.

This is very much an album track, part written by the pianist on the session, C. W. Kendall junior, who normally lined up as part of The Big Beats, a Dallas group fronted at one stage by Trini Lopez.

Musically the number has a very unusual structure and it is hardly surprising that it has seldom attracted covers. Jimmy Gilmer put out a very different interpretation on his album 'Buddy's Buddy'.

The Holly version was issued during his lifetime on his first solo album and posthumously included on the second volume of the 'Story' album to make up the standard twelve tracks. (Other unreleased material had not been fully collected together at that point).

'Lonesome Tears'

Recorded at Norman Petty Studios, Clovis, New Mexico, 25th May 1958.
Personnel: Buddy, Jerry, Joe plus Tommy Allsup, lead guitar.

Both sides of The Crickets' follow-up to 'Think It Over' were recorded at the same May 1958 session, with backing vocals added by the Roses. It failed to chart and, coincidentally, happens to have been the last Crickets single released during Holly's lifetime.

Both melody and lyrics were written by Holly and despite the fact that it is an attractive number, it has hardly ever had any exposure. For years it was not available on album in the UK, a situation remedied by the release of the 'Remember' album in 1971.

One of the very few covers was by folk artist Carolyn Hester on her Dot LP, 'That's My Song' released in the 1960s.

'Look at Me'

Recorded at Norman Petty's Clovis, New Mexico Studios, December 1957.
Personnel: Buddy, Jerry and Joe. Vi Petty, piano.

Recorded just after Niki Sullivan left the group, this heavily piano-based number was used on Holly's first solo album and was not considered obvious single material. But it did get a posthumous release on 45rpm in this country late in 1961 when it was used as the

121

follow-up single to 'You're So Square'; unfortunately, it didn't reach the Top 40. The trade magazine of the day, *World's Fair*, had a Top 100 chart listing into which the record just crept.

The UK Coral single Q72445 is worth seeking out as it has been run through an echo chamber and is therefore different to the original master recording for this reason.

The number was part composed by Buddy Holly and whilst his songbook has been heavily plundered over the years this is one of those tracks that gets overlooked.

Trini Lopez

Trini Lopez was born on 15th May 1937, in Dallas, Texas, where he first started performing at the El Pango Club while still a teenager. In the early 1960s, just before Trini Lopez hit the big time, he looked poised to join The Crickets as lead vocalist, but it never happened. The story was that The Crickets were sidelined for several months after J.I. broke a bone at the same time as things started happening for Trini.

Trini Lopez is usually labelled a Chicano artist (along with Valens, Romero, etc.)

Holly and Lopez were certainly contemporaries with Lopez heading a Dallas group called the Big Beats, who also used Norman Petty's studios around 1957–8. If Trini had later become involved with The Crickets the Tex Mex sound label first used in Holly's day would surely have been revived, even if the term is a relatively meaningless one.

It is believed that Holly and Lopez first met in December 1957, introduced by their mutual friend, Snuff Garrett.

'Love is Strange'

Taped at Holly's New York flat, January 1959. Buddy and acoustic guitar.

This is one of a batch of tunes Buddy left on tape at his New York flat just before embarking on the final tour. Of the five numbers, two were released in 1963 ('Reminiscing' LP) while the remainder had to await the release of the 'Giant' album in 1969.

The song was part written by Mickey Baker, one half of the Mickey and Sylvia duo, who had a No.2 hit with it on the US R&B charts. Ten years later Peaches and Herb took it back into the charts while in the UK The Everly Brothers did a very powerful interpretation that got to No.11. Earlier still the song got to the top of the charts courtesy of Lonnie

Donegan although only as the flip of 'Cumberland Gap'. The Holly version only made the charts in the USA where it crawled to a lowly No.105.

Holly's version, issued as a single to coincide with the release of the 'Giant' album, failed to chart here, which, in retrospect was surprising. The shortened, undubbed recording eventually appeared on the MCA box set. The dubbed version has Buddy's short vocals repeated to produce a full-length commercial release.

Although official composer credits are Baker/Ethel Smith it has been rumoured over the years that it was co-written by Bo Diddley, Ethel Smith being the name of Bo's wife. In fact, Chess had turned down Bo's original composition 'Paradise', on which Mickey and Sylvia had based their number. 'Love Is Strange' was later to figure in a lawsuit in connection with the Billy Stewart number 'Billy's Blues'. The Bear family CD 'Love Is Strange', by Mickey and Sylvia details all the convolutions and is highly recommended.

In 1987 the Mickey and Sylvia version was used as part of the soundtrack of the *Dirty Dancing* film.

'Love Me'

First Nashville recording session at Bradley's Barn, 26th January 1956. Take 10. Personnel: Buddy, Sonny Curtis, Don Guess plus Nashville session men.

Buddy's first real commercial attempt at recording and it duly became the flip of his first Decca 45, 'Blue Days, Black Nights' in 1956. The number was written by local songwriter, Sue Parrish, who offered it to Buddy. He had performed it several weeks earlier at a demo session in Wichita Falls. (This earlier more ragged attempt has been released over the years on bootleg-type albums.)

The composition itself is not a memorable one and has not attracted cover versions. The Buddy Holly Nashville recording was reissued in 1984 with vocal embellishments by The Picks.

'Love's Made a Fool of You'

Recorded at Norman Petty's Clovis, New Mexico studios, July–August 1958. Personnel: Tommy Allsup, lead guitar; Jerry and Joe replaced by session men.

One of Holly's greatest recordings, it was put down as a demo for the Everlys in Norman Petty's studios during the summer of 1958. The Everly's evidently felt they couldn't improve on Buddy's demo and

123

passed on it. Thereafter, it remained unissued because of legalities to do with Holly's estate and it only turned up six years later as part of the 'Showcase' album. Months later, chosen as a single, it crept into the Top 40.

Discographical details show the recording as being overdubbed. In fact, recently, an undubbed version, which seems to lack hand claps only, was released on a European album and should be sought out by all genuine collectors. Its also on a Vigotone CD box set.

The sheet music for this Holly composition reads 'moderately with a strong beat', which seems a reasonable instruction. Buddy's dual-tracked vocal is quite gentle. The feeling that this was recorded as a demo for the Everlys is quite striking.

Strong rock'n'roll versions of the number, which make it almost seem a different composition, were hits for the Bobby Fuller Four, Matchbox and the post-Holly Crickets themselves.

Lubbock, Texas

Birth place of Charles Hardin Holley, which is described as the Hub City of the South Plains. Certainly Lubbock is far bigger in size these days than it was during Holly's brief lifetime. One thing is for sure, anyone visiting that part of Texas gets the feeling that the country is still new and evolving. Remember, Texas didn't get annexed by the USA until 1845, an act that probably triggered off The Mexican War.

One of the nicest aspects of the Holly story is that he was always very proud of his roots and never made any attempt to distance himself from Lubbock, even though he had temporarily based himself in New York. The signs were that he was going to gravitate back to Texas and make that his main centre. Perhaps, as a successful artist he could have kept a foot in both Texas and New York?

For years there was little recognition of Holly's achievements in his home town but these days the civic authorities certainly acknowledge their famous son, whose family still mainly live in and around Lubbock. Things probably got rolling in 1980 when the statue of Buddy Holly was unveiled and, in later years, the civic authorities acquired a substantial amount of Holly memorabilia, which it hopes to house in a permanent exhibition site.

There have been a string of artists from the Lubbock area that have followed in Buddy Holly's footprints over the years. Amongst these have been The Maines Brothers, Joe Ely, Mac Davis and Jimmy Velvet. There's a flourishing 1990s music scene in the area these days by all accounts.

Why this musical pedigree? Well, it's been said that there's not that much to do in that wide expanse of land except to sit around and pick on your guitar!

Rod Lucier

No other details to hand, but Rod Lucier was the road manager on the final 1959 Winter Dance Party Tour. It is believed he was an employee of General Artists Corporation and, as such, is sometimes listed as actual promoter of the tour.

Robin Luke

This US singer was somewhat of a one-hit wonder and has seldom been heard of since. But the hit 'Susie Darlin'' was a monster (peaking at No.5 in Billboard) and one of the best Summer hits of 1957.

Several years back Robin Luke was located (he was a doctor practising his vocation in Hawaii) and interviewed about his involvement with Buddy Holly. It seems the two met up on some tour and Holly spent virtually an entire day showing Robin Luke his guitar style and passing on quite a lesson in the art of playing the instrument.

Certainly 'Susie Darlin'' seems to have a Hollyish feel to it, and it did lead to Luke being termed a copyist, something, perhaps, he would not deny. Luke is now believed to be a professor and resides in Missouri.

Bob Luman

Talented country musician and singer born Nacogdoches, Texas on 15th April 1937 who had a brief period of national success in 1960 with the huge-selling chart record 'Let's Think about Living'. A Boudleaux Bryant composition, it was the answer to all the death discs that had clogged the airwaves back in 1960.

Both Holly and Luman got a kick start in the business after seeing Elvis on his early Southern tours *circa* 1955. Both signed record contracts shortly thereafter. A minor coincidence is that Holly and Luman

125

both cut Ben Hall's 'Blue Days, Black Nights' at their earliest recording sessions.

Luman became a member of the Grand Ole Opry before dying much too early, aged 41, in Nashville on 27th December 1978.

M

'Mailman Bring Me No More Blues'

Recorded at Norman Petty Studios, Clovis, New Mexico on 8th April 1957. Personnel: Buddy, Jerry, Joe B. plus Vi Petty, piano.

Apart from having blues in the title, the sheet music exhorts any would-be musician to adopt a blues beat on this unusual number. Partly written by Bob Thiele (see separate entry) under the *nom de plume*, Stanley Clayton, it was pushed to Buddy, who cut it early in 1957. It subsequently came out in the USA as the B side of the 'Words Of Love' single, but the record flopped. Whether for this reason or not it didn't get a single release here at the time.

1950s balladeer Don Cornell (see entry) was also on Coral Records and cut his own interpretation. Curiously, his version was released, both here and in the USA but it didn't manage to revive his flagging chart career.

Holly's UK single, 'Look At Me' with 'Mailman' as the flip was a posthumous release but didn't chart. But it is collectable as both sides of the single had a strong dose of echo added to it for the British market – presumably to give it a more commercial sound.

Hank B. Marvin of the Shadows

This legendary UK guitarist was born Brian Marvin in 1941. His early image was certainly modelled on that of Buddy Holly. Perhaps Hank B. got his name from The Crickets' Joe B.? Hank certainly played a strong lead guitar on the Fender Stratocaster and even wore heavy hornrims to make himself look very much like Holly. He even tried to buy Buddy's guitar from Mr and Mrs Holley at one point. The

Shadows' material in the early 1960s was peppered with Buddy Holly numbers and Cliff himself was also fond of using The Crickets' material, including three tracks on the live 'Cliff' album, which came out in 1959. In 1983 he recorded 'True Love Ways' live at The Royal Albert Hall for his 87th single. It was a major hit.

There is a further link with the Shadows: guitarist Bruce Welch, a keen fan of Holly's music, was chosen to be musical consultant for the *Buddy* musical from the moment it was first launched in 1989.

Joe B. Mauldin

Joe Benson Mauldin, bass player with The Crickets, was born 8th July 1939, and joined the group early in 1957, just after 'That'll Be The Day' was recorded. He was a mainstay in The Crickets for the next 18 months until the split with Buddy (probably temporary only) occurred. Joe B. had previously played bass with the Four Teens, a Lubbock group who featured Terry Noland as their lead singer.

Although he is most recognizable playing stand-up bass, photos came to light several years back showing him backing Buddy on stage on electric bass. This came as a belated shock to UK fans familiar with the group image from the days of the 1958 British tour. It's also interesting to reflect that on that legendary tour Joe didn't have an amplifier and the bass sound would have been picked up by whatever mike was nearby – a different era!

It's well documented that Joe teamed up with friend Jerry and others from late 1958 onwards having a fair share of success as the post-Holly Crickets. The group eventually disbanded and Joe went into musical production and engineering, working with his friend Snuff Garrett in Studio City, California. Believe it or not, he even helped Phil Spector create his legendary Wall of Sound, before being lured to Nashville to help a friend set up a recording studio. He's been based near Nashville ever since.

Joe is still performing and recording with The Crickets (Sonny Curtis, Jerry, Joe) and looks in good shape. He has even helped out on vocals occasionally in recent times. He spoke eloquently of his association with Holly on the definitive *Arena* television documentary of Buddy's life several years ago.

In 1996 he's been involved with recording a new Crickets album under the aegis of expatriate Stuart Coleman, and was also roped in to play on some of Nashville's 40 years' tribute CD, which was issued by Decca. Joe shows no sign of retiring.

'Maybe Baby'

Hit version recorded on the road, Tinker Airforce Base, Oklahoma City, late September 1957. The Crickets were a quartet at that time: Buddy, Jerry, Joe and Niki, second lead.

Released on the eve of The Cricket's March 1958 UK tour, the single rocketed up the charts and peaked at No.4 staying in the hit parade for close to three months. Apparently Mrs Holley (mother) had some input into the lyrics, although the number is credited to Holly and Petty.

The hit version has a drum pattern similar to the Richard Penniman hit 'Lucille', and the overall sound, including The Picks' overdubbed backing vocals, is unique. Six months earlier the quartet had cut a version of the same song, using a totally different rhythm pattern, which was held back from release.

It was not until 1966 that, in a quite unheralded move, the alternate version was released in the UK. It received no promotion and failed to chart. What was little known at the time was that this new version was itself heavily overdubbed, virtually obscuring Niki Sullivan's harmony vocals.

Although more than 20 different versions of 'Maybe Baby' have been recorded over the years it is still almost impossible to improve on the unique sound of the original. The flip side, 'Tell Me How', is felt by many to be almost the equal of the main side so the pairing was strong. A back-to-back biggie was the descriptive slang term used at the time.

The Crickets performed a good live version of 'Maybe Baby' on TV's *Off The Record* in 1958, of which an audio tape still exists. It is to be hoped that it is one day given an official release.

Paul McCartney

Former Beatle, born June 1942, who has never denied his indebtedness to Buddy Holly from his earliest, formative years when growing up in Liverpool. The entry under Buddy Holly in *The Ultimate Beatles Encyclopaedia* (Virgin Press) makes this clear and should be read.

In the 1970s McCartney bought the Nor-Va-Jak music publishing catalogue from Norman Petty, which comprised titles ranging from 'An Empty Cup' to 'You've Got Love'. One assumes that the move was a good one on both an emotional as well as on a business level. Spasmodically, since 1976, McCartney has promoted a Buddy Holly

Week each September, celebrating the anniversary of Holly's birth (7th September) in a host of different ways.

There is no doubt that McCartney's involvement with the memory of Buddy Holly is quite genuine. In 1986, McCartney's company co-produced the definitive film biography of Holly's life, a formidable project, whilst just a few years ago McCartney both produced and played on the single 'T Shirt' for the still-active Crickets group.

The songwriting talents of Lennon and McCartney certainly drew some inspiration from the simple melodies, rhythms and lyrics that Buddy and The Crickets forged in the late 1950s.

Echo McGuire

Echo McGuire was one of Buddy's girlfriends during his High School years in Lubbock. They first started dating soon after they met at the age of 15. Although both came from a churchgoing background, Echo was apparently much more conservative than Buddy and while she didn't hold back his musical ambitions, she gradually became less than comfortable with her role in his life.

The relationship continued for a while, even after she began to attend a Christian college in Abilene around 1955, and they kept in contact for a year or two thereafter. Echo eventually married a preacher and no longer lives in the Lubbock area. But she was recently traced and interviewed extensively for a Channel 4 documentary on the singer's life.

In the film biography of Holly's life he leaves his Lubbock girlfriend (presumably Echo), explaining his decision to her with those immortal words: 'Just Tell Them Bula-Bula.'

Don McLean

This great singer/songwriter was born on 2nd October 1945 in New Rochelle, New York and came up via the folk route, finally surfacing in 1971 when his hit 'American Pie' went into the charts in both the UK and the USA. Both the single and the resultant album went gold in 1972.

Like Dylan, Don McLean seems to carry the music of the 1950s around in his head and has recorded his own interpretation of several of the best numbers from that era, which truly is a surprising fact as literally all of his remaining recordings are self-penned. Although he no longer has chart records he seems able to tour regularly, appearing

129

mostly at major venues.

An intensely honest man, he has said his aim is to combine the diverse musical styles of Woody Guthrie and Frank Sinatra and doesn't worry if that offends purists along the way.

See also 'AMERICAN PIE'.

Dutch McMillin

Dutch was born in North Carolina around 1916 and died in August 1995. For years it was thought that the session man playing sax on Holly's last Nashville recordings was the Yakety Sax man Boots Randolph. However, recent research has proved that Boots did not get to Nashville until 1958 some two years after the date in question. Instead, it was the veteran musician Elbert Raymond McMillin who was used by boss Owen Bradley on this session and others over the years with Brenda Lee, Roy Orbison, Webb Pierce, Mitchell Torok, etc. Prior to this he had been a DJ on a Nashville station. In later years he headed up a life assurance agency.

Joe Meek

Born Robert George Meek in Newent, Gloucester in 1929, Joe Meek became an avant-garde record producer in the late 1950s, and was responsible for some of the most innovative sounds in British pop music. But it has to be added that he also worshipped Holly's music and, consequently, often attracted soundalikes to his tiny London studio.

His biggest hit was with the Tornadoes' 'Telstar', although his association with John Leyton was equally impressive. In 1961 he produced the classic 'Tribute to Buddy Holly' by Mike Berry, which was leased to HMV and became a minor hit. The number was written by the enigmatic Geoff Goddard, who claimed, controversially, to have made spiritual contact with Holly. Not only that, but according to Meek biographer John Repsch, Joe Meek had had a premonition that Holly would die on 3rd February and had a note passed to Holly to this effect during the singer's UK tour. Needless to say this is unconfirmed!

Eventually, Joe's career went into a downward spiral and he committed suicide in bizarre circumstances on 3rd February 1967, the eighth anniversary of Holly's death.

'Memories'

Buddy and Bob performance at radio station KDAV, circa 1954–5.

Composed by Bob Montgomery this is one of the batch of early country-style performances that dates from Buddy and Bob days, which was eventually released in the 1960s on the 'Holly In The Hills' album. 'Memories' was one of three tracks that did not get an official US release until the box set came out in 1981.

An undubbed version of the song has been released on the little-known Vigotone label in 1996. Sound quality is quite good.

Mickey and Sylvia

Holly was a big fan of this duo, who had a million-seller on Groove in 1957 with 'Love Is Strange'. The group comprised of McHouston Mickey Baker (born 15th October 1925) and Sylvia Robinson (born 6th March 1936), who first met in 1955 and had a productive partnership that remained active for 10 years. Incidentally, both had solo recording careers before and after their days as a duo.

Buddy Holly left two Mickey Baker compositions (they were also Mickey and Sylvia recordings) on tape in his New York flat, these being 'Love Is Strange' and 'Dearest'. The latter is surely one of Holly's best vocals and an alternative performance has surfaced on bootleg-style albums lately.

Often called Mickey Guitar Baker, he remains a proficient guitarist up to the present time, having moved from the pop realm to the jazz arena.

'Midnight Shift'

First Nashville recording session at Bradley's Barn, 26th January 1956. Personnel: Buddy, Sonny and Don Guess plus Nashville session men.

This excellent rockabilly track from Holly's first Decca session under Owen Bradley had been passed to Buddy by Jim Denny. It didn't get a US single release at the time but was the posthumous follow-up on Brunswick to 'It Doesn't Matter Anymore' in the UK; it made the charts in the summer of 1959.

The principal composer was Earl Lee, a pseudonym for country singer/songwriter Luke McDaniel. The other co-writer, evidently, did not actually contribute any input to this song. Despite memorable lyrics and a good melody, the track has seldom attracted cover versions, although Sonny Curtis has perennially featured it in his act and committed it to wax on a Ritz album. The song itself seems to be a derivative of the 'Annie' songs that Hank Ballard and the Midnighters popularized in the 1950s. Such was the impact of these records that an answer series of 'Henry' songs were started by Etta James.

There is a version of the Holly recording overdubbed by The Picks that came out a few years ago. Opinions vary amongst fans as to the wisdom of the project, which involved 21 dubbed recordings in all. See entry THE PICKS.

Gary Miller

This little-remembered UK balladeer, real name Neville Williams, had numerous single releases to his name in the 1950s and 1960s but is probably best remembered for his cover of 'The Story Of My Life'. His only Top 10 hit was another cover, 'Robin Hood', in 1956.

In 1958, he appeared on the same UK tour bill as The Crickets and there are pictures extant of Miller with Holly from those days. By coincidence, he released a Pye single, 'Maria Elena', in 1963, which was not an allusion to Buddy's widow but rather a vocal version of the instrumental hit by Los Indios Tabajaros.

Gary Miller died suddenly from natural causes in the mid 1960s when only in his forties. His recording material is seldom reissued these days, which seems a harsh judgement on one of Britain's better balladeers. He deserves to be rediscovered and have his material back in catalogue.

Mitch Miller

Born in 1911 and with a classical background Mitch Miller, his orchestra and chorus, were a big success during the 1950s and even had a No.1 disc, 'The Yellow Rose Of Texas', for Columbia in 1955. In addition, Miller was A&R man for the label and it was hardly surprising that Norman Petty (whose Trio were signed to the label) should contact him and seek to place 'That'll Be The Day' with Columbia. The label was not exactly famous for its roster of rock'n'roll artists, and Mitch Miller was to forgo his chance to sign the group.

Mitch is famous for passing up on a few of the rock greats in the

1950s and always seemed more at home with artists like Frankie Laine and Rosemary Clooney. Shortly thereafter Murray Deutch and Bob Thiele entered the picture and we have to accept that everything that happened was for the best. Mitch Miller retired from the active music business many years ago.

'Modern Don Juan'

Final Nashville recording session at Bradley's Barn, 15th November 1956. Personnel: Buddy and Don Guess plus Nashville sessionmen. See below re take number.

This track formed the A side of Buddy's second US Decca single but it failed to make any impact. Perhaps being released on Christmas Eve (1956) didn't help. The number was written by Lubbock friends Jack Neal and Don Guess. The latter actually played bass on the session and was the only musician there who was not part of the Nashville set-up. The recording features a prominent saxophone thought to be that of the legendary Boots Randolph. It was later to come out that Boots didn't start to do session work in Nashville until 1958 and that, in fact, it was another famous session man, E.R. Dutch McMillin, who had a notable career in music, and who recently died. (See separate entry.)

Perhaps the most surprising fact about the recording is that it's supposedly Take 76! Alternatively, the engineer himself develops a hiccup in trying to say 'Take seven' or 'six'.

'Mona'

Rehearsal at Norman Petty Studios, Clovis, New Mexico, probably late 1957 or early 1958.

It is only in the last few years that nearly 10 minutes of tape has been discovered of Buddy, Jerry and Joe rehearsing this famous Bo Diddley number. If the session had been completed to everybody's satisfaction the track could well have ended up on Holly's first solo album, which was in preparation at that time. Whilst Holly's vocals are off mike, the bonus is to hear some excellent practice guitar. Jerry Allison is also heard strumming guitar during part of the lengthy workout.

These rehearsals have been unofficially released on bootleg-type albums in recent years, along with similar workouts of 'Fool's Paradise', 'Think It Over' and 'Take Your Time'.

133

'Mona' was eventually taken high into the charts in 1990, courtesy of Australian soap star, Craig McLachlan.

Bob Montgomery

Bob Laroy Montgomery was born in Lamasas, Texas, and he and Buddy Holly were firm friends from early school days in Lubbock, Texas.

Buddy had initially teamed up with Jack Neal, who was replaced by Montgomery in the Buddy and Bob duo (see BUDDY AND BOB entry). During 1954–5 they cut several demo-type recordings, either at nearby Nesman Studio, Wichita Falls or at radio KDAV, where they performed weekly on the Sunday Party. Although heavily influenced by country artists such as Hank Williams and Bill Monroe, the boys were not just parodists, and, in fact, they performed many of their own compositions. It is interesting to listen to these early 'country' attempts but frustrating that the overdubbing robs them of some of their authentic sound.

Although Bob travelled to Nashville when Buddy got his first beak, he did not perform on any recordings. Bob was based in Clovis for a time, working as Petty's assistant and even working as a session guitarist, appearing on several recordings, including those by The Fireballs.

Montgomery moved to Nashville in 1962 and eventually teamed up with Earl Sinks, calling themselves The Holidays, to release a single. Bob was to become a backroom boy and worked his way up the ladder, eventually owning House of Gold for many years. He also helped Jerry Chestnut run Passkey Publishing.

Among the many artists Bob produced in the 1960s and 1970s, by far the most successful was Bobby Goldsboro, who had a string of major hits. Moving into the 1980s he had hits with Janie Fricke and Razzy Bailey.

Montgomery's wife Carol was, for years, a Nashville session singer and in later years his son Kevin joined the business, helping on a duet in 1996 on the Nashville tribute to Holly, 'Not Fade Away'.

'Moondreams'

With the Dick Jacobs Orchestra; recorded in stereo at Coral Record Studios, Pythian Temple, New York, 21st October 1958.

Buddy was familiar with this Petty composition as he had played

134

guitar on a 1957 session with the Norman Petty Trio when an instrumental version was cut. Holly handles the melancholy number well, in a performance fans tend either to dislike or to rate highly.

The number was written by Norman Petty and although he was not the producer on this last studio session he may have been present in New York. If so, perhaps he contributed some input. Ultimately, the recording became a posthumous release as the flip of 'True Love Ways' in 1960.

All four songs from the October session have eventually seen release as both mono and stereo masters.

Motorcycles

In addition to driving his parents' cars Buddy owned a Cushman Eagle scooter in high school and one of his non-musical ambitions was to acquire a high-powered bike.

The opportunity came up at the end of a Big Beat tour of the USA in mid 1958. Fired up after watching the famous Brando film *The Wild One*, Buddy, Jerry and Joe had flown into Dallas *en route* to Lubbock and decided to go shopping – big time! Having got a cool reception at the Harley dealership they called in at Millers' bike shop nearby and purchased three new machines. Each picked a different model.

Holly got himself a new 1958 maroon and black Aerial Cyclone, around 650cc, whilst Joe picked a red 58 6T Triumph Thunderbird. Jerry settled on a red and white TR6A Trophy, also in the Triumph range.

After the purchase only one thing was left to do: ride the machines the 500 miles back to Lubbock! For the three musicians, life in 1958 must have seemed like a dream become reality.

The Arthur Murray Party

The Crickets performed live on this regular TV show back in December of 1957, just after Niki Sullivan left the group and they became a trio.

The film clip of their performance is often screened (they sang 'Peggy Sue') and was used on a Dick Clark video release as his own footage of The Crickets on *Bandstand* had been destroyed sometime in the late 1960s. Kathleen Murray introduced Buddy, Jerry and Joe, who sang to a backdrop of motionless dancers. The programme was transmitted in colour but black and white film only survives.

'My Two Timin' Woman'

Recorded at home 3315 36th St, Lubbock, on a wire recorder around 1949.

This is undoubtedly the first recording of Buddy, which dates from 1949 when he was 13 years of age. Not surprisingly his voice had not yet broken.

The song was written by country great, Hank Snow, and was pretty popular in the South around that time. Buddy's version was eventually released by brother Larry Holley, on his own label.

N

The Nashville Sessions

Listed alphabetically in this volume are details of the 12 song titles that Holly recorded in Nashville during 1956. The recordings took place over three sessions, spread throughout the year – January, July and November. The personnel backing Buddy were different on each occasion except for bassist Don Guess. Owen Bradley was the producer and Bradley's Barn is usually listed as the venue. At the time only two Decca singles were released in the USA and the songs only achieved fame in retrospect. Some of the music is quite potent rockabilly and it's particularly interesting to hear an early attempt at 'That'll Be The Day' (sung in a different key) as well as two different interpretations of 'Rock Around With Ollie Vee'.

Of the various Nashville session men, Grady Martin, guitar, recorded with Elvis, Johnny Horton and many others, while Floyd Cramer was also a session man with Elvis before he went on to a big solo career.

Any reader not familiar with The Nashville recordings should seek them out. While the output is uneven there are some excellent recordings amongst them.

TRACK LISTING:

- 1st session, January 1956:
  Love Me / Don't Come Back Knockin' / Midnight Shift / Blue Days, Black Nights
- 2nd session, July 1956:
  Rock Around With Ollie Vee / I'm Changin' All Those Changes / That'll Be The Day / Girl On My Mind / Ting A Ling

• 3rd session, November 1956:
  Rock Around With Ollie Vee (Sax Version) / Modern Don Juan /
  You Are My One Desire

Jerry Naylor

Jerry Naylor Jackson was born in Stephensville, Texas on 6th March 1939. Naylor was in The Crickets' line-up during the early 1960s, although he tended to give the impression that he was a member of the original quartet, when Holly was the lead singer! Despite his memory having occasional lapses, he has nevertheless done his best to promote the name of Buddy Holly via documentary-style programmes in the past.

Naylor was the lead voice on a whole string of post-Holly Crickets Liberty recordings before being sidelined for a while with heart problems in his twenties. He toured USAF bases in the UK in the late 1960s eventually cutting several records under both his own name and as Jackie Garrard on a variety of labels.

He later became a DJ on radio KLAC in Los Angeles and has continued in the music business down the years.

Jack Neal

Jack Neal lives in New Mexico these days and can boast that he was the first person to team up and make music with Buddy Holly as the Buddy and Jack duo back in 1951–2. A fine guitar and piano player he was born in Fort Worth, Texas in 1934 and actually still owns two unissued gospel-style recordings that Buddy is playing on, dating from 1957. These are 'I Heard The Lord Calling For Me' and 'I Saw The Moon Crying Last Night'.

Jack left the music industry and has spent most of his life as an electrician. See also BUDDY AND JACK entry.

Ricky Nelson

Born 8th May 1940, this late, great star lost his life in a Texas plane crash on New Year's Eve, 1985. The members of his backing band also

perished in the tragedy; only the pilot and co-pilot of the recon-
ditioned DC 3 survived.

Although Buddy Holly and Ricky Nelson only met once, evidently,
it is believed that Nelson rated Holly very highly and usually featured
'Rave On' in his stage act. On 30th December 1985 he played his final
concert in Guntersville, Alabama, performing 'Rave On' as his last
song to the full-house audience. If so his final words would have been,
'Rave on for me.' Not a bad epitaph for a singer.

Ricky Nelson left a long and varied recording output. Although
stories suggest that he only drifted into singing, he came from a
highly musical background and was a professional musician through
and through. (His father Ozzie Nelson made dozens of big band
recordings.) Ricky was a real modern day troubadour. His versions of
Holly's 'Rave On' and 'True Love Ways' were recorded in 1979 and
released in the year following his death on the Epic label.

New York

The tee-shirts proclaim that Buddy Holly was a good ol' boy who was
about as Texan as you can get, with his parents having also been born
there. Remember that, although part of the Union, Texas, which is
267,300 square miles in area and 938 miles from the Northern border,
to the Rio Grande on the edge of Mexico, is as near to a country as you
can get.

But after marrying in Lubbock in August 1958, Buddy and Maria
headed for New York and settled in an apartment in The Brevoort
building on 8th Street, which is within the area commonly known as
Greenwich Village. That was his base for the six months up to his
death and whilst he retained business contacts in Texas, he may well
have shuttled between the two localities.

Certainly Buddy was no stranger to The Big Apple (the phrase had
not been coined then by the way) having stopped off at venues there
on most tours at least a dozen times. Several of his major TV appearances had also been in New York and, of course, he had recorded studio sessions both at Bell Sound Studio in 1957 and twice at the Pythian
Temple in 1958. If we include the apartment tapes material, then
Buddy recorded around 20 numbers overall in New York – one-fifth of
his total musical output.

As he also met his wife in New York, it's fair to conclude that his
brief contact with the city was highly significant both in musical and
in personal terms.

The Nighthawks

It is often mentioned, but has not been confirmed, that Holly plays guitar on a track recorded at Clovis in 1958 by this Amarillo band. Fronted by vocalist Eddie Reeves, they had cut the original version of 'When Sin Stops', composed by band member Bob Venable and later to be recorded by Waylon Jennings in a session produced by Holly.

Listening to the guitar solo the aural evidence would seem clearly to indicate that Buddy did not play on this track. Since his death, numerous claims have been made for his involvement in recordings, and as composer, when it is patently obvious that he wasn't involved.

Eddie Reeves has gone on to carve out a career in music as composer, publisher and eventually as a producer. Kenny Rogers and Kim Carnes are amongst those artists he produced.

Terry Noland

Born Terry Noland Church on 17th November 1938 in Abilene, Texas, Terry joined the Four Teens group in 1956, the personnel of which included a very youthful Joe B. Mauldin and Larry Welborn. Noland was a friend and contemporary of Buddy Holly but sadly no photo of the two together exists.

Noland recorded several solo sessions at Norman Petty's Clovis studios during 1957 and at one of these Trini Lopez (The Big Beats) played lead guitar. As can be seen from this book there were a lot of good musicians passing through Clovis.

Terry Noland and Buddy Holly kept in touch after Holly hit the big time and there is correspondence between the two dated late December 1958. In it Buddy suggests Noland consider using notable record producer Jesse Stone (see separate entry). This and other projects were left to wither on the vine when fate stepped in on that February night. Certainly Terry's own career virtually went on hold and he was eventually to quit the music business.

But Terry Noland did make many excellent records in Clovis, Nashville and New York during the years 1957 and 1958. Fortunately, most of these recordings have now been collected onto one CD by Bear Family Records, which is a highly recommended buy.

The author has been in touch with Terry Noland, who these days is semi-retired and living in Oklahoma City. He has spent the bulk of his working life in real estate but has warm memories of all the tours he made and all the legendary artists he was fortunate enough to meet.

Nor-Va-Jak

Norman Petty used Nor-Va-Jak Records and Nor-Va-Jak Publishing as names for two of his business enterprises. The name was taken from the name of The Norman Petty Trio (Norman, Violet, Jack) to produce a highly distinctive identity.

These were both based at the Petty's 7th Street recording headquarters in Clovis, New Mexico. This studio, where Holly and The Crickets recorded their most famous numbers, has been restored and is regularly opened to visitors who are fascinated to get a glimpse behind the scenes.

Later, the Pettys also purchased a theatre nearby in Clovis, which became their main headquarters in later years. See entry NORMAN AND VI PETTY.

Not Fade Away – Film

This is the Buddy Holly film that never was. The basic story was written by Tom Drake and Jerry Allison and revolved around the events surrounding the Texan group being booked onto an otherwise all-black bill at the Apollo theatre. Shooting actually got under way sometime around 1975 before things were aborted. Of course, the later Holly film biography included a classic sequence using the very same events. Interestingly, Gary Busey was actually cast in the part of Jerry Allison for this movie.

'Not Fade Away'

Recorded at Norman Petty Studios, Clovis, New Mexico, 29th May 1957. No bass on session but Jerry Allison played cardboard box percussion and sang backing vocals. Buddy, guitar and backing vocals, with Niki Sullivan.

Q: When is a B side not a B side?
A: When it's 'Not Fade Away'

An interesting recording that was first released tucked away on the flip of 'Oh Boy!'. Although a Crickets recording it is only one of three tracks that doesn't feature a dubbed vocal backing by either The Picks or The Roses. This has Buddy, Jerry and Niki doing the honours –

140

Niki's only involvement with the track. Also noteworthy is the percussion, which is courtesy of Jerry beating upon a cardboard box.

The Holly/Petty composition is something of a steal of the Bo Diddley beat although it doesn't infringe any copyright. If Bo Diddley was upset he's never shown it and has dignified the situation by recording his own excellent version of 'Not Fade Away'. Incidentally, while Norman Petty's name is on the composer credits, it's certain this is a drummer's number that J.I. Allison helped compose.

There is also no doubt that the Holly/Crickets recording has grown in stature over the years and the phrase has almost entered our language. Perhaps the earliest impetus was The Rolling Stones' decision to record the song in 1964 (it became their first major UK hit). In the Holly film biography the number is the last song in the Clear Lake Medley, providing a dramatic climax to the film.

An undubbed first take of 'Not Fade Away' by The Crickets has been released but differs little from the well-known version, part of which has been spliced into the tape.

The song was a minor country hit for Tanya Tucker in 1979 while The Crickets and The Band joined forces in 1996 as part of a Nashville tribute to record a powerful version.

The song has long been a favourite stage number for a whole roster of musical greats that we can edit down to three; Bruce Springsteen, The Grateful Dead and the post-Holly Crickets themselves.

O

Phil Ochs

A brief, sad entry for this US folk artist who brought out a lot a material in the 1960s, part of which was categorized as protest music. Although based in the North at that time he was born in El Paso on the Mexican border in 1940.

Seemingly a misunderstood figure he became deeply depressed after a mugging incident badly affected his vocal chords. He was to commit suicide in 1976, aged 35.

He is included here because, in the early 1970s, when Holly seemed to be forgotten in his homeland, Ochs dared to sing medleys of Holly material in his Carnegie Hall concerts risking the boos of the audiences in the process.

Ochs is probably best remembered for composing the Joan Baez classic 'There But For Fortune'.

See also JOHN DENVER AND OTHER FOLKIES entry.

Des O'Connor

This English comic's career started as a post-war redcoat at Butlins. The general public first became award of him when he acted as compere on variety shows that proliferated during the 1950s. The most famous of these was to be the March 1958 tour, which was headlined by Buddy Holly and The Crickets and which had been organized by Lew and Leslie Grade. His billing stated that he was the comedian with the modern touch! He has been quoted as saying he received £100 per week for the tour.

Later, he had a highly successful career as a singer during the 1960s, raking up a string of hits, which ultimately led to his becoming a regular sight on UK television screens.

In recent years he has stated that he bought a Hofner President guitar at Buddy's request and it has been in his possession ever since. In 1990 it was included in a sale of Holly memorabilia and bids were requested in the £40,000–£60,000 range. It failed to find a buyer.

Off The Record

This typically staid 1950s UK TV show was hosted by former big band artist Jack Payne. Before the Second World War Payne had hosted the BBC Dance Orchestra, which, at one time, also included Jack Jackson, that granddaddy of DJs, in its ranks. The fact that Jack Payne had been in the record business since the 1920s surely made him a doubtful choice to host a topical music programme. However, in 1958 youth culture was not yet all pervasive.

Off The Record was one of the few television vehicles for visiting US rock artists and one suspected Jack Payne tolerated the music, even if he seldom waxed enthusiastic. The Crickets' performance was telerecorded and for a long time there was doubt as to whether they mimed their number ('Maybe Baby') or performed live. The question was settled in 1994 when an audio recording came to light finally confirming that Holly sang live vocals on the programme. Hopefully, the tape, when cleaned up, will eventually get released in some way, if it can be legally arranged.

It has often been mentioned that The Crickets appeared on the TV show *See You in Soho*. Although this was advertised it didn't actually happen. But Buddy was interviewed on *Cool For Cats* on 28th February that very first day he arrived in Britain. No film of that appearance survives.

'Oh Boy'

Recorded at Norman Petty's Clovis Studios, New Mexico, between 29th June and 1st July 1957. The Crickets were a trio on this recording: Buddy, Jerry and Joe. The Picks' overdubbed backing vocals were added later.

It is intriguing to think that when the group recorded this number, 'That'll Be The Day' was still in the can and a release date had not yet been scheduled. 'Oh Boy!' was to become a monster hit for the quartet although rhythm guitarist Niki Sullivan didn't actually play on the session. Also recorded on the same day were 'Listen To Me' and 'Peggy Sue' – three classic numbers.

Even today, the recording of 'Oh Boy!' comes over as a high-energy performance that would be difficult to better. Sonny West and Bill Tilghman were the main writers on both this and 'Rave On' with Norman adding his name, although one senses the songs were basically written before being brought to Clovis. Evidently, Sonny West, who was a rockabilly artist himself, recorded it little thinking that Holly would pick up on the song. Sonny's version was not a hit but it's interesting to learn that his demo of the song was entitled 'All My Love'.

'Oh Boy!' became a major hit on both sides of the Atlantic for The Crickets and with 'Peggy Sue' still on the charts Holly was established as anything but a one-hit wonder. A label to be avoided at all costs, both then and now.

In the last few years an unauthorized release of 'Oh Boy!' by The Crickets, with The Picks' backing vocals omitted, has cropped up. It is to be hoped that an official release will follow at some point. Similarly, The Crickets' televised Palladium appearance has come out on record but not on official release via MCA. (The three tracks performed, 'That'll Be The Day', 'Peggy Sue' and 'Oh Boy!' are poorly recorded and of interest only from the point of view of nostalgia.)

An earlier live performance of 'Oh Boy' by The Crickets as a trio on *The Ed Sullivan Show* is available on a videogram and the sound is much better. 'Oh Boy!' has been heavily covered over the years with Mud taking it to No.1 in 1975 with their own distinctive interpretation.

Johnny O'Keefe

Johnny O'Keefe was one of the very small group of 1950s Australian rock'n'roll artists, and was virtually unknown in both the UK and the USA. He eventually carved out a career that lasted about 26 years. Born in 1935, he became the Antipodean answer to Elvis before a 1960 car crash laid him low. It was to be the start of a turbulent period in his life. Despite this he continued to record and perform.

Although not listed on most posters, he opened The Crickets' Australian tour shows (see separate entry) and presumably included his domestic hit recording 'Wild One', which came out on an EP rather than as a single. It is this song that Jerry Allison took a liking to and cut as Ivan with the amended title 'Real Wild Child'. (A few years earlier the controversial Brando film *The Wild One* had been partly banned, so retitling the disc was no doubt prudent.)

By the 1970s he had totally changed his image and became Chairman of the Australian Variety Artists Committee, a post he held until he died, unexpectedly, of a heart attack in 1977.

Roy Orbison

Roy Kelton Orbison was born in Vernon Texas on 23rd April 1936 and died on 6th December 1988, aged 52. The towns of Vernon and Wink in Texas both claimed him as their native son after fame struck. His earliest attempts at music involved forming a group, the Wink Westerners, while still at school.

This first attempt was a fairly short-lived affair. With the passage of time we think of Orbison and Holly as direct contemporaries but Roy had only regional success in the early years and did not blitz the charts until almost 18 months after Holly had died. Their paths seldom crossed although Orbison did briefly record as the Teen Kings in Clovis during 1956 before making his way to Memphis and Sun Records. Certainly two Orbison compositions ('An Empty Cup' and 'You've Got Love') were passed on to The Crickets via Norman Petty and made their way on to 'The Chirping Crickets' album. In an interview, Roy Orbison spoke fondly of spending a day in Holly's company and forming a fast friendship.

Had Holly lived, one wonders if there would have been room for two heavy-spectacled Texan singers in the business. Certainly, their images do overlap somewhat both in life and in death. Like Holly before him Orbison has had a highly successful posthumous career.

Little else links the two; however, Orbison's first wife, Claudette, used to attend Lubbock High School in the 1950s, and we can add that Ellis Amburn has written controversial biographies of both singers in recent years.

P

Larry Page

Larry is probably most famous as founder of Page One records and also as manager of The Troggs. But he was actually a performer and back in the 1950s he was known as Larry Page, the Singing Rage. If that description doesn't date him nothing will.

In fact he has the honour of being the first UK artist to cover a Holly/Crickets number when he recorded 'That'll Be The Day' for Columbia. Larry's version was very different from The Crickets and featured Geoff Love and his Orchestra as well as The Rita Williams singers. It didn't really sell.

The Palladium, England

Buddy Holly and The Crickets achieved the accolade of playing the London Palladium when they were over here on their only UK tour. On Sunday 2nd March 1958 they closed the first half of the televised show, the headliner being another American, Bob Hope, whom they met only briefly. That same day they also fitted in two shows at Kilburn, which meant a quick dash around the postal districts of London.

Memories of their first national TV appearance are mixed. They rushed through three numbers in just over six minutes and the aural evidence that survives on bootleg albums is less than impressive. But the London Palladium was *the* venue and undoubtedly one of the most prestigious shows of their career.

Thirty-two years later in 1990, The Crickets played The Palladium again. This time there was no Robert Morley as compere and this time they topped the bill instead of supporting Bob Hope. For Jerry and Joe the occasion must have been brimming with nostalgia.

145

The Paramount, New York

Probably equivalent to the London Palladium, the Brooklyn Paramount theatre was the mecca for American rock'n'roll performers during the 1950s. The aura of these times was lovingly recreated on screen in 1978 when Alan Freed's film biography *American Hot Wax* was released (by Paramount Pictures no less).

The Crickets actually appeared at The Paramount in both 1957 and 1958 as part of major rock'n'roll package shows that crisscrossed the country. The superb colour shot that adorns the cover of 'The Chirping Crickets' album was actually taken on the roof of that same theatre during their first appearance there.

If anyone points out that there were two Paramount theatres (Brooklyn and New York) he could be right.

Colonel Tom Parker

This legendary individual, an honorary colonel only, was manager of the late, great Elvis Presley from 15th March 1956 up until his client's premature death in August 1977. Born Andreas Cornelius Van Kujik in Holland, 1909 he kept a tight grip over Presley's affairs that was only relinquished after courtroom litigation ruled against him following Elvis's demise.

There is speculation that at some time in 1955, Colonel Parker was sounded out as regards managing the career of Holly, still Buddy Holley at that time. This would seem improbable, but not impossible, although to imagine such a pairing is too bizarre. Buddy and the Colonel just doesn't have the same ring to it!

Sue Parrish

Sue Parrish was a local Lubbock songwriter who collaborated with Holly in the early years by penning two of the numbers that he recorded in Nashville on his first visit there in January 1956. These were 'Love Me' and 'Don't Come Back Knockin''.

Buddy hardly knew of her before she wrote to him offering him some songs she had written. Sue Parrish eventually moved away from Lubbock and settled in the California area. It seems pretty certain that Buddy's name is only included as co-writer because he was able to get the songs exposure.

146

Gram Parsons

This legendary country rock artist who died back in 1973, aged just 26, was briefly linked with The Crickets in the time immediately prior to his death.

It was when The Crickets themselves were turning to country rock material and J.I. Allison and Sonny had been augmented by a bunch of other musicians to form a six-man outfit that eventually put out a new album 'Remnants'. It seemed that Parsons would join the group but it was not to be. Instead, he composed 'Ooh Las Vegas', which was used on the album. His own version of the song didn't appear until after his death.

Parsons is probably best remembered for his brief period with The Byrds, whom he quit in 1968 to help form The Flying Burrito Brothers with Chris Hillman. There is a fine biography out on Parsons entitled *Hickory Wind*, which is the name of his most enduring composition.

Gordon Payne

From Oklahoma, USA, Gordon Payne was lead singer with The Crickets from 1985 to 1994 and whilst not a household name he held the position for longer than Holly himself ever did. Whilst Joe B. Mauldin and Jerry Allison remain with the group, the personnel has seen numerous changes over the years, but with Jerry remaining very much the common denominator.

Gordon played a powerful lead guitar, a Stratocaster of course, and managed to avoid plagiarizing Holly's style. He started with J.J. Cale before becoming a member of Waylon Jennings's back-up band while also cutting solo records without notable success.

He really gave The Crickets a lift by bringing them back to a three piece for a while, and they performed several popular tours of the UK and Scandinavia. Sadly, Gordon decided that he needed more regular income and he now runs a vacuum cleaner business in the USA.

Bobby Peeples

This is an obscure name except to the most fanatical Holly followers. Bobby Peeples was one of Holly's school friends at Lubbock High School and had access to an acetate disc cutter in the early 1950s, which was a godsend to Holly and Montgomery, who were anxious to make demos in their quest to get a break.

All the undubbed garage-type material on the 1986 'Something Spe-cial' Rollercoaster album was recorded by Peeples, who drifted out of sight at some undetermined point. It was thought he may have recorded a live concert in Carlsbad, New Mexico, but trying exactly to determine his whereabouts has been a matter of extreme frustration for fans. He was located in Texas a few years ago by English superfan Ray Needham, who confirmed that no 'live' footage was lying around waiting to be unearthed.

Peeples did add that Buddy liked to drive hot rods, a remark not heard publicly before. If correct, it is yet another link with Bobby Fuller!

Peggy Sue Gerron

Peggy Sue Gerron is the former wife of J.I. Allison, drummer and co-founder of The Crickets. They married in 1958 and jointly went on honeymoon with Buddy and Maria to Acapulco, Mexico.

She remains famous for inadvertently giving her name to one of the most seminal of all rock'n'roll anthems, 'Peggy Sue'. However, she has no connection with the music industry and these days runs a plumb-ing business.

Peggy Sue visited the UK a few years ago to promote the showing of a short TV feature, which told of her part in the Buddy Holly leg-end. By an amazing coincidence it was found that she and Donna Ludwig, the ex-beau of Ritchie Valens, were actually living close to one another in the same town. Remembering that Ritchie and Donna came from California whilst she was from Lubbock, it seems a big coincidence.

'Peggy Sue'

Recorded at Norman Petty studios, between 29th June and 1st July 1957. Personnel: Buddy, Jerry and Joe. Niki Sullivan, see below.

This most famous of compositions was attributed to Buddy, Jerry and manager Norman Petty. Recorded in pretty quick order it started out as 'Cindy Lou' but ended up instead with the name of Jerry's girl-friend. The story goes that when practised in its original state it had more of a calypso rhythm.

'Peggy Sue' became Holly's first solo hit and was high in the Top 10 on both sides of the Atlantic. At the time the track was laid down, The Crickets were a quartet but all Niki Sullivan got to do was to flick the treble switch on Buddy's fender to facilitate that great guitar solo. The recording the world is familiar with is Take 2 but the first take has been released on a European album and differs little. Holly's vocal mannerisms probably include fewer hiccups. The Picks have also overdubbed Holly's vocal on a recent reissue and whilst this style works well on some of the Nashville tracks, it is less successful on classics such as 'Peggy Sue' and 'Everyday'.

J.I.'s unique sound was achieved by his concentrating on the snare drum while Norman Petty switched the drum in and out of the echo chamber, thus creating a rolling sound.

Three separate live versions of 'Peggy Sue' are in circulation. In chronological order these are from the first *Ed Sullivan Show, The Arthur Murray Show* and from their UK performance at the London Palladium. Finally, Holly recorded a 28-second radio jingle (to the tune of 'Peggy Sue'), which is worth seeking out.

There have been hundreds of cover versions of 'Peggy Sue ' over the years but not many are that noteworthy. Beyond doubt, Holly recorded the definitive version, and it is a song that will always be associated with him. Worth a footnote, however, are two other interpretations: an instrumental going under the name of 'Reggae Sue' and, more recently, Connie Francis's version, the first by a female artist. (She changes the lyrics in the process.)

Believe it or not the 'Peggy Sue' rhythm is linked with the entry for Sir Andrew Lloyd Webber.

Buddy, Maria Elena, Jerry and Peggy Sue pictured on their joint Mexican honeymoon, 1958. (Courtesy of Bill Griggs.)

'Peggy Sue Got Married'

Taped at Holly's New York flat, 5th December 1958. Buddy with acoustic guitar.

This is one of six tracks recorded at home on Buddy's Ampex tape recorder in the run-up to Christmas 1958. All are penned by Holly but this one is a cleverly constructed sequel to 'Peggy Sue'. Evidently Buddy's father had suggested the basic idea for the song.

Heavily overdubbed by Coral's Jack Hansen within months of Holly's death, the single made the Top 20 in the UK but did little in the USA. Later, both the undubbed version and a second dubbed version masterminded by Norman Petty, very similar instrumentally to 'Peggy Sue', were released and formed part of the MCA box set.

As with 'Crying, Waiting, Hoping' a stereo master was probably not made and the Hansen dubbed performance is available in mono only.

The song itself has seldom been covered; however, Mike Berry used it (as Kenny Lord and the Statesmen) when cutting a 1959 demo record for submitting to Joe Meek. If it has been neglected it got a real shot in the arm a few years ago when it was used as the title and theme tune for the much-acclaimed film of the same name, starring Kathleen Turner, which was set in or around 1962.

Carl Perkins

Carl Lee Perkins was born on 9th April 1932 in Lake City, Tennessee, and is one of the all time greats of 1950s rock'n'roll, principally through having written and recorded 'Blue Suede Shoes'. In fact, that was his one and only major hit record and it's really hard to believe that he hasn't had a whole string of them, such is his fame.

Apart from 'Blue Suede Shoes', Carl has written a series of rock'n'roll standards, three of which were recorded by The Beatles, which doubtless swelled Carl's bank account. (He bought his parents a farm, or so the story goes.)

Carl's greatest recordings were on Sun, but he also cut a lot of fine sides for Columbia. Holly and Carl only met once or twice and the Tennessean has spoken movingly of their immediate warm empathy.

He has been involved in Holly tributes over the years and has also penned a song, 'Take Me Back', which reflects on those days. He survived a cancer operation a few years ago but still keeps touring.

Peter and Gordon

This UK vocal duo had a string of British hits in the 1960s before going their separate ways: Gordon Waller into eventual obscurity whilst Peter Asher, who almost became Beatle Paul's brother in law, stayed in the music business over the years with significant success.

The duo scored well in the USA, where they had a string of hits as part of the British invasion. Their interpretation of Holly's 'True Love Ways' was a Top 20 hit there but in the UK it got to No.2 to notch up the greatest level of success to date for the song. Asher had an affinity with Holly's music and it is not surprising that he produced a whole series of Holly-associated songs for Linda Ronstadt, two of which ('That'll Be The Day' and 'It's So Easy') were major chart records for her in the 1970s.

Rare photograph of Roger Peterson, charter pilot on the ill-fated last flight. (Courtesy of Bill Griggs.)

Roger Peterson

Roger Arthur Peterson was the 21-year-old pilot of the Beechcraft Bonanza aircraft that crashed five miles northwest of Mason City in the early hours of 3rd February 1959, killing all four of the plane's occupants. Roger left a widow, De Ann Peterson.

Remembering that the loss must have been as great for Peterson's family, it was gratifying to learn that his name was in- cluded on the permanent memorial to Holly, The Big Bopper and

Valens that was erected a few years ago at The Surf Ballroom, Clear Lake, Iowa.

See also CIVIL AERONAUTICS BOARD REPORT.

Norman and Vi Petty

Norman Petty set up a recording studio in Clovis, New Mexico in 1950, the year after he had formed The Norman Petty Trio, which comprised of his wife Vi Petty, Jack Vaughn and himself. Buddy Holly gravitated to the studio in 1956 and eventually recorded that most famous of all demos, 'That'll Be The Day' in Clovis, late February 1957.

Earlier, The Norman Petty Trio had achieved quite a bit of success themselves selling half a million copies of the Duke Ellington classic, 'Mood Indigo', in the early 1950s. Not long after they were voted the most promising new group of 1954 by US Cashbox. One feels, however, that with the days of sweet music becoming numbered, the Pettys were happy to turn to recording others and to put their own careers on hold. (Vi Petty was a fine vocalist and also played keyboards). They did this to such good effect that Petty was to become one of the first independent producers of the rock'n'roll era and one of its most successful.

Norman was to soon become manager of The Crickets and produce those famous 1957–8 sessions that, in retrospect, have to be Buddy's most fertile recording period. Petty's name is shown as part composer on many of the most famous Holly numbers despite the fact that he himself didn't read music. However, he was exceptionally musical and doubtless contributed something to various compositions, but just how much will always remain unclear. Both Norman (piano/organ) and Vi (piano) occasionally played on Holly recording sessions.

The Norman Petty story is a long and involved one. He produced major hits with a variety of artists over the years, the best known of which are The Stringalongs and The Fireballs. It's sad that Petty never got the recognition he deserved and was totally omitted from the 1970s Hollywood film biography that purported to show Holly's life.

Tragically Norman Petty succumbed to leukaemia in 1984, having been hospitalized in Lubbock Methodist Hospital. He was 57. Coincidentally, Jack Vaughn, guitarist with the Trio, died the same year while the last member of the group, Vi Petty, died in 1992.

Violet Petty was always known affectionately to Buddy and the boys by the nickname Pansy. Although the Pettys have been heavily criticized in later years it is perhaps significant that most contemporaries from Lubbock and Clovis unfailingly speak of them with affection.

Charlie Phillips

This country artist was born close to the Texas/New Mexico border in July 1937. He wrote and recorded the popular number 'Sugartime' back in 1957, a song that the McGuire Sisters had a US No.1 record with the following January. Phillips was eventually to have two Billboard country singles in the 1960s.

At the time Charlie recorded 'Sugartime' in Petty's Clovis studio, Buddy was always about and it was natural for him to play lead guitar on the session. Jack Vaughn of The Norman Petty Trio also helped out instrumentally on the track.

Apart from playing lead on the flip, 'One Faded Rose', Buddy also performed harmony vocals. Both tracks are virtually impossible to find in their original 45 rpm state.

For many years Charlie Phillips was a DJ in Amarillo and was even voted DJ of the year in 1964. He has remained in the music business all of his life even appearing on the Grand Ole Opry.

Sam Phillips

Born Alabaman Sam Phillips in 1923, Sam formed the Memphis Phillip's International label in 1950 and its more famous associate, Sun records, just two years later. In the early explosion of rock'n'roll, dozens of Southern artists gravitated to the door of his Union Avenue studio to try and persuade Sam to record them, with varying degrees of success (and not too many from Texas).

Elvis, Jerry Lee and Johnny Cash were three of the names that did achieve fame in a big way, but others, such as Roy Orbison, achieved little but regional success via Sam. Other notables, such as Johnny Burnette and his Trio, were rejected at the outset. Rumours did arise that Buddy may have tried the Sun route but with the superb facilities on his doorstep in Clovis it is debatable. Then again Buddy did get a Nashville contract in 1956, so he was frequently in Sam's home territory of Tennessee.

Phillips has attained his own special niche in rock'n'roll by nurturing his great discovery, Elvis, before pointing him on the way to everlasting stardom with RCA. Sam's brother, Judd Phillips, who did so much to help Sam distribute his records in the early days, passed away in 1994.

The Picks

Bill and John Pickering had started out from their youngest days as part of a family gospel group before eventually teaming up with an acquaintance, Bob Lapham, to form a vocal trio that Norman Petty was to use frequently for overdubbing sessions during 1957 in Clovis. It was there that the group met up with The Crickets. The actual vocals on those early classics ('Oh Boy!', 'Maybe Baby', etc.) were dubbed on weeks later when Buddy was not usually present.

The Picks were not used from early 1958 when Petty decided to drop the group at short notice and turned to another trio, The Roses. For years in the 1960s and 1970s the brothers performed as a duo, The Pickerings and recorded in a variety of styles achieving some local success. John Pickering was eventually to change direction and become an oil geologist. Brother Bill had a somewhat chequered career doing DJ work in the early 1950s, but he developed personal problems that eventually affected his health. He died in 1985, aged 57.

The year before the trio had reformed and completed a major project to dub backing vocals onto a whole host of Holly recordings in an attempt to give them a more distinctive Chirping Crickets sound. Twenty-one tracks in all were given the treatment, including classics such as 'True Love Ways' and early efforts such as 'You are my one Desire'. Interestingly, they chose once more to create mono master recordings, as was done with Chirping Crickets material, rather than use a second (stereo) channel for their vocals.

The posthumous overdubs were done with great love and affection but they have met with a very mixed response from longtime fans. Having been familiar with recordings over a period of nearly 30 years it is exceptionally difficult for fans to judge such amended recordings dispassionately. Interestingly, whilst the overdubs were submitted to MCA in the 1980s, they were eventually released on The Picks' own record label, Pick Records.

The trio think that maybe they were the best vocal group of 1957, rather than Jerry, Joe B. and Niki, who were instrumentalists only at that time. It's rather academic really but no one can grudge The Picks their efforts to achieve belated recognition for the part they played in Holly's recording career.

Plays

Prior to the launch of the phenomenal musical *Buddy* other attempts had been made at producing shows that one way or another incorporated Holly's music or segments of his life.

In the USA during 1980 *The Adventures of Buddy Holly* was premiered in Dallas and got favourable press reaction. Members of Holly's family attended the opening. Around 1985 a UK musical by Phil Woods entitled *Buddy Holly at the Regal* toured the country fairly extensively. There have been many provincial shows, including one put on many times in Rotherham by Peter Piper and his travelling theatre.

In retrospect, all seem mere curtain raisers for the international *Buddy* musical.

Brian Poole

This UK 1960s hitmaker is still performing all over the UK and the Continent with his current group, The Electrics. He had a run of great chart hits that stretched over a three-year period.

He started out in the 1950s and was heavily influenced by The Crickets even to the extent of fronting his group wearing heavy frames. He corresponded with Buddy's manager, Norman Petty, and in 1964 this eventually led to Brian and the Tremeloes covering The Crickets' 'Someone, Someone', which was their first release after the split with Holly. Petty played both guitar and piano on the hit. Norman was also to play piano on two other Brian Poole recordings. 'Three Bells' and 'After A While'.

Fans who learnt of Brian's link-up with Petty had not been surprised as a year or two earlier the group recorded 'Twist Little Sister', which sounded like a recording straight out of Clovis.

Interviewed for this book, Brian Poole spoke warmly of his involvement with Norman Petty, whom he remembers as being hugely talented.

Postage Stamps

In June 1993 a commemorative postage stamp was issued in the USA showing a likeness of Buddy Holly. It was part of a series honouring early artists and included Elvis, Bill Haley, Clyde McPhatter and Ritchie Valens. Coming 34 years after his death the honour was overdue.

A few years earlier, a likeness of Holly had actually appeared on a German stamp, one of a set of four. The other legends were Elvis, Jim Morrison and John Lennon. Holly was in rarefied company. Most recently there have been several Holly stamps issued by the island of Grenada. Perhaps the UK will one day join in.

Meanwhile, his likeness has also cropped up on long-distance telephone cards, so no doubt this short list will gradually be extended.

Elvis Presley

Buddy Holly and Elvis first met when Presley was on one of his frequent tours of the southern states in 1954–5. Lubbock, Texas was often part of the itinerary. Holly is said to have picked up Elvis in his car and shown him the sights – such as they were! There is a 1955 photo of Elvis (probably taken at The Cotton Club) with Buddy and Bob Montgomery in close proximity. Buddy, Bob, and Larry Welborn performed as opening spot on one of Elvis's earliest Lubbock concerts and there is no doubt that Holly was heavily influenced by Elvis in the composition of his backing group and in his material. Interestingly, Presley's first dates described him as The King of Western Bop. Buddy's visiting card stated Western and Bop.

The bootleg-style Atlas album 'Elvis and Buddy' alternates Buddy's and Elvis's versions of seven songs, and makes for interesting comparisons. However, the Elvis recordings were all studio performances, whilst Holly's are largely demo-type efforts. Elsewhere, there is one recording to be avoided at all costs, an apparent duet by Elvis and Buddy of 'Ready Teddy'. It is nothing more than the two records played simultaneously. Unfortunately, they were recorded at different tempos!

Although Presley and Holly never met after 1955, there was a bond. Elvis sent a telegram to Buddy's parents from Germany at the time of his death and, in later years, he was quoted as saying that Buddy was his favourite rock'n'roll singer. Holly was to say that without Elvis none of them would have made it.

Certainly both are now legendary figures.

Johnny Preston

This US singer, born in Port Arthur, Texas in 1939, was to become the Big Bopper's protégé during 1958. The Bopper had been impressed when he first saw Johnny perform at a night spot in Beaumont, Texas as a member of a group called The Shades. He subsequently lined up a Mercury recording audition.

Initially, nothing much happened but later the Bopper took a demo of 'Running Bear' to Preston, who was persuaded to record it despite the fact that it was a change of style. It was set for an early 1959 release, but held back when news of the February crash broke. It eventually came out in July but didn't make it to No.1 until the end of the next year in the UK. It was fascinating to discover that backing vocal grunts were courtesy of The Bopper himself and the great George Jones.

Preston achieved far more success in the UK than back home but even here it was to be shortlived. By 1961 he was little more than a footnote in music books and left the scene for many years.

Johnny Preston had one of the most melodic voices of the era and his recordings are worth seeking out.

Prism Records

This is the name Buddy chose for a new record label that he hoped to get off the ground at some point. It is one of several projects that was embryonic at the time of his death. Maria Music, for publishing, was another.

Buddy Holly would have been president of Prism, which would have been based in Clovis, New Mexico. Ray Rush (one of The Roses) was slotted in as promotions manager while Norman Petty was to be responsible for sales. This format was mooted prior to Buddy's split with Norman, so what the final format of Prism Records would have been we will never know.

A few years ago 'The Apartment Tapes' were issued on a bootleg-style album: Prism Records, 819. So a very different Prism label has come into existence, via the back door.

The Pythian Temple, New York

The wonderful name of the building that housed the Coral studios on 80th Street in New York. It was the scene of Holly's last studio session in October 1958, which produced four numbers, the final one of which was the ballad, 'Moondreams'.

A few years earlier Billy Haley and his Comets recorded their hit version of 'Rock Around The Clock' at that same venue. That single was to sell well over 16 million copies worldwide and become one of the largest-selling singles ever.

A cavernous venue, the Temple was ideal to house sessions where a large number of musicians were involved. But it was to go out of fashion within few years and become little used.

Q

'Queen of the Ballroom'

Buddy and Bob performance of radio station KDAV, circa 1954–5.

Believed written by Lubbock bassist Don Guess, this was one of the compositions that was eventually issued posthumously under the Buddy and Bob banner. In the UK this came out in 1965 on the 'Holly In The Hills' album, but it was omitted from the US album of the same name.

A fairly routine countryish number, the mono release of this item has some instrumental overdubbing. It has not been released in its original format and seems unlikely to be put out commercially.

There is a 1955 tape of the same song by Sonny Curtis, which features Buddy Holly on guitar. It has not been officially released.

R

'Raining In My Heart'

With the Dick Jacobs Orchestra. Recorded in stereo at Coral Record Studios, Pythian Temple, New York, 21st October 1958.

One of Holly's greatest ever solo recordings that continues to get airplay to the present day despite not achieving hit status. Instead, it was the flip of 'It Doesn't Matter Anymore', which became a major posthumous hit on both sides of the Atlantic in 1959. 'Raining In My Heart' was written by the legendary songwriting duo of Boudleaux and Felice Bryant and was presumably passed to Buddy via The Everlys for what was to be Holly's final studio recording session.

Although recorded in stereo, the single was a mono master and for a great many years the track was not readily available in its stereo format except in the USA, where it had appeared on a compilation LP. (It was not until 1986 that a commemorative UK release in stereo came about.)

Holly's version has often been plagiarized in TV adverts and the phrase now seems to have entered the public's general consciousness. Buddy's brother Larry always quotes this number as his favourite, and it's easy to understand why. In recent years Larry produced a version of the song by his daughter Sherry on his Cloud Nine Label. The song has been much covered over the years, including a version for Dot by the composer Boudleaux Bryant, who died in 1987, aged 67, just months after being inducted into the Songwriters' Hall of Fame, Nashville. Leo Sayer had a minor hit with it in the 1970s.

'Rave On'

Recorded at Bell Sound Studios, New York, 25th January 1958. Personnel: Jerry and Joe B. on backing instrumentals with Al Caiola and Donald Arnone (guitars) and Norman Petty (piano); background vocals by session singers.

This is the 1950s track that has the dubious honour of being described as 'music to steal hubcaps by'. Surely one of the silliest quotes to emanate from a paranoid older generation that felt threatened by the unfamiliar music they were hearing for the first time. The phrase 'Rave On' was first heard in 1956 as part of the lyrics of the Carl Perkins number 'Dixie Fried', which is doubtless how Bill Tilghman and Sonny West got the idea for their song.

'Rave On' is an absolute gem from the West/Tilghman partnership that was also responsible for the hit 'Oh Boy!' just a few months earlier. Buddy and the boys had travelled up to New York for TV dates after Christmas 1957 and managed to fit in the session at the end of a tour that had been headlined by The Everly Brothers. It is worth mentioning that, although Milton de Lugg is listed as producing the session, his boss Bob Thiele insists that it was he who masterminded the proceedings.

It is worth briefly reflecting that the composer Sonny West recorded his own version of the song for Atlantic and it is probable that if it had become a hit then Buddy would not have cut it. But he did and it was a Top 5 hit in both the USA and the UK, and became one of Holly's best-remembered recordings. Whilst there have been several laudable versions of 'Rave On' over the years, none has the impact that Holly's stretched opening syllable gives his recording. Knowing that Holly started off singing a capella in his school choir he would doubtless have been delighted with the unaccompanied version released by Steeleye Span.

In discographies of Holly recordings it is often noted that there are two unissued takes of 'Rave On'. If the unissued tapes ever were returned to Norman Petty in Clovis, they have not been found and must be assumed lost.

Mike Read

One of the UK's great DJs, Mike Read has always acknowledged his liking for Holly's music. He has endeared himself to pop fans over the years by exhibiting a deep knowledge of all musical tastes.

He has also dabbled in recording, and in 1981, as The Grasshoppers, he recorded The Crickets' 'Teardrops Fall Like Rain' on Polydor, which didn't chart. In the USA 'That'll Be The Day' and 'Oh Boy!' came out on the Promenade Label. It is little known that he also cut a version of 'Midnight Shift' backed with 'I'm Gonna Love You Too' and although given a catalogue number by Pinnacle records, it remains unissued.

He is currently working on several diverse projects that include a biography of the legendary English poet Rupert Brooke. Earlier this year (1996) he penned the sleeve notes on a Connie Francis Holly tribute CD. See acknowledgements section.

'Ready Teddy'

Recorded at Norman Petty Studios, Clovis, New Mexico, May–July 1957. Solo release. The Crickets were a quartet of Buddy, Jerry, Joe and Niki Sullivan, with Vi Petty on piano.

'Ready Teddy' was written by John Marascalco and Bumps Blackwell and had been a No.1 record for Little Richard in 1956 on the R&B charts. Elvis recorded his version later in 1956 and frequently featured it, as did Buddy, in live performances.

Holly's version was recorded with his first solo album in mind but he made few concessions in cutting the number. It is anything but a filler in an all-out vocal performance that matches Little Richard in its power. The instrumentation is also first rate in what is a very tight group sound. Overall the record is probably as dynamic as any Buddy ever recorded but anyone interested in lyrics should give it a miss. It's a prime example of the 1950s' 'Go, Cat, Go' genre.

Latterly, a grotesque duet of 'Ready Teddy' between Elvis and Buddy was released on a foreign album but it is not recommended. (Literally both artists' recordings are played simultaneously).

'Real Wild Child'

Recording by Ivan. Backing musicians: Buddy Holly, guitar, Joe B. Mauldin, bass, and Bo Clarke, drums.

160

Ivan was the middle name of Jerry Allison, who gave up his drumkit to record the vocals on this Johnny O'Keefe number, which was released on Coral in 1958. Jerry's vocals were evidently a parody of actor James Cagney's delivery, whilst the flip, 'Oh, You beautiful Doll', was simply a novelty recording. It was the old standard delivered in a unique doubletalk style.

The A side reached No.68 in the USA, and evidently Jerry occasionally performed it during the 1958 Biggest Show of Stars tour. He recorded one other single, 'Frankie Frankenstein', but Holly was not on that session.

These days, as drummer with The Crickets, Jerry Allison can be occasionally lured to the mike but only rarely will he attempt his sole chart entry. 'Real Wild Child' became a US hit again in the 1980s for the outrageous Iggy Pop.

Record Collection

It is difficult to analyse exactly what recordings Buddy owned as some listed were not even issued at the time of his demise! But he did have a collection of singles including six by Ray Charles at a time when the singer was not in the pop charts. Next on were a handful of records by The Midnighters and by Jimmy Reed. Singles by black artists predominate and include favourites such as Bo Diddley and Little Walter but, surprisingly, not Fats Domino. (He was able to listen to hit singles down at the local radio stations, which presumably curtailed his need to purchase somewhat.)

The very few ballads that are listed appear to have 1960 release dates according to researchers! But singles by old friends the Everlys are in evidence as well as his favourite, 'I'll be Alright', by The Angelic Gospel Singers.

Anyone wanting more information should search out back issue 138 of rock'n'roll magazine *Now Dig This*. See SOURCES section for contact address.

Record Labels

Buddy Holly's first recording contract was as a solo artist for the US Decca label and his complete output for them was recorded over three sessions in Nashville during 1956. It was at this stage that his name was misspelt as Holly (not Holley) and was to remain that way. The producer on each occasion was Owen Bradley. See separate entry.

With his career going nowhere, Buddy, now part of The Crickets, signed with Brunswick and their subsequent recordings were released on that Decca subsidiary. Meanwhile, Petty arranged for solo recordings by Holly, usually featuring the same personnel, to be released through Decca's more prestigious label, Coral. This is the label that Buddy was contracted to at the time of his death while The Crickets, with replacement lead singer Earl Sinks, had recorded a new single in November 1958 that was released on Coral Records both here and in the USA.

In the UK, Holly/Crickets recordings during 1957–8 were all released on Vogue Coral or Coral, with Brunswick being the vehicle for the Nashville recordings only. The Vogue prefix was gradually phased out. Holly product has, over the years, been leased by his recording company (now styled MCA) to a whole collection of labels. Bootleg-style releases have also proliferated in recent years, with MCA apparently unable or unwilling to issue fresh material.

The continuing absence of a definitive box set collection of all Holly/Crickets recordings on compact disc remains a major oversight bearing in mind the wealth of additional material that has surfaced over the last 15 years. CDs themselves have been about since 1982 and there are still Holly recordings that are not officially available in that format.

In the 1960s, an article in the music press discussed Holly releases under the heading 'The Long Waiting Game'. Despite the appearance of a vinyl/cassette box set in 1979, the situation remains frustrating and disappointing to hard-core Holly fans. The waiting game continues.

'Reminiscing'

Session at Norman Petty Studios, Clovis, New Mexico, 10th September 1958. Personnel: Buddy, Joe B. and Jerry plus King Curtis on saxophone.

The background to this recording is fully described under the heading of King Curtis elsewhere in this book.

A posthumous single release for Holly in 1962, 'Reminiscing' acted as a trailer for the album of the same name, which belatedly hit the shops the following year. Both the single and the album had chart success in the UK but made little impact in the USA.

Although this is listed as a King Curtis composition, it was learnt recently that it was written by Holly himself. In retrospect this makes sense because, whilst Curtis Ousley was a talented musician, and composed scores of instrumental numbers, he wasn't noted for his lyrics! Over the years the song has attracted few covers, although The Beatles' version from their Hamburg days has been released. A second-wave San Francisco group, The Flamin' Groovies, also recorded the song in the 1970s.

The Holly version we are familiar with includes dubbed instrumentation courtesy of The Fireballs. The undubbed version has only been released to date as bootleg material.

For completists the original UK 45 release has a guitar line omitted. It was added for the album release only. This means that there are three different versions available, all with the same vocal. All three are virtually indistinguishable.

'Reminiscing'

UK album: CORAL LVA 9212.

Various Buddy Holly singles began to chart in 1962–3 and several contained material that had not been released in the singer's lifetime but had apparently been held up in the tangled legal situation that arose following Holly's unexpected death.

Eventually, 11 tracks came out on the above album, all of which were overdubbed by The Fireballs under the direction of Buddy's former manager, Norman Petty. The majority of the tracks were demos from 1956–7 and were overdubbed by The Fireballs to create stereo masters.

The album reached No.2 in the UK charts and was to remain in the Top 20 for almost the whole of the year. It helped to bring Holly a whole new body of fans as some four years had passed since the singer had been near the top of the charts.

The distinctive colour photo on the album sleeve was taken by Norman Petty and pictured Buddy looking out of a plane window while *en route* to Hawaii. The touching sleeve notes were penned by Buddy's parents.

Listing: Reminiscing / Slippin' and Slidin' / Bo Diddley / Wait 'til The Sun Shines, Nellie / Baby, Won't You Come Out Tonight / Brown-Eyed Handsome Man / Because I Love You / It's Not My Fault / I'm Gonna Set My Foot Down / Changing All Those Changes / Rock a Bye Rock

Tim Rice

An unlikely entry perhaps but Sir Tim Rice has never hidden his affection for several of the 1950s' singers, usually singling out Rick Nelson, The Everly Brothers and Buddy Holly. Although a lyricist, he has gone for melody.

In fact, before he was knighted he recorded a powerhouse version of 'Not Fade Away' on the Chrysalis label. It came out in the 1970s but didn't chart. Coincidentally, Sir Andrew Lloyd Webber also qualifies for inclusion in this volume although few will guess the connection.

Little Richard

Little Richard was born Richard Wayne Penniman on 25th December 1932, and it is quite certain that Buddy Holly was a big fan. The two met back in Lubbock well before Holly hit the big time. For almost three years from late 1955, Richard was almost constantly in the US charts. When he gave up rock'n'roll (and found God) the event was listed as a watershed in rock'n'roll.

It is sometimes hard today to remember just how influential Richard was on his fellow performers. Elvis led the pack with three Penniman hits ('Rip It Up' / 'Ready Teddy' / 'Long Tall Sally') on his second album release and others followed. While artists such as Holly and Vincent recorded powerful versions of Richard material, Pat Boone went for sanitized covers – perhaps to appeal to the mass market. Strangely, the biggest influence that Richard had on Buddy was on the latter's guitar style, which often incorporated Little Richard's straight eight rhythm. The influence on Jerry Allison was to be equally profound.

While Holly never commercially recorded a Penniman composition ('Slippin' And Slidin" was a practice tape), he certainly performed his material routinely on stage with 'Keep A Knockin'' and 'Tutti Frutti' being especial favourites. Holly's own recording of 'Well... All right' was inspired by Richard's frequent exclamation to the audience of those three words.

It is disappointing that the linked memory of Holly/Richard has been tarnished by dubious quotes from the veteran singer about Holly that cannot be readily challenged 30 years on. The quotes continue to get repeated without corroboration.

What is certain is that Holly and Richard met up frequently from 1956 onwards and the Georgia Peach even visited Holly's home during one tour that included Lubbock. Little Richard still performs even though he is now in his sixties. He's one of the real survivors of a bygone era.

'Rip It Up'

Practice tape. Recorded at the Venture Studio in Lubbock, Texas, probably late 1956. Personnel: Buddy, Jerry Allison and others unknown.

Composed by erstwhile Little Richard chauffeur, John Marascalco and Speciality producer, Bumps Blackwell, 'Rip It Up' was a hit for both Richard and Bill Haley in 1956 and would have been standard bandstand material for most rock'n'rollers of the age.

Certainly Holly was no exception and his rehearsal-style version, also from 1956, was not a studio performance as such.'Rip it Up', together with a mixed bag of material, was released in 1964 as part of the 'Showcase' album, albeit heavily overdubbed instrumentally. The untouched mono recording wasn't released until two decades later.

Fans of 1950s music will remember Little Richard performing this song in the movie *Don't Knock the Rock*. An enduring image of the era.

Marty Robbins

Charismatic country artist who died prematurely in 1982 at the age of 57, just shortly after appearing in Clint Eastwood's film *Honky Tonk Man*, for which he also performed the title track.

It is well known that Marty Robbins's manager, Eddie Crandall, helped in getting Buddy the chance to cut demo records that were subsequently sent on to Nashville and which led to his first recording contract.

Certainly Marty Robbins recorded very much in the rockabilly vein himself back in 1955–6 even covering the Elvis release of 'That's All Right'. He later became a country superstar but was always ready to reminisce and discuss the early days when Buddy, Jerry and Joe hung around his office. He had fond memories of Buddy, whom he remembered as being completely besotted with the music, style and appearance of Elvis Presley.

The paths of Marty Robbins and Holly rarely crossed after those early days but both are major artists who contributed much to the music scene that they both left much too early.

Marty was born on 26th September 1925 and died 8th December 1982. His last studio recording 'Some Memories Just Won't Die' was produced by Buddy's childhood friend Bob Montgomery.

Marty Robbins was inducted into the Country Music Hall of Fame in 1982 as a singer and, in 1975, as a composer.

Jim Robinson

This Texan singer was born in Littlefield in 1926. Sadly, he never achieved national success but at least three of his recordings ('Whole Lotta Lovin'' / 'It's a Wonderful Feeling' and 'A Man From Texas') feature Holly on lead guitar, having been cut at Norman Petty's studios in early 1957. On a couple of the tracks Jerry Allison uses a cardboard box instead of his drumkit, a forerunner to the session at which they cut 'You're So Square', when Jerry used the same technique.

Robinson had a successful songwriting partnership with Peanuts Wilson in the 1960s but eventually left the music business and became a senior electrical engineer.

Jim Robinson currently lives in Odessa, Texas. He hails from a musical family and was a cousin to Johnny Horton.

Red Robinson

Unknown on these shores, Red Robinson was Canada's premier DJ back when rock'n'roll ruled the airwaves. He did a lengthy interview with Holly backstage at the Georgia Auditorium, Vancouver, 23rd October 1957, at a time when interviews with rock artists tended to be both banal and brief. His interview, which we first heard in 1980, is lengthy and less superficial than, for example, the Dick Clark Bandstand interview. It was to be several years before rock stars were interviewed in greater depth and the music started to be dissected and analysed almost *ad nauseam*.

There is a wonderful 1957 photo of Red with Buddy, where the singer has not yet acquired his solid-framed specs, nor had his teeth capped. Robinson himself looks much like Jerry Lee. Holly would have tied for third in a lookalike contest using this picture.

There is no doubt that Red Robinson was one of the few important Canadian figures in rock'n'roll during the 1950s when the scene was dominated by the USA. From the outset Red championed 'That'll Be The Day' at a time when the record was going nowhere and certainly helped it to break out in Canada and the border area.

Red Robinson is alive and well and still heavily involved in

Buddy with Red Robinson, Canadian DJ, on tour with The Biggest Show of Stars, 23rd October 1957. (Courtesy of Red Robinson.)

entertainment. In 1983 he published *Rockbound*, a book cataloguing his life in music, during which time he met everyone from Elvis to the Beatles. He did it all.

'Rock A Bye Rock'

Demo recorded at Norman Petty Studios, Clovis, New Mexico, February–April 1956. Personnel: probably Buddy, Sonny Curtis, Don Guess and Jerry Allison.

A perfect example of the Buddy Holly knack of singing a patently rock'n'roll number while at the same time endowing the lyrics with a most plaintive vocal delivery.

A self-composition that has been likened to 'Sexy Ways', it was one of a batch of demo-style recordings that didn't see the light of day until the 1960s when a series of albums came out. ('Reminiscing', 'Showcase', etc.)

Again the released recording was heavily overdubbed *à la* The Fireballs in order to produce a commercial, stereo release. It was

167

later released (mono/undubbed) on the 1986 LP 'For The First Time Anywhere'.

The Holly recording with dubbed backing vocals by The Picks has also been released.

'Rock Around with Ollie Vee'

Versions recorded at second and third Nashville recording sessions, Bradley's Barn, 22nd July (Take 8) and 15th November 1956 (Take 12). July: Lubbock personnel. November: Nashville session men and Don Guess.

Sonny Curtis wrote this most rhythmic of numbers and has featured it in his own stage act through to the present day. He was present playing lead guitar on Holly's July recording but not on the later version when the song was transformed into a sax-based number. This sax cut of 'Ollie Vee' was released as a Decca single in the USA during September 1957, probably as a direct result of 'That'll Be The Day' going to No.1. If record buyers bought it, and few did, they were in for a shock as the B side was the much earlier recording of 'That'll Be The Day', vastly different to the slick, commercial hit waxing.

The alternative, saxophone version of Ollie Vee remained unissued in this country until 1975 when all the Nashville material was released on one album, 'The Nashville Sessions'. Whilst the number has never been a hit it has always remained a favourite to jive to and has featured prominently in both the stage show and the film biography of Holly.

The Picks did vocal overdubs in 1984 of the guitar version of the number. Ollie Vee, by the way, is the unusual name of a local person that Sonny knew back on his father's farm in Meadow, Texas.

It is now known that Boots Randolph did not play sax on the November cut. It was, in fact, E.R. Dutch McMillin.

'Rock Me My Baby'

Crickets recording cut on the road, Tinker Airforce Base, Oklahoma City, September 1957. Personnel: Buddy, Jerry, Joe and Niki Sullivan.

One of the greatest examples of The Crickets' work as a quartet. It was recorded with three other numbers at the Tinker Air Force Base,

Oklahoma City whilst the group were taking an enforced break from touring because of segregation problems. The whole thing is a gem, from the vocal itself through the ringing lead guitar solo to the perfect backing vocals of The Picks.

Written by songwriters Shorty Long and Susan Heather, the recording formed part of 'The Chirping Crickets' LP. Album charts didn't arise until the *Melody Maker* printed a Top 10 in November 1958, so the album, statistically, was not a hit. But it was in every other respect and has often been included in all-time top-100 album lists down the years.

Tommy Roe

Born Thomas David Roe on 9th May 1942, Atlanta, Georgia, Tommy Roe had a whole cluster of hits in the USA during a term that lasted some 10 years. Not only did his vocals lean somewhat on Holly's style but he virtually took over the 'Peggy Sue' rhythm, especially with his first No.1, 'Sheila' in 1962 and several years later with 'Dizzy'.

He has never been afraid to acknowledge his debt to Holly and during his stage act often includes a medley of Holly's hits. Strangely he has not recorded a full-blown tribute album, but has recorded the occasional track ('It Doesn't Matter Anymore' / 'Raining In My Heart') at random times.

See also SOUNDALIKES entry.

Chan Romero

Chan was a Cricket for a day or so back in the post-Holly years when Jerry and the boys were doing a midwest tour. Based in Los Angeles at the time they often drafted in fellow musicians at short notice. At this time, Jerry Allison and Larry Trider formed the nub of the group, usually augmented by one or two others – as the venue demanded.

Although often linked with Valens, the vocals of Chan Romero were quite dissimilar. Instrumentally their styles were alike, with Romero often using the same set of musicians in the studio.

Chan is most famous for writing and recording 'Hippy Hippy Shake' when he was with Bob Keane's Del Fi label back in 1959. Royalties from the song, which even The Beatles recorded, have been a consistent earner for him through the years.

Wesley Rose

Wesley was the son of Fred Rose, one of the early giants of the country scene who founded the Hickory label and also started the Acuff Rose publishing house with Roy Acuff.

Wesley Rose was groomed to follow his father and expanded his enterprises by going into record production in the early 1950s largely in the country field. But he did help launch the career of The Everlys via the Cadence label.

It's possible that Rose was instrumental in rejecting two Holly demos that the singer pitched to the duo in 1958. Even if true it didn't seem to affect the relationship of the artists, who were to remain friends until the end of Holly's life.

After an honourable career Wesley Rose died age 72 in 1990. In an odd coincidence Archie Bleyer, Rose and his top songwriter, Boudleaux, all passed away in a three-year period commencing 1987.

The Roses

The group hailed from the towns of Andrews and Odessa in Texas, and had originally backed Roy Orbison on some of his Sun material. As we know, Roy also used the Clovis studios and it was through this that the trio were introduced to Norman Petty and, ultimately, became session vocalists there for several years.

The Roses were later used as the backing vocal group on The Crickets' recordings, replacing The Picks, who had been used from early 1957 through to the end of that year. The group consisted of Bob Linville, Ray Rush and David Bigham, and their involvement differed significantly from The Picks in one respect: they actually toured with The Crickets on a unique occasion in 1958. (Despite this fact, Norman Petty still preferred to overdub backing vocals on The Crickets' material without the backing singers being present on the session. Consequently, whilst Holly had met all the various backing vocalists they didn't exactly hang out together.)

Later Ray Rush acted as A&R man on several David Box recordings, and, it seems, he had been lined up during late 1958 to act as promotions manager with Holly's embryonic Prism record label. He stayed on in the music business and later worked with B.J. Thomas. Robert Linville is a supermarket manager in Clovis while the whereabouts of David Bigham are not known.

Ray Ruff who recorded the Hollyish 'I took a liking to you' in Clovis with Norman Petty should not be confused with Ray Rush of The Roses.

Royal Teens

Little-remembered group from the 1950s that had just one big record 'Short Shorts' a disc that, in the trade, would have been called a novelty number. Their other claim to fame was that Bob Gaudio was, briefly, a member before joining The Four Seasons.

In 1958, lead singer Joey Villa was instrumental in introducing Lou Giordano to Buddy and Giordano became the protégé of Holly and Phil Everly, who co-produced his Brunswick single 'Stay Close To Me'. See LOU GIORDANO.

Rumours

Over a period of almost 40 years all sorts of rumours have come and gone concerning undiscovered Holly performances and most are hardly worth repeating, but a random sample are given below.

In the early days it was rumoured that a song title existed called 'So Rare', which was a 1957 instrumental hit for Jimmy Dorsey, but was unconnected in any way with Holly. For even longer the title 'I Tried To Forget' was said to exist until it was realized it was just an alternative title for 'I Guess I Was Just A Fool'.

In the 1960s fans learnt through the musical press that the unkown Rutland Records intended to put out a whole collection of unreleased material. It never happened. This was similar to publicity surrounding a US Live Gold release that eventually turned out to be a virtual re-release of tribute-type material. It certainly contained nothing devastatingly original.

A Dutch compilation album, 'His Kind Of Music', has three tracks attributed to Buddy Holly and Larry Welborn but minimal research shows that these are 1960s recordings.

Back in 1959–60 it was even rumoured that Holly hadn't perished after all, but was just badly mutilated! Also, as more and more posthumous material came to light, it was suggested that all Holly releases might not be 100 per cent authentic.

Coming up to date we do know that there are odds and ends of Holly material that could still come out, but all studio masters have long since been released – unless, perhaps, a piece of tape still exists somewhere amongst all the reels of recording paraphernalia in Clovis? With new Glen Miller material being discovered who knows? And of course computer technology might lead to Holly's voice being recreated in the laboratory!

S

Tommy Sands

This little-remembered Capitol recording artist's other claim to fame is that for five years he was Sinatra's son-in-law, being married to daughter Nancy. When the marriage finished so did his career, and for years he worked as a tour operator in Hawaii.

A few years ago it came to light that, Graham Turnbull, aka Scotty Turner, had turned up several songs that he had composed with Buddy Holly and of which at least one was being offered to Tommy Sands. Incredible as it may seem the songs had lain neglected in a guitar case for around 30 years!

In another twist to the story the late actor Audie Murphy was listed as a co-writer. But it does seem as though Murphy was a songwriter and a producer, so perhaps this does check out.

According to Scotty Turner the handwritten lyrics had been verified as being Holly's, and it was hoped that the songs would be recorded by US group, The Razorbacks, and put out on release.

Teenage crush Tommy Sands never made the Top 40 over here but, by coincidence, he entered the US Top 40 in 1957 on the very day that The Crickets were in Clovis recording 'That'll Be The Day'. Golden days for the older reader.

Frankie Sardo

This obscure New York singer of Italian extraction helped complete the bill on the final Winter Dance Party Tour. He had an ABC Paramount release, 'Fake Out' that was described in 1959 as a fast-rising hit but certainly never got near the US Top 40 singles chart.

He is rumoured to have gone into film production after his singing career failed to ignite, but has never been traced since. Equally, biographical information appears non-existent.

Saxophones

By virtue of The Crickets' line up Buddy Holly rarely came into contact with the most inspired of musical instruments, the saxophone, but when he did the results were memorable.

The last of Holly's Decca sessions in Nashville (November 1956) was believed for years to feature the Yakety Sax man, Boots Randolph, but it was established recently that it was, in fact, Dutch McMillin, brief details of whom are given under a separate entry. Of the three tracks recorded in November there is prominent sax on 'Ollie Vee' and 'Modern Don Juan' but it seems not to be present on the ballad 'You Are My One Desire'.

Buddy next used a saxophone at his mid 1958 session in New York when he cut 'Early In The Morning' at short notice using much the same set-up as Bobby Darin used for his version. The marvellous searing sax is probably courtesy of Sam 'The Man' Taylor, whose pedigree included working with Louis Jordan, and who himself released a string of instrumental albums on US Decca over the years. Holly and Taylor were on the same tour bill the month before.

Within three months Buddy had recruited the legendary saxophonist King Curtis to perform a one-off Clovis session which produced both Waylon Jennings first single as well as two tracks by Holly himself, although they were not to be released in his lifetime.

Finally, at Buddy's last Coral recording session, Boomie Richman played a mellow tenor sax, which only comes through as a solo on one of the four tracks, 'True Love Ways'. It is hard to imagine the solo being bettered and invariably other versions have reproduced his solo, note for note.

As Buddy Holly continually experimented musically he would doubtless have tried further work with this most famous of reed instruments.

Schools

Buddy's First school was the Roscoe Wilson Elementary school. Eventually, he transferred from there to the Roosevelt Elementary School.

In later years he first attended the J.T. Hutchinson Junior High (with Bob Montgomery) and finally Lubbock High School from where he graduated, in the American sense, in 1955. His only full-time paid job was to be in the world of music.

Incidentally, all the above schools were either in Lubbock itself or Lubbock County.

The Searchers

This UK group are still in existence well over 30 years after they made their chart debut, and are frequently voted the best 1960s act still performing. It is often forgotten that they started their life at The Cavern in Liverpool.

They have occasionally performed Holly material on stage but, recording wise, they have only committed 'Listen To Me' and 'Learning The Game' (as 'Led in the Game') to wax. Founder member Mike Pender has always been quick to pay tribute to the influence of Holly and The Crickets' sound from the earliest days.

The Searchers – Film (1956)

This famed western featured John Wayne and was recently named as one of the 10 movies that shook the world in the 20th Century.

Certainly it shook two young friends, Buddy Holly and Jerry Allison, who came out of their local State Theatre in Lubbock uttering the phrase that dominates the movie: 'That'll Be The Day'.

Within a short space of time they had collaborated on a song that would become a classic and is still popular some 40 years later.

'Send Me Some Lovin''

Recorded by The Crickets (quartet) on 12th July 1957 at Norman Petty studios, Clovis, New Mexico. Personnel: Buddy, Jerry, Joe and Niki Sullivan.

Written by John Marascalco and singer, Lloyd Price's brother Leo, and was first recorded by Little Richard in 1956, being released as the flip of 'Lucille' on Speciality 598. The B side entered the Top 100 in the USA during 1957, but it was not until 1963 that it became a Top 20 recording, courtesy of Sam Cooke.

The Crickets' recording features the dubbed vocal backing of The Picks and became one of many great tracks used for 'The Chirping Crickets' album in 1958. The original recording, without The Picks, has been released on bootleg versions. The quality is, however, substandard.

'Shake Rattle and Roll'

Practice tape; recorded in Lubbock, Texas, late 1956. Personnel: Buddy, Jerry Allison and others unknown.

Written by Jesse Stone aka Charles Calhoun, this song is rock'n'roll through and through. First charted as an R&B hit for Joe Turner in 1954 in the USA, it was then used by Bill Haley as his follow-up to 'Rock Around The Clock'. (In the UK the Brunswick single of 'Shake' actually beat Haley's earlier single of 'Clock' into the charts.)

The number is one of a handful of rock'n'roll numbers that would have been included in most self-respecting rockers' stage acts. Holly's version, from his earliest days, uses a compromise of the overtly sexual lyrics of Big Joe Turner's version and the sanitized Haley rendition.

The posthumous release of the Holly recording is heavily over-dubbed instrumentally, and has since seen release on Rollercoaster Records in its original basic mono format – in vinyl to boot.

Del Shannon

Del Shannon was born Charles Westover on 30th December 1939 and was, sadly, to die a suicide victim on 9th February 1990. He was evidently taking anti-depressants, which, it was suggested, may have contributed to his shotgun death.

If Holly was one of the earliest rockers, perhaps Del was one of the last real rock'n'rollers? Playing a ringing Fender lead he always seemed somewhat of a throwback having not actually hit the bigtime until 1961 with the phenomenal 'Runaway'. This featured a new instrument known as a musitron, an organ-based instrument.

The organ was highly unfashionable in the rock'n'roll era with only Norman Petty keen to use it and Dave Baby Cortez having an isolated hit or two. Whether Shannon got the inspiration for his sound from either source is a matter of conjecture.

Del Shannon had appeared in Holly tributes in both Lubbock and at Clear Lake over the years and is fondly remembered by fans for a string of dynamic hits in the 1960s at a time when the British invasion had almost completely taken over.

'Showcase'

UK album: Coral LVA 9222.

Released in June 1964 this followed in the wake of the 'Reminiscing' album and comprised material largely unreleased up to that point. Again it proved to be a hit album reaching No.3, and a single release from it, 'Love's Made A Fool Of You', crept into the Top 40.

After 1964 Buddy Holly was to have no further singles in the charts except for reissues and his name in his homeland was becoming very much a distant memory. It was to be the 1970s before his name was to reappear Stateside.

Listing: Shake Rattle and Roll / Rock Around With Ollie Vee / Honky Tonk / I Guess I Was Just A Fool / Ummm, Oh Yeah / You're The One / Blue Suede Shoes / Come Back Baby / Rip It Up / Love's Made A Fool Of You / Gone / Girl On My Mind

Earl Sinks

This Texan singer was born Earl Henry Sinks on 1st January 1940. He became a member of the post-Holly Crickets in 1958 and was lead singer on some of their very best material even if he is, naturally, somewhat overshadowed by the legacy of Buddy Holly.

In 1959 The Crickets' version of 'Love's Made A Fool Of You' was often mistakenly thought to feature Holly, such was the similarity in styles. (Backing vocals were by The Roses, as in earlier days and The Crickets' sound differed little from their first hits.)

Earl Sinks also recorded as Earl Richards and Sinx Mitchell in a long low-key career, although he did have the occasional country hit in the USA over the years. At one time he was a session guitarist and songwriter with MGM/Hickory. He also owned the small US country label Ace of Hearts at one point.

Holly and Sinks are said to have met at The Clover Club in Amarillo, introduced by their mutual friend, Hipockets Duncan.

'Slippin' and Slidin''

Taped at Holly's New York flat, January 1959. Buddy with electric guitar (fast) and acoustic guitar (slow).

The song evidently went under various names until Little Richard adapted the lyrics and it became a minor US hit as the flip of 'Long Tall Sally', which went Top 10.

Holly experimented with slow and fast versions of 'Slippin' and Slidin'', using both acoustic and electric guitar in his attempts. Later, it came to light that the slower version was probably meant to be played at double time so as to reproduce The Chipmunks' sound! If this sounds far-fetched remember Alvin and gang were No.1 in the US charts at that time. See THE CHIPMUNKS entry.

A slow version, overdubbed by The Fireballs, came out on the 'Reminiscing' album while the faster version came out years later on the 'Giant' LP. The undubbed versions as well as other takes have also been released (unofficially) over the years.

It is always debatable as to just how many versions of this song there are where Holly's vocal differs. There are probably three; however, taking into account false starts, overdubbings, etc., I have seen as many as seven listed!

Ronnie Smith

Ronnie Smith headed a group in the 1950s, Ronnie Smith and the Poor Boys, which included Carl Bunch, who was to be seconded by Holly for the Winter Dance Party Tour after Jerry and Joe had decided to go their own way. In the Poor Boys at the same time was Tommy Allsup, who also temporarily left to join Bunch and Jennings backing Buddy.

There was no acrimony in these arrangements and Ronnie Smith, from Odessa, Texas, and Buddy were well known to each other. It's quite probable that Buddy was at the group's Clovis sessions even though he didn't perform. In an ironic twist Smith was reunited with his sidesmen in early February 1959, when he was hired by the tour organizers to front Jennings/Allsup/Bunch and fulfil the remaining tour dates. Thereafter, they became The Jitters, for a very brief period of time.

Ronnie Smith was always a minor artist although he recorded for several labels before he died a drugs related death in the 1960s.

'Smokey Joe's Cafe'

Taped at Holly's New York flat, January 1959. Buddy and electric guitar.

A classic composition by the songwriting team of Jerry Leiber and Mike Stoller, 'Smokey Joe's Cafe' was recorded by The Robins for Spark in 1955 and eventually released via Atco. It crept into the US Hot 100 at No. 79. But it has been termed a Coasters' record ever since and is on most of their compilations.

Just before Holly left on his final, ill-fated tour in January of 1959, he recorded several numbers that had been early favourites of his; 'Smokey Joe's Cafe' was included. It was finally released, heavily overdubbed both instrumentally and vocally, on the

'Giant' album (1969).

Only in the last few years has the undubbed version been heard via bootleg-style releases.

'Soft Place in My Heart'

Buddy and Bob performance at Nesman studio, Wichita Falls, Texas, circa *1954–5.*

One of the earliest recordings that dates from the days when Buddy and his school pal, Bob Montgomery, were playing fairly regularly at the Sunday Party on Radio KDAV, Lubbock, Texas. Composed by Montgomery, the released track is overdubbed somewhat in an attempt to give the track a commerial sound. In fact, having both fiddle and steel guitar on the original performance indicates that Buddy and Bob were heavily country orientated at the time. Certainly the audiences they were performing for on local Texas radio would have been expecting mainly country material.

Another version of 'Soft Place In My Heart' exists dating from the same time and is of poor quality.

'Something Special from Buddy Holly'

UK Album: Rollercoaster ROLL 2013. Vinyl only, released 1986.

As mentioned several times during this book, this was a largely unheralded album that was put out by John Beecher of Rollercoaster, apparently containing previously released material that MCA were quite prepared to lease.

In fact, while the titles were familiar to Holly fans, they were all undubbed and even contained some session talk together with unreleased alternate takes. All this with sleeve notes by Holly expert John Ingman and a previously unseen colour photo on the sleeve.

Not a hit album but a real collector's item and it's a pity it's no longer in catalogue. The tracks have been lifted by Vigotone on their recent four-CD boxset.

Listing: Gone (2 tracks) / Have You Ever Been Lonely (3 tracks) / Brown-Eyed Handsome Man / Good Rockin' Tonight / Rip It Up / Blue Monday / Honky Tonk / Blue Suede Shoes / Shake Rattle and Roll / Bo Diddley / Ain't Got No Home / Holly Hop

Soundalikes

Let's hope not too many singers read this entry as to be termed a Holly soundalike might not seem to be entirely complimentary. In fact the time has long gone when a series of artists did seem to be following in Holly's shoes and, of course, he was no longer part of the scene and there was a void. Many of the singers so categorized (Adam Faith, Bobby Vee, etc.) have outlived the stigma and carved out long and distinguished careers. Many are the subject of separate entries scattered throughout the text.

There are many other singers who weren't to emerge from the Texan's shadow and they are best remembered for covering his material or else performing numbers that really seem directly descended from Holly/Crickets material.

It's only possible to be selective here and readers will no doubt have names of their own to add. Buddy Britten and The Regents came on the scene in the early 1960s with a style and image very like The Crickets. Looking back with hindsight over a 30-year timespan, Britten would have been ideally cast in the Buddy musical had it arrived earlier than it did! Terry Jacks ('Seasons In The Sun') recorded Holly covers in a similar voice whilst UK record producer Mickie Most had a series of South African hits with Holly/Crickets material.

Many other minor figures have either used the Holly hiccup or else adapted the Peggy Sue rhythm in their attempts at fame. In the USA Ray Ruff's 'I Took A Liking To You', Bob Osborn's 'Bound To Happen' and Don Webb's 'Little Ditty Baby' were three that achieved no more than brief local success.

Buddy Holly himself had always striven to take the music forward so it was little surprise when artists who did little more than ape his early, initial style didn't stay the course.

A few more to finish? Matlock, Lee Diamond and the Cherokees, Pilot, Familee, Trident, Bunch, Esquires, Hullaballoos, etc., etc., etc.

See also INFLUENCES entry, which includes some overlap.

Sources

A list of acknowledgements appears elsewhere and amongst those names are several who have kindly provided material for this book. In addition, reference books, musical periodicals and fan-club publications have been invaluable sources of information. They are all thanked even if a selective few only are listed here with permission:

The British Buddy Holly Society, run by Trevor Lailey of Bramwell, Roke, Nr. Benson, Oxon OX10 6JD.

Buddy Holly and Crickets Fan Club (a somewhat smaller club), run by Alan Jenkins of 142 Burns Avenue, Feltham, Middx TW14 9HZ.
Crickets File, run by John Firminger of 412 Main Road, Sheffield S9 4QL.
Bill Griggs, P.O. Box 6123, Lubbock, Texas 79493 USA.
Holly International, run by Jim Carr of 45 Westfield Road, Tickhill, Doncaster DN11 9LB.
Now Dig This, monthly rock'n'roll magazine, c/o 19,South Hill Road, Bensham, Gateshead, Tyne & Wear NE8 2XR.
Rollercoaster Records of Rock House, London Road, St Mary's, Chalford, Gloucs GL6 8PU.

Return postage or an international reply coupon are suggested if contacting.

Tommy Steele

Tommy Steele is an accomplished all-round entertainer who was born in Bermondsey, London, the same year as Holly entered the world in Texas. Tommy was to spearhead the UK challenge to rock'n'roll supremacy, and had major British chart success in 1956 whilst Holly was still searching for a breakthrough.

Steele and Marty Wilde ensured that the great Ritchie Valens would never enjoy major chart success over here by respectively taking Valens's compositions 'Come On Let's Go' and 'Donna' into the Top 10.

It seems Tommy Steele rated Buddy Holly highly and often featured a medley of his songs in stage or TV shows. These tributes eventually took some poetic licence with Tommy's accompanying monologue describing Buddy as a gangling giant of 6' 4! (He was actually a shade under six feet.)

For many years Tommy talked of recording an album of Holly material but eventually his career veered away from recordings into musicals or production numbers. As a postscript Tommy Steele is still featuring Holly numbers on his nationwide tours and claims that he met Buddy in the USA during 1956 when the latter was a little-known artist on country tours and Steele was in the merchant navy.

Stereo

Essentially, these are a layman's comments that might clarify the picture where Holly's recordings are concerned. The first point is that stereo was only just coming in during the late 1950s and many independents who leased product, such as Norman Petty in Clovis, solely recorded in mono until around the early 1960s. Then again, if majors used stereo equipment, the tracks were often mixed down to produce a mono single and tracks often didn't surface in stereo until released on albums years later.

Buddy Holly only did one session – his last – in true stereo and four tracks were recorded, of which the best known are 'It Doesn't Matter Anymore' and 'Raining In My Heart'. In fact, confusingly, both stereo and mono masters were created of all four titles. (If the 'Early In The Morning' session was recorded in experimental stereo, tapes have not been found.)

The wealth of Holly's 1956–7 demos and later apartment tape material was overdubbed by Norman Petty, who opted to create stereo masters from what were totally mono tapes. However, all the Buddy and Bob material, although also overdubbed by Petty, was mastered in mono perhaps to help cover imperfections in the tapes, which had often not been recorded under studio conditions and which dated back to 1954–5.

An exception to the above were the Hansen overdubs, which were not all in true stereo; both 'Peggy Sue Got Married' and 'Crying Waiting Hoping' are in mono. (I'm not sure whether stereo masters were ever created.)

A brief footnote to the above: it is best to obtain true stereo recordings where they exist or, if not, to go for basic monaural. Unfortunately, material was often reprocessed for stereo in the past and the fidelity obtained left a lot to be desired. This was compounded by companies unwilling or unable to seek out first-generation master tapes.

'Pappy' Dave Stone

Dave Stone, real name Dave Pinkston, helped start the local Lubbock radio station KDAV on 19th September 1953 and remained part owner for several years thereafter. Like Hipockets Duncan and Ben Hall he had defected from radio KSEL to start the new venture. He also had a hand in getting Buddy his first big break, which led to him obtaining a Nashville recording contract with Decca. Briefly, he was able to get the trio of Buddy, Bob and Larry on a Lubbock concert bill and this resulted in Eddie Crandall acting as the catalyst (see separate entry).

A minor coincidence is that another Pappy (Pappy Daily, a Houston distributor), was instrumental in getting the Big Bopper his original Mercury recording contract.

Dave Stone has been involved in the country music scene during a long life that has also seen him owning several radio stations in the South.

Jesse Stone

Jesse Stone is a legendary name from the early days who, apart from being a superlative arranger, also composed a number of classic rock'n'roll songs under the pseudonym, Charles Calhoun. Pick of the bunch is probably 'Shake, Rattle and Roll' followed closely by 'Money Honey' and 'Two Hearts, Two Kisses'.

He was arranger for Ray Charles in the 1950s and, according to a letter Buddy wrote to Terry Noland on 14th December 1958, Holly was already using Stone for arrangements. More likely is that Buddy was trying to line this up as we know that a gospel album was an unfulfilled project and Jesse Stone would have been the man for this.

It was almost certainly one of several projects that got permanently sidelined by the events of 3rd February 1959. Others included forming his own music company (Maria Music) and his record company (Prism Records). It is also suggested that he may have tried to set up a state-of-the art recording studio, perhaps with the help of his friend Snuff Garrett and others.

Jesse Stone retired to Florida and is in his nineties.

The Stringalongs

This instrumental group produced by Norman Petty in Clovis had a million-selling single in 1961 with the catchy 'Wheels'. Although composer credits were shown as Jimmy Torres and Richard Stephens, both guitarists with the group, in fact it was a Norman Petty composition and became one of his biggest-earning numbers.

As we know Petty's career didn't end in 1959 and his engineering skills were used to good effect in helping groups such as The Fireballs and The Stringalongs achieve hit status. He was involved in producing hundreds of recordings over the years usually leasing product to major labels but occasionally using his own small labels. See NORMAN AND VI PETTY entry.

Ed Sullivan

Host of the major US TV series, *The Ed Sullivan Show*, Ed Sullivan was a monolithic anchor man who introduced a coast-to-coast show that was equivalent in many ways to the UK's *Sunday Night at the London Palladium* shows.

The Crickets made two guest appearances on the show, the first as a quartet in New York late in 1957 when they performed 'That'll Be The Day' and 'Peggy Sue', and early in 1958, as a trio, they performed 'Oh Boy!'. The surviving film clip is generally felt to be the best footage of Holly that exists.

It is interesting to compare both clips, which were only filmed some eight weeks apart. Not only had Niki Sullivan departed the scene but

Holly is by now sporting his trademark horn rims and looks a more confident TV performer. (The story is that the group performed 'Oh Boy!' against the wishes of Sullivan.)

Niki Sullivan, one of the earliest Crickets, in a rare publicity shot taken shortly after he left to perform solo. (Courtesy of Bill Griggs.)

Niki Sullivan

Born 23rd June 1937 in South Gate, California, Niki was a member of The Crickets almost continually during 1957 and his main role was in playing rhythm guitar. In early photographs of the quartet Sullivan looks uncannily like Buddy, and both wore spectacles. However, with Holly able to play both lead and rhythm guitar there was not much of a role for Sullivan, who for a while had his own musical aspirations. For example, during the recording of 'Peggy Sue' Niki didn't actually get to play but instead switched a lever on Buddy's guitar so that Holly could go into the instrumental break without pause.

Sullivan was later to form his own group, The Plainsmen, who met with only limited success. After Buddy's death Niki teamed up with Gene Evans and recorded at Clovis under the name of The Holly-hawks. The group were managed by Lawrence Holley, Buddy's dad, for a short period in the 1960s. Niki also had releases on the Joli label before heading up a new group, The Four Crickets. No recordings were made and it seems Sullivan left the music scene around 1967 when he just happened to get married.

Sullivan remains a warm, emotional man who has the fondest memories of his days with the group. His input into The Crickets has been musically modest, but for a while he was an essential ingredient in the group's sound and visual presentation. He received belated recognition in 1986 when, along with Jerry, Joe and Sonny, he was inducted to Lubbock's Walk of Fame. Like those three, his part in the group was omitted from the film, although he was probably relieved not be called Jess or Ray Bob.

It seems Niki and Buddy were distant cousins by marriage but didn't actually realize it at first. In recent years Niki has put in occasional appearances at the Surf Ballroom reunion concerts.

He spent years in sales before eventually joining the Sony Corporation for whom he now works in research.

Sun Records

Whole books have been written on the subject of Sun Records, the Memphis label started by Sam Phillips back in 1952. See entry under SAM PHILLIPS.

Buddy never knocked on that particular door, even though he was from the South and close, in US terms, to Tennessee. But he often drove through Memphis during 1956 *en route* to his Nashville sessions from his Lubbock home. Perhaps he did try and make contact. Meanwhile, his friend and idol, Elvis, had temporarily transferred his own recording operations up to New York for the famous 'Hound Dog' session.

Sun Records holds a quite unique place in the history of rock'n'roll and will not be forgotten while the music itself lives.

The Surf Ballroom, Clear Lake, Iowa

The scene of Holly's last stage appearances on the evening of Monday, 2nd February 1959 when fans got to see the Dance Party troupe perform, having paid their $1.25 admission charge. The show was advertised for entrants aged 12 to 21. Life really was different back then!

It wasn't until 20 years after the crash that annual tributes started at The Surf to commemorate the deaths of the three stars. Evidently radio KZEV jock Mad Hatter started the tradition, and it is still going strong in the late 1990s.

Usually a weekend of events are arranged that culminates in a concert at The Surf and over the years a wealth of talent has put in an appearance, including: Rick Nelson (1980), Del Shannon (1979, 1982 and 1987), Carl Perkins (1981 and 1991), Jack Scott (1991), Bo Diddley (1992) and many others.

Not surprisingly, Bobby Vee, who lives nearby, has been an almost constant presence and is always assured of a great reception. The Crickets themselves avoided the gig for many years, but, since 1992, they have made the long trek North from their Nashville homes.

Both Tommy Allsup and Waylon Jennings, who backed Buddy on the night, have also made their way back evidently feeling a huge mix of emotions in the process. Because The Surf has been lovingly restored over the years they both felt a strong sense of *déjà vu*. Waylon was to say that the trip back exorcized his guilt for not having caught that plane.

It was Holly fans Bruce and Sue Christiansen who really made it all possible when they took over the largely derelict Ballroom in the 1970s and worked hard to make it a living thing. Darrel Hein took over for a while until, in the 1990s, a local family, the Snyders, set about fully restoring the venue.

There is now a monument to the singers at the ballroom and in addition many fans visit the crash site each year to stand in silence at 1.07 a.m., the exact time of the accident.

1st February 1959, the day before Buddy's last appearance at the Surf Ballroom, he was photographed with twins Judy and Joan Bender, backstage at Green Bay, Wisconsin. (Courtesy of Larry Matt.)

Billy Swan

Singer, writer and even on occasion producer, Billy was born Billy Lance Swan in Missouri on 12th May 1942. He acquired a liking for country icons such as Hank Williams and Lefty Frizzell whilst equally influenced by Fats Domino and Clyde McPhatter. An upbringing not that much different from the older Buddy Holly.

His first break, in 1962, was to write McPhatter's hit 'Lover Please', a number he went on to record himself. These days he's probably remembered either for his brilliant slow version of 'Don't Be Cruel' or perhaps for penning 'I Can Help', which Elvis also recorded. In fact, he's recorded an impressive body of work, including reworking 'You're The One', a Holly number that has hardly ever been covered, if at all.

He has always cited Holly as a major influence and inspiration. He still performs and frequently visits the UK.

T

'Take These Shackles From My Heart'

Home recording by Buddy Holley and Bob Montgomery, circa 1952.

One of the very earliest Holly vocal attempts in duet with his school pal, Bob Montgomery.

The recording takes the form of a very rough acetate indeed and jumps badly in places. It is almost certainly a number performed by The Maddox Brothers and Rose, whom Holly admired when he was growing up. The Maddox brothers described themselves as The Most Colourful Hillbilly Band in the Land. They were pure country and, just before they disbanded in 1956, they recorded a number called 'The Death Of Rock'n'Roll'!

'Take These Shackles' has been released on an unauthorized Vigotone collection

'Take Your Time'

Recorded following Niki Sullivan's departure at Norman Petty Studios, Clovis, New Mexico, probably 14th February 1958. Personnel: Buddy, Jerry and Joe.

Released as the flip of 'Rave On', this song was not recorded at the New York session but several weeks later in Clovis after the group had returned from their highly successful Australian tour.

The number was written by Holly in collaboration with Norman, who plays a prominent organ throughout. A Holly discography reveals that Jerry was keeping the moderato tempo going via a cardboard box, and the overall sound is a good one.

As most fans know Crickets and Holly recordings are virtually indistinguishable, and at this particular recording session the other two numbers ('Fool's Paradise' and 'Think It Over') were released under The Crickets' banner, the subtle difference being the dubbing of background vocals from The Roses.

Rehearsal tapes of 'Take Your Time' – not *alternative* takes as such – have been put out as unsanctioned releases and make for interesting listening as they are interspersed with occasional studio chat that allows the listener to be a fly-on-the-wall eavesdropper.

A fact seldom recorded by others is that Carolyn Hester, the folk singer, did a version at Clovis in 1958 on which Buddy Holly plays guitar and George Atwood played bass. It remains unissued.

Homer Tankersley

Homer deserves inclusion simply by virtue of his wonderful name! More seriously, under the pseudonym Ken James, he did vocal overdubs on 'If I Had Known', on which Buddy plays acoustic guitar (*circa* June 1958).

In the 1960s Homer was used by Petty to help out on backing vocals with the major overdubbing that was carried out on several recordings. (Norman was to overdub around 50 Holly tracks but backing vocals were only needed on a handful of these.)

The present whereabouts of Homer Tankersley is not known.

'Tell Me How'

Recorded at Norman Petty Studios, Clovis, New Mexico between May and July 1957. The Crickets as a quartet: Buddy, Jerry Allison, Joe B. Mauldin and Niki Sullivan.

This has to be one of the greatest B sides ever released (as flip to 'Maybe Baby') and is an example of The Crickets at the very height of their creativity. Holly's unique lead guitar solo appears to be played on the bass string of his Fender and it's one of those small changes that, to a layman, smacks of pure genius.

Writing is credited to Holly, Jerry Allison and Norman Petty, and instead of the sheet music ending up under the MPL banner it remains with Sherwin Music. I'm not quite certain why but the history of publishing rights (except those owned by MPL) is extremely complex.

The number has seldom been covered by other artists and it remains one of those gems that has surely deserved greater airplay over the years. We all know that if a Holly/Crickets number is played on the radio it is invariably one of a select few. This number is rarely featured.

Tex Mex

Early reviews of Holly/Crickets material in the USA occasionally used the term Tex Mex to label the music. Indeed, the memorial album that appeared after Holly's death used the expression that he was a wild and frantic rockabilly with the Tex Mex sound. But is the term genuine?

Well, of course the music did originate in both Lubbock and Clovis, which straddle the borders of Texas and New Mexico respectively, the area itself being less than 250 miles from Mexico. The music produced by Holly, Buddy Knox, Jimmy Bowen and others was certainly different and perhaps Tex Mex was as descriptive a title as anything else.

But there is in fact another distinct category of music that perhaps better deserves the genuine label of Tex Mex. This is genuine border music and features artists such as Hermanas Mendoza, Flaca Jimenez and others from that area close to the Mexican border. In other words artists who are much more ethnic and who usually feature lyrics in Spanish.

Texan-born country artist Freddy Fender, alias Baldemar Herta, could probably be described as a Tex Mex artist using either set of criteria for selection. Certainly, much vibrant music continues to emanate from that corner of the globe.

With Buddy married to the Spanish-speaking Maria, there was talk of his taking lessons on the Spanish guitar. So perhaps he would have become Tex Mex using either definition?

'That'll Be The Day'

Hit version recorded as a demo at the Norman Petty Studios, Clovis, New Mexico, 24th–25th February 1957. See below re personnel. Belatedly certified gold in 1969.
Nashville version 22nd July 1956. Personnel included: Jerry Allison, Sonny Curtis and Don Guess (Take 19).

Generally acknowledged to have been written by Buddy and drummer

188

Jerry Allison shortly after attending a John Wayne movie (see entry THE SEARCHERS) 'That'll Be The Day' was first recorded in Nashville and came out in the USA as the flip of 'Ollie Vee' just two weeks after The Crickets' hit version entered the US charts. The composition had been offered initially to Roulette in 1956 but rejected as the label had just signed Buddy Knox and Jimmy Bowen. Instead Holly was initially to cut it for Decca and if any US fan somehow purchased both versions (Holly/Decca, Crickets/Brunswick) in the 1950s they would have been faced with two distinctly different recordings. The earlier version was more ponderous and seemingly in a higher key whereas the Holly performance was totally slick, even if only a demo.

The Nashville version had been cut at the July 1956 session when Buddy was backed up by his Lubbock cohorts, which included Sonny Curtis. The hit version also featured Buddy and Jerry, with old friend Larry Welborn on bass; Joe B. had not yet joined. Niki Sullivan and the Tolletts performed back-up vocals that were not overdubbed as was to be the case with later Crickets material.

Norman Petty had to really peddle hard to get the hit demo released and tales are legion that companies such as Columbia and RCA turned it down before, eventually, Bob Thiele of Coral and Brunswick persuaded his superiors at Decca to put it out. (The irony of all the above is that both Brunswick and Decca for whom Buddy recorded 'That'll Be The Day' were basically one and the same company!)

But there are other performances of the same number that have been captured for posterity even if they weren't recorded under studio conditions. Two live versions are available: the first from The Crickets' 1957 appearance on *The Ed Sullivan Show* and a poorly recorded version from their UK appearance at *The London Palladium* in March 1958 when they raced through three numbers on their UK TV debut. (Film of the latter appearance has not survived.)

Also available on bootleg-style albums are short jingles sung by The Crickets with the words of the hit song adapted as a 'thank you' to Bob Theile and Murray Deutch, who had done so much to help launch and promote the disc. These 32-second jingles are fun to hear and should be sought out by keen fans.

'That'll Be The Day' doubtless inspired the 1973 film and book by Ray Connolly that became a very popular release despite not being able to use the hit record in the soundtrack. Bobby Vee's version was included instead. The Ronco soundtrack album was to top the charts in 1973.

Earlier in 1957 The Tunettes did the usual Embassy (Woolworths) version whilst a UK cover by Larry Page got nowhere. Years later the Everlys had a 1960s UK chart hit and Linda Ronstadt had a huge hit in the USA the following decade. The song has been covered by a diverse variety of recording artists over the years and is one of the most covered of all Holly recordings.

Strangely, an unsuccessful US lawsuit was brought in the 1980s claiming that Holly's version plagiarized a song others had written but the plaintiffs apparently waited 30 years too long before bringing the case. This was surely taking the slogan 'If there's a hit there's a writ' to the extreme!

Finally, the song has been given a lift recently with the release of a version by The Beatles – their first genuine studio recording.

'That'll Be The Day'

UK album: Ace of Hearts AH3.

With the posthumous fame of Holly continuing to grow over here in the 1960s, most keen fans began to realize that the singer had recorded a whole series of numbers in Nashville sometime before achieving stardom. UK Brunswick had rushed out eight of the recordings on two EPs, but that presumably left other numbers still in the can.

Matters were largely remedied in 1961 with the release of the above album until, eventually, word got around that two distinctly different versions of 'Ollie Vee' had been recorded. The second sax-based version eventually came out in the UK in 1975 as part of 'The Nashville Sessions' album.

The 'Ace of Hearts' album was one of the earliest to come out on what were to be termed budget labels. These usually specialized in recycling material that had come out earlier but fully priced. (The Holly album was not therefore representative of the genre.)

The album reached No.5 on the UK charts during a 14-week spell. Its distinctive sleeve artwork was to endear it to a generation of fans.

Listing: You Are My One Desire / Blue Days, Black Nights / Modern Don Juan / Rock Around With Ollie Vee (guitar version) / Ting A Ling / Girl On My Mind / That'll Be The Day / Love Me / I'm Changing All Those Changes/ Don't Come Back Knockin' / Midnight Shift

'That Makes It Tough'

Recorded at Holly's New York flat, 8th December 1958. Buddy and acoustic guitar.

Another of the half-dozen compositions that Holly sang into his Ampex tape recorder just before Christmas 1958. The Ampex had been bought from Norman Petty, who had used it commercially so it was by no means the run-of-the-mill domestic machine.

'That Makes It Tough' ended up a posthumous release as the B side of 'Learning The Game', which became a short-lived hit single in late 1960. (With Buddy far more popular in the UK than in the USA the LP – infuriatingly for fans – had been released many months earlier in the USA.)

The original single version was the Jack Hansen overdub and the later overdub engineered by Norman Petty did not have an LP release here until the 'Remember' album came out. All three versions, including the undubbed one, came out as part of the MCA box set several years back.

Not long ago US fan Bob Dees did an in-depth interview with Tommy Allsup, who said that he actually played acoustic guitar on this track. As both he and Waylon Jennings visited Holly at his New York flat this does seem possible.

'That's My Desire'

Recorded at Bell Sound Studios, New York, 25th January 1958. Personnel: Jerry and Joe B. backing musicians with Al Caiola and Donald Arnone (guitars) and Norman Petty, piano; background vocals, session singers.

Written by Carroll Loveday and Helmy Kresa in 1931, this ballad has become an evergreen, and Holly was by no means the only rock artist to try it. Eddie Cochran recorded it in 1956 while Elvis had sung it during his Million Dollar Quartet session. Earlier, both Frankie Laine and Sammy Kaye had versions that entered the Top 10 US Billboard charts, the strong lyrics not falling foul of the censor unlike some much more innocuous material in the 1950s.

Holly's version was recorded at the same session as 'Rave On' but was to remain unreleased for eight years until it emerged (over-dubbed by Norman Petty) as the flip of the alternative 'Maybe Baby'. Buddy Holly's version didn't appear to do him or the song justice and it was largely ignored. Interestingly, it was a minor revelation years later finally to hear the undubbed version, which seems to lack the slightly discordant sound of the original dubbed release.

Outtakes of Buddy singing the number, prior to completing the finished take, have been released in recent years but not on MCA. One final footnote: although the session listing indicates Milton de Lugg was producer, Bob Theile – in his wonderfully irreverent autobiography – insists that he masterminded the recordings.

'That's What They Say'

Taped at Holly's New York flat, 3rd December 1958. Buddy and acoustic guitar. Take 2.

This was one of the new compositions that Holly recorded with simple acoustic guitar accompaniment in his New York flat, late 1958. It appeared in 1960 overdubbed by Jack Hansen, as part of the 'Story Volume 2' LP before being used as the flip of 'What To Do' in 1961, which became a minor hit. The Petty dubbed version came out years later on the 'Remember' album while the undubbed version has never had an official release.

Thirty-seven seconds only of an alternate take exists but has not been released. Even the bootleggers haven't caught up with that item yet!

Bob Theile

It's almost a case of saying see the entry under MURRAY DEUTCH as their names are always linked when Holly's name comes up. In fact, Bob was the A&R man for the record company Coral, whereas his compatriot was on the music publishing side of things over at Peers Southern. While both had a hand in getting Holly's career launched, Bob Theile seems to have been the major player.

Bob was born in Brooklyn, New York, and spent a lifetime in the recording industry briefly as an embryonic jazz musician, writer and broadcaster before joining Decca in 1952. Theile had a jazz pedigree and when rock'n'roll began to saturate the airwaves things couldn't have been harder for him – and others. Coral's roster of stars included million-selling artists such as Teresa Brewer, The McGuire Sisters and Don Cornell but, nevertheless, the times were changing and they (Decca/Coral) strove to obtain their market share of the new sound via Holly, Haley, The Kalin Twins and the Johnny Burnette Trio.

It is interesting to speculate whether Buddy would have remained with Coral (now MCA). Certainly, MCA have been criticized for releasing Holly product that has been very uneven indeed over the years, and, as we know, Holly had plans to open his own studio in Texas and had even purchased a parcel of land in readiness.

Bob Theile died 30th January 1996, aged 73, leaving a widow, singer Teresa Brewer and a son, Robert junior, from an earlier marriage. His autobiography *What A Wonderful World* came out in 1995 and was named after his most famous composition.

A minor footnote: Theile persuaded Holly to record the blues-styled 'Mailman Bring Me No More Blues', which, it so happens, he had composed under the alias, Stanley Clayton.

'Think It Over'

Crickets recording, following Niki Sullivan's departure, at Norman Petty's Studios, Clovis, New Mexico, probably 14th February 1958. Personnel: Buddy, Jerry, Joe with Vi Petty on piano.

Attributed to Buddy, Jerry and Norman Petty this was the last Crickets recording to go Top 40 in the USA, reaching a lowly No.27. In the UK the record was much more popular, reaching No.11 and spending virtually two months in the charts.

Interestingly, Holly, ever innovative, moved away from the standard guitar break and instead Vi Petty treated the record buyer to a fascinating piano roll solo. Even now I can remember Luxembourg DJ Pete Murray spinning the record again and again just to listen to the unique piano sound.

The finished hit recording was transformed into a Crickets release courtesy of The Roses' added backing vocals. In the last few years studio outtakes of this number in rehearsal have been (unofficially) released and studio dialogue helps to show how they would often creatively work up an arrangement as they went along.

Although this is seldom covered, it is worth looking out for the Bobby Fuller Four version; the vocals are similar but a stinging guitar solo galvanizes the recording midway, and the change works well.

This song is typical of so many of the 1957–8 Holly recordings where it is impossible to really discover quite who wrote what. For example, Jerry feels pretty sure that this was originally one of his songs that got changed around.

Hank Thompson and His Brazos Valley Boys

This legendary Texas band were voted the top country outfit every year from 1953 to 1966. What's more they had country hits from the 1940s through to the 1980s (perhaps a record that may never be beaten).

Born on 3rd September 1925 in Waco, Texas, Hank's group and Buddy were on several tours together during 1956 and early 1957. Although Hank was the star at that point, they were always fans of one another's music, and Thompson has been quoted as saying that Holly had what it took to succeed.

As often occurs in this A–Z names link up and it so happens that Wanda Jackson, mentioned elsewhere, used to sing with Hank Thompson and met with Holly on those same tours.

Hank is alive and well.

'Three Stars'

If 'Tribute To Buddy Holly' is the definitive paean to Holly then surely 'Three Stars' is the most memorable where the triumvirate of artists is concerned (but see TRIBUTE RECORDS entry).

The US hit version was by DJ Tommy Dee of Radio KFXM, San Bernadino. He was moved by the tragedy to pen the number the day after the accident. His recording was made at Gold Star and had vocal accompaniment by Carol Kay and Teenaires, who were session musicians with the label (Crest). In the UK Ruby Wright, last in the charts with 'Bimbo' 1954 (!), had the hit on the Parlophone label. Although the British have tended to follow American trends we have not really latched onto the 'death disc' genre. 'Just Like Eddie' by Heinz is, however, the exception that proves the rule.

Surely the most heart-rending version of 'Three Stars' is that by Eddie Cochran, which was also cut at Gold Star (5th February 1959) with the finished master said to be made up from eight separate takes. Perhaps too traumatic to release when recorded, it came out as a posthumous single in 1966 on the Liberty label.

On the subject of stars did you know that one of the myriad stars in our constellation was literally named after Buddy several years ago? That's official and Larry Holley has the paperwork to prove it.

The Three Tunes

This was one of the early band names for the musicians who backed Buddy. Apparently the name was not used on the bandstand but it did end up on a record label (US Decca single 'Ting A Ling').

Before The Crickets became an established quartet in 1957, various local Lubbock musicians had played back-up and the whole situation tended to be a bit fluid. Amongst the names used in addition to the above were The Two Tones, Buddy and Bob and The Rhythm Playboys.

Most of the above names don't need explanation but Sonny Curtis has observed that The Two Tones name came about when the two musicians both turned up wearing blue pants and white shirts and needed names.

'Ting A Ling'

Recorded at second Nashville recording session, Bradley's Barn, 22nd July 1956. Personnel: Buddy, Sonny, Jerry and Don Guess. Take 7.

One of the best of Holly's largely abortive Nashville sessions was his different interpretation of the old Clovers 1952 hit 'Ting A Ling'. Holly's release was eventually credited to Nugetre (Ahmet Ertegun, Atlantic mogul's name reversal) and was belatedly issued as a single in the US as an obvious attempt by Decca to jump on the Holly/Crickets bandwagon, their fame being at its peak in mid 1958. Strangely, the single was released with the description 'Buddy Holly and The Three Tunes' (see previous entry).

Its first UK release was a posthumous one on a Brunswick EP. It then ended up on the budget-priced Ace of Hearts' album 'That'll Be The Day'.

With Earl Sinks on vocals the post-Holly Crickets also did a particularly powerful version of the number in 1959. In the muddled world of composer credits the song was listed as composed by Cedarwood's Jim Denny before, eventually, getting its rightful Nugetre accreditation. (In mitigation the Holly recording bears only passing resemblance to The Clovers' version.)

Gary and Ramona Tollett

Gary Dale and Ramona Tollett were born 13th December 1932 and 19th December 1936 respectively. They had a brief but significant part to play in the Buddy Holly story. In February 1957 Gary Tollett recorded a couple of Clovis demos under the name of Gary Dale. Playing lead guitar and drums on the date were, respectively, Buddy Holly and Jerry Allison. Gary's wife Ramona and Niki Sullivan helped out on backing vocals, and it seemed fairly logical for the Tolletts to reciprocate a few days later when Buddy and Jerry were cutting their own demo, 'That'll Be The Day'.

In March 1957 the Tolletts recorded a further session. The tracks from this session remained unissued until recently when they appeared on a European album, again under the name Gary Dale. The tracks are quite collectable, featuring as they do Buddy and Jerry as backing musicians. Although tracks recorded as Gary Dale were originally unreleased, Gary Tollett did release a single 'Dynamite' on Gone, which was also recorded in New York in 1957.

Sadly the Tolletts themselves lost a son a few years ago, the victim of a light plane crash. They have had further family tragedies since that time.

George Tomsco

Lead guitarist with The Fireballs instrumental group that had a number of US hits in the 1960s all of which were recorded under the direction of Norman Petty at Clovis. Jimmy Gilmer joined the group as vocalist/guitarist in 1961 and they had a massive hit with 'Sugar Shack' (see entry under JIMMY GILMER).

In the 1960s Tomsco helped on 'The Buddy Holly Songbook' project with Tommy Allsup and also assisted The Fireballs with a whole

195

series of posthumous overdubs of Holly material. This ranged from the earliest Buddy and Bob material through to the tapes Holly had left in New York on his portable tape machine, just days before he joined up with the 1959 Winter Dance Party Tour.

George had met up with Holly briefly when The Fireballs were at Clovis to record their 'Fireball' single. Tomsco is a talented musician and he also found time to compose much of the instrumental material that both The Fireballs and The Stringalongs issued. See separate entries.

Tomsco was born on 24th April 1940.

Tours

As a member of a group, though never on a solo basis, Buddy Holly toured almost continuously from the time he hit the charts in August 1957 with 'That'll Be The Day'. He undertook three tours during 1956 and early 1957, playing dates in Southern states with a roster of exclusively country-based artists. (Needless to say without a hit to their name Buddy and The Crickets were very much a support act.)

There were two major overseas tours during 1958 (UK and Australia) and, as we know, a 1959 tour of Britain was felt to be a certainty with exploratory talks having taken place between Leslie Grade in this country and US tour promoter Irving Feld.

One ironic footnote: when researching this book it was discovered that the Winter Dance Party was Holly's thirteenth tour.

See also AUSTRALIAN TOUR and UK TOUR entries.

Peter Townshend

Lead guitarist with The Who, Peter Townshend is an unlikely entry perhaps but Townshend got to play lead guitar on the 1970s' Crickets recording 'Can I Make You Feel It' as part of the 'Bubblegum, Bop, Ballads and Boogie' album. As such that gets him in as an honorary Cricket.

Later, Who vocalist Roger Daltrey starred in the TV series *Buddy*, which chronicled the relationship between an ageing Buddy Holly fan and his young son.

To complete a brief trio of entries for the group, drummer Keith Moon, who had appeared in the UK movie *That'll Be The Day* was to die tragically of a drug overdose the morning after attending the 1978 UK film premiere of *The Buddy Holly Story*.

Tribute Records

Many years ago a US publication listed more than twenty different tribute records that directly referred to the February 1959 Iowa plane crash. The majority of these were eulogies to Buddy Holly but some referred to all three stars ('The Great Tragedy' / 'Three Young Men' / 'Three Stars', etc.) There was also a sub-genre of records that were paeans not just to the three artists but just about every late great from Johnny Ace to Elvis.

Thicker on the ground have been tracks that mention Holly fleetingly in the lyrics. Probably the most famous of all tribute records is 'American Pie', which cleverly manages not to mention Holly's name at all, although Don McLean has always said that Buddy was the inspiration behind the recording (His 'American Pie' album is dedicated to Holly.)

Over the years records that have alluded to Holly in their lyrics have outnumbered those mentioning Valens and Bopper by about 10 to 1 although at the time of the fatal crash, Valens was arguably the major star by virtue of his having had a hit near the top of the charts.

One of the most interesting tribute records is 'Buddy's Song', which was recorded by Bobby Vee; Holly's mother is given composer credit whereas, in fact, the writer was Waylon Jennings. The idea was that royalties would go to the Holley family. Waylon recorded another tribute, 'The Stage', about the same time but he has said time and again that he was not happy with his recording. He made amends later with a much more subtle tribute, 'Old Friend', which didn't actually need to mention Buddy by name.

Although many people would claim to dislike tribute records they do seem to exercise a certain fascination.

Larry Trider

Larry is one of the least-known, one-time members of the post-Holly Crickets. He originated from Lazbuddie, West Texas, but didn't actually get to record with the group. Consequently, he rarely received a mention on sleeve notes pertaining to The Crickets. This has, however, been remedied in recent years.

Initially Trider had worked around both Clovis and Lubbock, where he had briefly met Buddy Holly. He cut his first record in Petty's studio back in 1961 but that failed to open doors.

When The Crickets were getting towards the end of their Liberty days (1965), and with Jerry Naylor sidelined, Larry and Jerry Allison got together to tour as The Crickets – sometimes supplemented by one or two friends. After some 18 months together they split amicably. Both, however, remained in the music business. Larry was to sign with Dot and later released an excellent album, 'Country Man Soul', but without great success.

Larry had a lengthy musical stint at the Golden Nugget casino in Las Vegas during the 1970s when he actually topped a bill that included Waylon Jennings! He returned to Texas at one point but is currently back working in Vegas. He is always mentioned as a greatly underrated performer.

'True Love Ways'

With the Dick Jacob's Orchestra; recorded in stereo at Coral Record Studios, Pythian Temple, New York, 21st October 1958.

Written by Buddy with the help of Norman Petty the song was apparently composed for Buddy's wife Maria. The melody was supposedly based on a gospel tune, 'I'll Be All Right', a particular favourite of Holly's recorded by The Angelic Gospel Singers. See separate entry.

This last session of Buddy's produced his only recordings with strings. In fact, he has often, mistakenly, been given credit as the first rock artist to use a full orchestral backing. Whilst he was ever innovative, acts such as The Platters had used orchestral backings from around 1956.

What is surprising is that although 'True Love Ways' did not make the UK Top 20 when released in 1960, it has subsequently been recognized as probably Holly's greatest vocal performance. The song has become an evergreen through the years and it briefly became a US country No.1 in 1980 courtesy of Mickey Gilley. (The recordings by Holly/Gilley were in the same key and tempo, and the tapes could have been used to construct a duet!)

Both stereo and mono masters were made from Holly's recording. The stereo cut was used in a Terry's All Gold TV advert in 1988 and, consequently, the single was re-released and spent four weeks in the Top 75 list.

Peter and Gordon (see entry) had the greatest success taking the song to No.2 in the UK while Cliff Richard made the Top 10 in 1983. Although this is one of Holly's most-covered performances, it is still hard to better the simple charm of his 1958 recording. Dick Jacobs remembers that the song was completed in only one or two takes.

The Picks have also released the Holly recording but with their dubbed vocal sounds the backing is intrusive and only recommended with reservations.

Rick Tucker

Rick was a contemporary of Holly's, born 8th July 1938 in Amarillo, Texas. He recorded two numbers at Clovis in 1957, 'Patty Baby' and 'Don't Do Me This Way', about which it is often said that Buddy played the guitar. (Another report even has Orbison on the session!)

The claim has been researched and it does seem unlikely that Holly is on the recordings although he and Tucker probably did meet in Petty's studio.

Tucker is a minor artist about whom little else is known.

Joe Turner

Born 18th May 1911 in Missouri, Big Joe Turner became one of the greatest pre-war blues shouters and appeared with such famous band leaders as Bennie Moten and Count Basie.

At the break-out of rock'n'roll, although well into his forties, he hitched his star to the trend, having already had a string of hits early in the 1950s in the R&B charts. 'Shake Rattle and Roll' on Atlantic 1026 then crossed over and became his biggest pop hit during 1954. Buddy's 1956 demo of the number appears to be a hybrid of Turner's raunchy version and the more antiseptic lyrics of Bill Haley.

It is not known whether Holly and Turner ever met. Biographical notes on Turner indicate that he undertook several Alan Freed tours in the mid 1950s.

Although Joe Turner really was a giant of rhythm and blues, he is sometimes mentioned as little more than a footnote in the history of rock'n'roll. Joe died 23rd November 1985, having continued to perform for several years despite deteriorating health.

'20 Golden Greats'

UK Album: MCA EMTV 8.

Worth a mention in passing is this 1978 collection, which hit No.1 in the album charts – remarkable considering that similar greatest hits compilations by Holly had already charted several times during the 1960s and 1970s. But this was TV advertised.

The album stayed on the UK charts for six months, and even made the US 100 album lists despite the fact that less than half the tracks on the album had ever made their Top 100 singles charts. But this sort of happening was by no means unusual. Ritchie Valens even had a greatest hits package released here, although he never had one recording enter the Top 20!

Listing: That'll Be The Day / Peggy Sue / Words Of Love / Everyday / Not Fade Away / Oh Boy! / Maybe Baby / Listen To Me / Heartbeat / Think It Over / It Doesn't Matter Anymore / It's So Easy / Well...All Right / Rave On / Raining In My Heart / True Love Ways / Peggy Sue Got Married / Bo Diddley / Brown-Eyed Handsome Man / Wishing

U

UK Tour, March 1958

The Crickets flew in to England late February for what was to be a most successful four-week tour. Always referred to as a UK, or British tour, it crisscrossed England, the only venue outside the country being on 24th March in Cardiff, Wales. For many years there were rumours that the group had stopped off in Ireland but this was not the case. They actually arrived in London on 28th February and Buddy – alone – was immediately rushed by taxi to appear with Kent Walton on *Cool For Cats*, the ATV weekly music programme.

Thereafter, they performed concerts that started 1st March and continued through to the final date on the 25th March at Hammersmith. In a typical three-day period they travelled from London to Hampshire to Yorkshire! In addition to that gruelling schedule they also fitted in a famous appearance at the London Palladium and telerecorded an appearance on BBC's *Off the Record*. There is a well-researched booklet, *Buddy in Britain*, available through The Crickets File and in addition we are promised an in-depth book on the tour by Julian Levene and Jim Carr in 1998.

On stage The Crickets always played a good proportion of their hits while in addition several numbers that they never recorded, including 'Money Honey,' 'Be Bop A Lula', 'Tutti Frutti', 'She's Got It' and 'The Girl Can't Help It'. Strange to say Holly hardly ever sang a ballad on stage.

The UK tour roster comprised Gary Miller, the Tanner Sisters, Des O'Connor and Ronnie Keene and his Orchestra. The Lew and Leslie

Grade bill was headed by Buddy Holly and The Crickets, the only US act on what was basically a traditional variety or music hall show. There are bill posters of the show listing Don Smith and his Orchestra but these are inaccurate; although Smith was provisionally booked, it was Ronnie Keene who actually got the job.

The tour was a landmark in musical entertainment in the UK and it is sad to think that a second tour was being lined up for the group in 1959.

Buddy, Jerry and Joe on their UK tour, City Hall, Newcastle, 6th March 1958. (Courtesy of Jim Carr.)

V

Ritchie Valens

Ritchie was born Richard Steven Valenzuela in Los Angeles on 13th May 1941. Probably the most startling fact in this whole book is that Valens was just 17 when he died. He is described as having had Mexican and Indian American ancestry, he came from a deprived but loving background. He attended Pacoima Junior High School, where he started singing, quickly becoming known as the Little Richard of San Fernando. He moved on from Pacoima to San Fernando High School in 1957, but by October the following year had already left as his first release 'Come on, Let's Go' was attracting attention and had become a Billboard Pick.

From that moment things happened in double-quick time for Valens. He was thrown straight into appearances on *The Dick Clark Show* and *Alan Freed's Christmas Jubilee*. Sometime in late 1958 he also managed to film his cameo appearance in *Go, Johnny, Go* before appearing on Ted Randal's 1959 *Cavalcade of Stars*. The highlight for Ritchie, however, was, returning to Pacoima to give a concert for his former friends – this time as a star. Fortunately, an audio tape of the appearance survived and formed the basis of an album that came out on Bob Keane's Del-Fi label. Next step was to sign for the Winter Dance Party Tour...

At the time of the fatal plane crash Valens was by far the hottest of the three artists in terms of chart action. His double-sided hit 'Donna' / 'La Bamba' had entered the lists in December and was at No.3 on 3rd February. It subsequently peaked at No.2 on the Billboard charts. By contrast, Holly's career in the USA was fairly moribund with his last real hit having been some six months previously.

Valens had a plaintive voice and played superb guitar, although on many recording sessions Rene Hall played lead and Ritchie played rhythm. Just days after the accident Del Fi released two of Valens's solo instrumentals on a single and for some reason used the pseudonym, Arvee Allens. The record failed to chart, which was no surprise. Bob Keane had put out a series of singles in 1959 and although they entered the Billboard 100 lists, none approached the amazing popularity of 'Donna'.

Ritchie has had a small renaissance in popularity following the release of the 1987 film biography *La Bamba*. This led to reissues of the very small catalogue of material Valens had recorded and also brought him his first UK hit for 28 years ('La Bamba' peaked at No.49). Much more exciting, for real oldies fans, was the recent discovery of numerous studio rehearsals by Valens, which were released on a CD entitled 'The Lost Tapes'. As if the discovery of thirty odd recordings were not enough, many were in rudimentary stereo.

Valens is remembered moderately well in this country, at least when he is not confused with the English singer, Ricky Valance, who had a brief chart success of his own in 1960. However, it is frustrating that portrayals of Valens invariably picture him as a hip-swivelling Latin Elvis, whereas photographic and celluloid evidence from the 1950s projects a totally different image. He also became a role model for other Chicano artists such as Chris Montez and Chan Romero because of the way he handled his success and for breaking down barriers that had previously plagued Mexican music. It was never mainstream until 'La Bamba' changed everything.

Who knows what would have become of Valens? Buddy's mother said he was going to visit the Holley family in the summer of 1959, and, of course, a Lubbock recording studio was in the offing. He might even have left Del Fi?

Some consider Valens the most overrated of all 1950s stars, but perhaps we have to judge everything in the light of his age. He achieved more than most, yet he never turned 18.

Ritchie Valens in reflective mood, backstage at Green Bay, Wisconsin, 1st February 1959. (Courtesy of Larry Matt.)

'Valley of Tears'

Recorded at Norman Petty Studios, Clovis, New Mexico between May and July 1957. Trio of Personnel: Buddy, Jerry and Joe supplemented by Norman Petty, organ, and Vi Petty, piano.

'Valley of Tears' was composed by Fats Domino and producer, Dave Bartholomew, and became a major hit for Fats in May 1957. Evidently, brother Larry Holley suggested that Buddy try the number and it went into the can to be released in 1958 as part of Holly's only solo album put out during his lifetime. It is one of two tracks where organ is featured prominently in the background.

In 1961 the song was released posthumously as the flip of 'You're So Square' – which, surprisingly, was a double-sided UK hit. (Surprising given that most fans would have already had both the Holly recordings in their collections.)

See comments under FATS DOMINO

Jack Vaughn

Jack Vaughn was the third member of the Norman Petty trio along with Norman and wife, Vi. Jack, a local musician, played guitar in the group, which had a half million-seller in 1954 with 'Mood Indigo' and a string of other releases on the Columbia label.

Sadly, Jack died in 1984, the same year as did Norman Petty.

Bobby Vee

Bobby Vee was born Robert Thomas Velline on 30th April 1943 in Fargo, North Dakota. Holly was actually flying to the town of Fargo at the time of the fatal crash. If any one person in the world believes in fate that individual is surely Bobby Vee. Not only did he and his group The Shadows make their professional debut on the Winter Dance Party Tour as a direct result of the fatal crash, but Bobby Vee performed for a while in a style that almost out-hiccuped Buddy Holly.

His performance on 3rd February 1959 at the Moorhead, Minnesota concert was to be a stepping stone to eventual fame and fortune. In fact, he became quite a teenage rage for several years in the USA, clocking up far more hits than Holly ever did, although he had a decade longer to try. Incidentally, in 1959 Bobby was to hire one Bob Zimmerman on piano – he who was later to become slightly better known as Bob Dylan. Evidently, he played about two gigs with Bobby and his group before moving on.

Bobby Vee is a genuine and sincere fan of Holly and has always been ready to give the Texan full credit. Bobby still performs but has more recently veered towards a cabaret-style act. He was to achieve a major ambition when he got to record in Clovis with Norman Petty in the early 1960s. On record the Snuff Garrett-produced 'Bobby Vee Meets The Crickets' album was a major hit in 1962 but his later LP, 'Tribute To Buddy Holly', did not chart. It has, however, been almost continually in catalogue. Always in demand for anniversary concerts, Bobby continues to link up with The Crickets on occasion, and, of late, he has recorded a superb Holly medley with them. Check out Roller-coaster 45 RRC 2009. He has continued to tour the UK on a fairly regular basis and these days has his son Jeff in the act as a group member and tour organizer.

Bobby Vee has active Fan Clubs in both the USA and the UK and really is one of the most approachable of all stars, an approachability that included helping in the production of this volume.

The Velvets

The Velvets, led by Virgil Johnson, were perhaps the only national black doowop act to hail from Lubbock, Texas. British fans will possibly remember their two minor 1961 hits, one of which was the old standard 'That Lucky Old Sun'.

Johnson was deservedly inducted into the West Texas Walk of Fame in Lubbock in 1994 in recognition of his services to music. He eventually went into education and retired as a Lubbock High School principal in 1993. In 1986, former Crickets Niki Sullivan, Jerry Allison, Joe B. Mauldin and Sonny Curtis were also inducted.

Gene Vincent

Vincent Eugene Craddock was born 11th February 1935 in Norfolk, Virginia and was surely one of the greatest of all rock'n'roll performers. His name is inextricably linked with that of Eddie Cochran for reasons any self-respecting fan is aware of (e.g. they toured together and almost died together). Even before that Easter 1960 accident when Eddie lost his life, Gene was quoted as being extremely depressed by the February 1959 air crash.

Vincent and the Blue Caps met Holly briefly when on tour in New Mexico and both artists are cited as having Eddie Cochran among their best friends. Both Vincent and Holly also cut their first professional sessions at the same studios in Nashville in early 1956. Any other links between Holly and Vincent are tenuous but the latter recorded the Johnny Burnette composition 'My Heart', which is very Hollyesque, while in later years Gene listed Buddy Holly's name when cataloguing the stars in Jim Pewter's 'Story Of The Rockers'. Certainly Holly and The Crickets sang 'Be Bop a Lula' as part of their stage act during 1957–8, but, probably, many contemporaries did too.

Only one musician was to be a member of both The Crickets and The Blue Caps, and that was Glen Campbell, albeit fleetingly with both outfits.

Gene never lost faith in rock'n'roll and it was a tragedy that he died too soon, on 12th October 1971 of bleeding ulcers. He is buried in the Eternal Valley Memorial Park near Los Angeles in California.

Violin

Early publicity information stressed that this was Buddy's earliest musical instrument before switching to guitar. In fact, he more often

205

practised on piano and drums from an early age eventually shifting to banjo, mandolin and guitar.

Apparently Holly sat in on drums with Dion and the Belmonts once or twice during the final tour after Carl Bunch caught frostbite and was sidelined. But his great love and talent was for the guitar. The makes he played are listed under a separate entry – GUITARS.

W

'Wait 'Til The Sun Shines Nellie'

Taped at Holly's New York flat between 1st and 22nd January 1959. Buddy and electric guitar.

Buddy strummed a short version of this oldie into his tape recorder just before setting out on his thirteenth and last tour in January 1959. This simple recording with electric guitar accompaniment lasted only just over one minute. Evidently, the number was a favourite of his mother's. It was composed by the songwriting partnership of Andrew Sterling and Harry Von Tilzer, and got a second lease of life in 1941 when Bing Crosby sang it in the film, *Birth of the Blues*. This is the version Ella Holley would have known.

Heavily overdubbed by The Fireballs and with ponderous backing vocals the number was released in 1962 as the flipside of 'Reminiscing', which scored heavily in the singles charts. This Coral single on Q72455 is worth seeking out as it has less instrumental overdubbing than the album release. (Extra guitar was added for the stereo LP release.)

The brief, undubbed recording is now available on bootlegs meaning that three different versions of the song have appeared, albeit with the same vocals.

Incidentally, is 'Wait 'Til The Sun Shines Nellie' the odd one out amongst those January recordings? Although the others were all from the R&B field and were possible early choices for material to use on an album Holly hoped to record with Ray Charles, is it possible 'Nellie' was too? It had been in *Birth of the Blues* after all. Or perhaps, quite simply, he was just experimenting with the number to please his mother.

Billy Walker

This country singer, was born Ralls, Texas on 14th January 1929. He formed a band back in the 1950s and embarked on what was to be a lengthy musical career. He got an early break on the Big D Jamboree before becoming a member of both the Louisiana Hayride and the Ozark Jubilee.

Before hitting the big time he made several recordings in Clovis and it was one of these sessions that he split with Buddy, Jerry and Joe in early 1957. Billy recorded 'I've Got You On My Mind' and 'Viva La Matador', which came out on Columbia. The Crickets are believed to have backed up the singer. It was at this time that Buddy was in the studio working on 'Words Of Love' and experimenting with overdubbing.

Walker eventually became a member of the Grand Ole Opry and had numerous country hits over a period that stretched from 1962 into the 1980s. He is still active in the business.

Don Webb

Don Webb was born in Lubbock, Texas in 1935. He hoped to follow a musical career and met up with Holly in 1958. He hoped that Holly would record him when the Winter Dance Party Tour was over. It wasn't to be.

Don Webb did, however, record a Hollyish number, 'Little Ditty Baby', backed with 'I'll Be Back Home' at Clovis in 1959. The single was released on Brunswick but it wasn't a hit. He left the music business and was last heard of in Dallas.

Andrew Lloyd Webber

Who would expect an entry on Sir Andrew in a book on Buddy Holly? But in fact the doyen of British musicals has taken his influences from many sources, one of which was the music of Buddy Holly, or, perhaps more accurately, the drumming of Jerry Allison.

Several years ago Lloyd Webber composed 23 variations on the melodies of Nicolo Paganini, which were released in album form. The twenty-third and final variation was to blend in the 'Peggy Sue' drum rhythm! Performed by Julian Lloyd Webber, cello, Rod Argent, keyboards, and with drumming honours going to Jon Hiseman, the overall work is quite a *tour de force*.

One of the early variations is known to millions as the popular signature tune for *The South Bank Show* TV series.

Larry Welborn

Born on 13th April 1939 in Pleasant Hill, Oklahoma, Larry moved to Lubbock as a teenager and met up with Holly around 1954.

He was bass player on the hit version of 'That'll Be The Day', and was a member of the Buddy and Bob line up. He is also on a whole stack of early tracks that predate both the Coral and Decca recordings, probably the best-known of which are 'Bo Diddley' and 'Brown-Eyed Handsome Man'.

In 1956 Larry co-founded The Four Teens with Terry Noland, and it was no surprise that he was called in to help Buddy record 'That'll Be The Day'. Whilst not well known as a solo performer he plays several instruments and was actually drafted into The Crickets for a period in the 1960s.

Eventually, he returned to Oklahoma but has put in appearances at Holly tributes in Lubbock over the years.

'Well . . . All Right'

Recorded at Norman Petty Studios, Clovis, 14th February 1958 (approximately). Trio included Jerry Allison, cymbals and Buddy Holly, acoustic guitar.

All three Crickets are listed as composers, along with Norman Petty, on this classic number. Only issued as a B side to 'Heartbeat' it is one of several numbers that would probably have charted if it had been released in its own right.

It was composed as a direct result of listening, backstage, to Little Richard continually shouting the phrase when performing at the Paramount theatre, New York. The lyrics are surprisingly introspective even if tearjerkingly simple. Surviving Crickets Jerry and Joe can't now remember who wrote what of this number.

It has been recorded by many artists, including Blind Faith and Santana, who had a very small UK hit with it in 1978. The Crickets have used it in their stage act over the years but have favoured a flat-out rhythmic interpretation, as did Bobby Vee when he re-recorded it a few years ago.

Of the 21 Holly recordings overdubbed by The Picks that were released a few years back, this one works well and is recommended.

The most recent reworking was in Nashville when Nanci Griffith (vocals) and The Crickets combined to record an exuberant version.

Sonny West

Joe Sonny West was born near Lubbock, Texas on 30th July 1937. A singer/songwriter, he collaborated with Bill Tilghman to write two of Holly's greatest numbers, 'Oh Boy!' and 'Rave On'. Sonny had several single releases himself over the years, including his version of 'Rave On' on Atlantic records. It is a likeable version but lacks the power and intensity of Holly's performance. As a performer West is best remembered for his classic rockabilly recordings of 'Rock-ola Ruby' and 'Sweet Rockin' Baby', which Norman Petty produced in Clovis at the Lyceum Theatre, and which came out on his Nor-Va-Jak label.

As a footnote it is worth mentioning that West sometimes adopted the Christian name spelling Sonnee. But he is not to be confused with Sonny West, a henchman of Elvis with his brother Red during the 1960s and 1970s.

'What To Do'

Taped at Buddy Holly's New York flat, 3rd December 1958. Buddy and acoustic guitar.

One of the half dozen of Buddy's own compositions recorded at home on his Ampex tape machine. It was given to Coral producer, Dick Jacobs, and was subsequently overdubbed by Jack Hansen with orchestra and chorus, and became a minor hit when released as a single in 1961 (Coral Q72419).

Two years later a much superior version (Coral Q72469), with instrumental overdubbing by Norman Petty and with Holly's vocal given more echo, was released and charted again. Meanwhile, the undubbed version has only been heard on bootleg releases.

Hank Williams

Born 17th September 1923, Hank Williams is probably the most legendary male country singer of all time. His immortality was assured following his early death at 29 on the first day of January 1953. Holly would have been an impressionable 16 at that time and was already performing locally around the Lubbock area.

Buddy was certainly influenced by Hank during those formative years, although unfortunately he never recorded any of Hank's material, unlike several of his Southern counterparts (Cash, Lewis, Orbison, etc.). Like Hank, Buddy was a fine yodeller but never used the technique in any recordings. It's even possible that the first rock'n'roll record was Hank Williams's 'Move It On Over'. Just one of many claimants.

One thing Holly and Williams do share is the heavy irony of their last studio recordings. For Hank it was the prophetic 'I'll Never Get Out Of The World Alive' while Buddy was more pointed, claiming 'It Doesn't Matter Anymore'.

It was strange to learn that Hank's widow, Billie Jean, was subsequently to marry Johnny Horton, only to be widowed a second time. Incidentally, both Hank Williams and Buddy have had Hollywood biopics immortalizing their career. If Busey was an unlikely screen Holly, then reflect that Hank was played by actor George Hamilton.

See also JOHNNY HORTON entry.

Larry Williams

Born Lawrence E. Williams on 10th May 1935, Larry Williams was one of the archetypal stars of primitive rock'n'roll, although his hit recordings were thin on the ground. He had two Speciality singles in the charts during 1957, but it was mainly downhill thereafter.

In 1958 he was on the Alan Freed *Big Beat* show along with The Crickets, Jerry Lee, Chuck Berry and others. An excellent photo of Williams with Holly exists from that time. In later years he drifted back to the R&B circuit, which he had deserted in 1955 when he joined the Lloyd Price band.

Almost all Larry Williams's Speciality recordings are self-penned, including one entitled 'Ting a Ling'. A quite different song to that of Holly or The Robins. Larry Williams and Little Richard are often linked and were certainly close friends. Both were with Speciality at a formative time in their respective careers. Holly was influenced by both singers and although he recorded some of Penniman's compositions he didn't get around to recording anything by Larry Williams despite occasionally performing his material on the bandstand.

Williams apparently committed suicide in 1980, at which time his age was given as 44. According to friends he was several years older. It has been alleged that his lifestyle was both flamboyant and tainted by involvement in racketeering.

Chuck Willis

Christened Harold Willis, Chuck was born in Atlanta, Georgia on 31st January 1928. Chuck was one of the few rock'n'roll artists to die before Buddy Holly. Johnny Ace, however, was probably the first. For many years the cause of his death was unknown but, on the definitive Chuck Willis boxset, the reason is stated quite clearly: he died of peritonitis following abdominal surgery on 10th April 1958.

The Crickets recorded a masterly version of the Willis composition, 'It's Too Late', but other connections between the artists are few. Chuck did use Jesse Stone (see separate entry) around 1956–7 as arranger on the sessions that produced 'Juanita' and 'C C Rider'.

If 'It Doesn't Matter Anymore' was a vaguely prophetic choice for Buddy Holly's final release, then Chuck Willis went overboard with his two-sided biggie 'What Am I Living for' and 'Hang Up My Rock'n'Roll Shoes'. It is also worth mentioning that King Curtis was involved on the last session that produced these numbers.

Incidentally, session men were often peripatetic, frequently being used by different recording companies. So we find on Holly's New York sessions for Coral, Al Caiola, guitar and Panama Francis, drums. They were also used by Atlantic on many Chuck Willis recordings.

Chuck Willis was one of the greats of rock'n'roll and it's somewhat sad that, as a footnote, he crops up most in the history of the music for having worn a turban on stage.

Bob Wills

This Texan band leader was rightly dubbed the King of Western Swing, and his style has been heavily influential throughout the years. Born on a farm in East Texas on 6th March in 1905, he was eventually to name his band The Texas Playboys. Among his acolytes can be counted such country luminaries as Merle Haggard, Waylon Jennings and Tommy Allsup (courtesy of Asleep at the Wheel).

There is little doubt that Holly was influenced by Bob Wills in his formative years, and, like Wills, he used a fiddle in his early line ups (not forgetting that Holly briefly used the name The Rhythm Playboys).

Waylon Jennings said it all when he composed and recorded 'Bob Wills Is Still The King'. Wills died 13th May 1975 in Fort Worth, Texas. He had appeared in over 20 Hollywood pictures and made 550 recordings during a lengthy career that spanned the years 1929 to 1975. He was deservedly elected to the Country Music Hall of Fame in 1968.

Peanuts Wilson

Johnny Ancil Wilson was born in West Virginia on 28th November 1935 and moved to Texas as an infant. He deserves a mention as joint composer, with Roy Orbison, of The Crickets' 'You've Got Love', the track often referred to as containing the best of all Holly guitar solos.

Johnny Wilson was a member of Orbison's group The Teen Kings in the early years before going solo and releasing the Brunswick single 'You've Got Love'/'Cast Iron Arm'. Never a national hit, the B side has, nevertheless, been recognized as a true classic of its era. Incidentally, it was, in fact, recording for Brunswick that led to Wilson adopting the nickname Peanuts as they already had another J. Wilson recording for them, the great Jackie Wilson, and they wanted to avoid any confusion.

In later years, Johnny became a songwriter of note composing 'Love The World Away' by Kenny Rogers, which was used in the *Urban Cowboy* movie, and 'Rock On Baby' for Brenda Lee.

Johnny Wilson died suddenly in Tennessee on 27th September 1980.

'Wishing'

Recorded at Norman Petty's Studios Clovis, New Mexico, July–August 1958. Personnel: Tommy Allsup, lead guitar; Jerry and Joe replaced by session men who included George Atwood.

Written by Buddy and friend, Bob Montgomery, 'Wishing' was one of two compositions that they hoped would be recorded by the Everly brothers, who had just hit No.1 with 'Bird Dog'. Unfortunately, this did not happen but fine demos were recorded by Buddy in Clovis and both eventually came out on UK singles.

Released in the UK in 1963, 'Wishing' was one of a hat-trick of posthumous Top 10 hits that Holly had that year. It's an absolutely amazing performance that more than answered back those critics who had said that interest in Holly's music would be short-lived morbid curiosity.

The UK single is worth searching out as it comes without the additional guitar overdubbing that was used on the album release, 'Holly In The Hills', and most subsequent reissues.

It is possible that Holly recorded the definitive version of 'Wishing' as it has seldom been covered with the memorable exception of the Mary Chapin Carpenter/Kevin Montgomery duet as part of the Decca Holly tribute.

'Words of Love'

Recorded at Norman Petty's Studios, Clovis, New Mexico, 8th April 1957. Personnel: Buddy, Jerry and Joe B. Mauldin.

One of Buddy Holly's greatest ever compositions it became his first US Coral release in 1957, but, incredibly, made little impact at the time. Instead, the Diamonds' cover version was briefly a hit, peaking at No.13 in the USA during July 1957. As this predated 'That'll Be The Day' hitting the charts it was actually Holly's first hit, albeit as composer.

'Words Of Love' didn't even rate a release over here and UK fans were left to discover it on side two of Holly's first solo album the following year. Four of these fans were embryonic singers known as The Quarrymen and eventually their 1964 recording was issued on their 'Beatles For Sale' album. Forever after it has been accepted as a song years ahead of its time and has been a perennial favourite. Its not being released here didn't stop it being included on the hit '20 Golden Greats' LP.

On his recording, Buddy used his own overdubbed harmony vocal, which was very innovative in those monaural days. Holly also used both acoustic and electric guitar on the track. A month before the April studio session, Holly had practised the number and a very substandard recording of part of his performance has been in circulation for several years.

According to Jerry Allison the vocal and guitar sound that they achieved on 'Words Of Love' was influenced greatly by the US duo, Mickey and Sylvia. The song itself bears more than a passing resemblance to their hit 'Love Is Strange'. In 1993 a compilation of Holly's/Crickets' greatest performances entitled 'Words of Love' came out here and went briefly to the top of the album charts.

Y

'You and I Are Through'

Buddy and Bob performance at radio station KDAV, circa 1954–5.

Although Jack Neal claims the honours, this was written by Bob Montgomery and was one of several country-style numbers released in 1965 on the 'Holly In The Hills' album. At the time it seemed to fans that the wealth of posthumous releases was exhausted. Years later, however, devotees were delighted by the release of several other recordings on the 'Giant' album.

The master recording of 'You And I Are Through' has unidentified overdubbing on it – in an attempt to give the record a better sound. A further poorly recorded version of the number by Buddy and Bob has circulated among fans for several years but has not been commercially released.

The undubbed original was released in recent years by Vigotone.

'You Are My One Desire'

Recorded at the third and final Nashville recording session at Bradley's Barn on 15th November 1956. Personnel: Buddy, Don Guess (bass) and other Nashville session men.

Written by bassist Don Guess, who played on the session, this was one of only two ballads that Holly attempted for Decca. None of the Decca material was successful apart from the posthumous UK release of 'Midnight Shift' on their Brunswick subsidiary.

The false start at the beginning of the issued Take 2 has been included on the bootleg albums and it is probably only of academic interest to even the most devout fans.

'You Are My One Desire' is rather a stark recording with prominent 'cling-cling' piano by Floyd Cramer. The Picks' dubbed vocal backings were added behind Holly's voice for a 1986 album release and gave the track a much better and fuller sound.

'You're The One'

Written and recorded Christmas 1958 at radio KLLL, Lubbock, Texas. Personnel: Holly (vocals), Waylon Jennings and Slim Corbin, handclaps.

Evidently written quite spontaneously when Holly met up with his friends, Waylon Jennings and Slim Corbin, who were connected with the local radio station, call sign K-Triple-L. The short number featured Holly accompanying himself on guitar whilst the others clapped a snappy rhythm. Fortunately, the tape was kept in its original form and released in 1964 as part of the 'Showcase' album. Much later a heavily overdubbed version was put out on the 'Giant' album.

This song is seldom covered, but Billy Swan, who has often recorded offbeat material, did a version some years back.

'You've Got Love'

Recorded on the road, Tinker Airforce Base, Oklahoma City, USA, late September 1957. The Crickets were a quartet at the time.

One of the many marvellous tracks that came out on 'The Chirping Crickets' album in 1958 in the days when The Crickets really did 'chirp' courtesy of The Picks or The Roses. The track was one of a quartet that The Crickets recorded when they met up on tour with Norman Petty, who borrowed a US airforce base to set up his mobile recording equipment. Later, the dubbed backing vocals of The Picks gave the track its finished sound.

Holly plays a ringing guitar solo on the number, which was written by fellow Texans Roy Orbison and Teen King member Johnny Wilson. Months earlier, Johnny 'Peanuts' Wilson had recorded his own version as the flip of 'Cast Iron Arm'.

The Holly/Crickets version got belated recognition as a minor UK hit single when released in 1964.

Z

Zager and Evans

Denny Zager and Rick Evans, recorded 'In The Year 2525' several years back and it was a giant hit.

It's been said that Holly's music is timeless and it certainly looks poised to live and flourish as we stand on the brink of the 21st Century. We can only hope that it's still being heard when the 26th one eventually rolls into view. Who knows?

What I little realized when first composing this final entry was that 'In The Year 2525' was actually recorded by Zager and Evans in the Tulsa studio owned by Tommy Allsup! And it was Tommy's wallet that was found in amongst the wreckage of the light plane on that famous day when the music almost died.

That'll be the day when it does.

The wreckage of the Beechcraft Bonanza at Clear Lake, Iowa, on the morning of 3rd February 1959. (Courtesy of Bill Griggs.)

The flat gravestone marker on Buddy's grave, Lubbock's main cemetery. The original marker disappeared shortly after it was put in place. (Courtesy of Bill Griggs.)

Acknowledgements

Sincere thanks are due to John Ingman, Jim Carr and John Beecher for the help and encouragement in completing this A–Z.

John Ingman's research does not end with Holly himself but has expanded to include West Texas and New Mexico music of the era. He opened his files for me and no query was too trivial or too obscure.

Jim Carr has retired and spends his days running the quarterly magazine *Holly International*. Jim constantly unearths previously unseen photos, or tracks down someone to interview and obtain a fresh insight.

To prepare a work on Buddy Holly and not involve John Beecher would be unthinkable. He has been supportive all the way and has penned the flattering introduction that opens this book.

Others who have helped are listed as follows: Lawrence Cross, Barry Holley, Bob and Sue Dees, Steve Derby, Peter Feast, Bill Griggs, John Firminger, Alan Jenkins, Peter Rodger, Eric White and Ian Westgate. A few celebs have helped, including: Ronnie Keene, Brian Poole, Sherry Holley, George Atwood, Mike Read, Bobby Vee, Red Robinson and George Hamilton IV. Apologies for any oversights.

My family have been vital in this project's success. My wife Pam has shown amazing fortitude as deadlines came and went while daughter Nikki has actually typed the manuscript. All the Mann clan are thanked, especially my artistic father, who is ultimately to blame.

Lastly, my thanks are reserved for Aurum Press and in particular Brian Burns. From the outset his enthusiasm has been above and beyond the call of duty.